PENGUIN EDITION

Unit Three
Resources

The American Experience

PEARSON

Upper Saddle River, New Jersey
Boston, Massachusetts
Chandler, Arizona
Glenview, Illinois

Copyright© by Pearson Education, Inc., or its affiliates. All Rights Reserved. Printed in the United States of America. This publication is protected by copyright, and permission should be obtained from the publisher prior to any prohibited reproduction, storage in a retrieval system, or transmission in any form or by any means, electronic, mechanical, photocopying, recording, or likewise. The publisher hereby grants permission to reproduce these pages, in part or in whole, for classroom use only, the number not to exceed the number of students in each class. Notice of copyright must appear on all copies. For information regarding permissions, write to Pearson School Rights & Permissions, One Lake Street, Upper Saddle River, New Jersey 07458.

Pearson® is a trademark, in the U.S. and/or other countries, of Pearson plc or its affiliates.
Prentice Hall® is a trademark, in the U.S. and/or in other countries, of Pearson Education, Inc., or its affiliates.

ISBN–13: 978-0-13-366464-5
ISBN–10:   0-13-366464-3

2 3 4 5 6 7 8 9 10   12 11 10 09

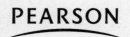

CONTENTS

For information about the Unit Resources, a Pronunciation Guide, and a Form for Analyzing Primary Source Documents, see the opening pages of your Unit One Resources.

"Luke Havergal" and **"Richard Cory"** by Edwin Arlington Robinson

"Lucinda Matlock" and **"Richard Bone"** by Edgar Lee Masters

"A Wagner Matinée" by Willa Cather

Name _____

Concept Map Unit 3

Division, Reconciliation, and Expansion: Literature of the Civil War and the Frontier (1850–1914)

Three Essential Questions serve as lenses through which to view the literature—

How does literature shape or reflect society?

What is the relationship between place and literature?

What makes American literature American?

Reflected in these selections:

Reflected in these selections:

Reflected in these selections:

Characteristics of the Period and Its Literature

which are demonstrated in these selections:

- The grim realities of the Civil War and of sprawling cities lead to new literary trends.
- The Civil War ends Romanticism; writers chart fateful forces at work in life.
- The nation expands rapidly, and writers record the local color of its many regions.
- As slavery divides the nation, African Americans testify to their experiences.

- A new African American literature emerges from song and oral traditions.
- War, including war against Native Americans, inspires charged persuasive works.
- Classic short stories reflect the nation's expansion into new territory.
- Writers use innovative techniques to explore war and daily life.
- Even as women agitate for their rights, new female voices emerge in literature.

Forms and Movements

- Realism
- Naturalism
- Regionalism
- Autobiography

Elements and Techniques

- Refrain/Rhyme
- Diction/Tone
- Humor/Conflict
- Point of View/Speaker
- Irony/Characterization

UNIT 3 STUDENT LOG

VOCABULARY	WRITING & EXTEND YOUR LEARNING	WORKSHOPS

Unit 3 Introduction
Names and Terms to Know

A. DIRECTIONS: *Write a brief sentence explaining each of the following names and terms. You will find all of the information you need in the Unit Introduction in your textbook*

1. Fort Sumter: _____

2. Homestead Act: _____
   _____

3. The Gilded Age: _____
   _____

4. Horatio Alger: _____

5. Muckrakers: _____

6. Local color: _____
   _____

B. DIRECTIONS: *Use the hints below to help you answer each question.*

1. How did the Civil War change American life?
   [Hints: How long did the Civil War last, and how many soldiers died in its battles? How did the war change the North? How did it change the South?]
   _____
   _____

2. How did the "Age of Electricity" make the lives of Americans both better and worse?
   [Hints: What were some of the inventions and other technological developments of the last half of the 19th century? In what way did these developments make life easier? What negative things did these developments bring about?]
   _____
   _____
   _____

3. Explain how the American frontier vanished a few decades after the Civil War.
   [Hints: What was the effect of the Homestead Act? What did the improved methods of transportation make possible? What replaced the American wilderness? What happened to the Native Americans?]
   _____
   _____
   _____

Unit 3 Introduction

Essential Question 1: How does literature shape or reflect?

A. DIRECTIONS: *Answer the questions about the first Essential Question in the Introduction, about the relationship between the writer and society. All the information you need is in the Unit 3 Introduction in your textbook.*

1. *Literary Forms for Expressing Social and Political Issues*

   a. What were spirituals and what did they communicate? _____
   _____

   b. Give examples of autobiographical writings of the period. _____
   _____

   c. Muckrakers focused on revealing _____
   _____
   _____

2. *Popular Literature*

   a. What do "rags-to riches" stories tell about? _____
   _____

   b. The surprise ends of O. Henry's short stories stress _____

   c. Give two examples of popular "escapist" writers. _____

3. *Realism, Naturalism, and the Social and Political Issues*

   a. How did the Civil War change American optimism? _____
   _____

   b. The fiction of Realism depicted _____

   c. Two poets who wrote of ordinary people were _____

   d. Writers of the Naturalist movement took Realism a step further by _____
   _____

B. DIRECTIONS: *Answer the questions that include the Essential Question Vocabulary words.*

   1. What did spirituals like "Go Down, Moses" *lament* in society? _____
   _____

   2. As *industry* grew, how did industrial-age American society feel about the western frontier?
   _____

   3. What level of society would Mark Twain's realistic *vernacular* dialogue portray? _____
   _____

Name _____ Date _____

Unit 3 Introduction

Essential Question 2: What is the relationship between place and literature?

A. DIRECTIONS: *On the lines provided, answer the questions about the second Essential Question in the Introduction, about the relationship between place and literature. All the information you need is in the Unit 3 Introduction in your textbook.*

1. *Northern Writers and the Physical Environment*

    a. Technological advances in the North encouraged people to _____
    _____

    b. What issues caused by urban growth did Civil-War-era writers focus on? _____
    _____

2. *Southern Writers and the Physical Environment*

    a. How did the Civil War change the physical environment in the South? _____
    _____

    b. In contrast to Northern writers, Southern writers focused more on _____
    _____

3. *Expressions of Place in Civil-War-Era Writing*

    a. "Local color" writing featured _____
    _____

    b. Give examples of local color writers. _____
    _____

    c. Give examples of writers who used urban settings. _____
    _____

B. DIRECTIONS: *Complete the sentence stems based on the Essential Question Vocabulary words.*

1. Mining California's *resources*, Bret Harte wrote _____
    _____

2. Edith Wharton wrote *urban* novels about _____
    _____

3. Two *regional* writers exploring Midwestern rural society were _____
    _____

Name _____ Date _____

Unit 3 Introduction

Essential Question 3: What makes American literature American?

A. DIRECTIONS: *On the lines provided, answer the questions about the third Essential Question in the Introduction, about what makes American literature American. All the information you need is in the Unit 3 Introduction in your textbook.*

1. *Literary Elements Contributing to the American Style*

   a. Give examples of the types of settings to be found in American literature at this time.
   _____

   b. What two types of speech were typical of American writing? _____

   c. In American writing, humor often served the purpose of _____
   _____

2. *Roles of Civil-War Era Writers*

   a. In contrast to Romantic writers, Realistic writers _____
   _____

   b. What did writers who specialized in local color depict, and how? _____
   _____

   c. What were some European influences on Naturalistic American writers? _____
   _____

   d. Naturalistic writers believed that human behavior was controlled by _____
   _____

3. *Turn-of-the-Century America as Portrayed in Literature*

   a. The Romantic beliefs of the American Renaissance had given way to _____
   _____

   b. What view of war replaced the idealism of "Old Ironsides"? _____
   _____

   c. Emerson's self-reliance was succeeded by _____

   d. Exceptional heroes were being replaced by _____

   e. What attitude toward science is revealed in the millions visiting the 1893 World's Fair in Chicago? _____

B. DIRECTIONS: *Complete the sentence stems based on the Essential Question Vocabulary words.*

1. Expressing *pessimism* about self-reliance were _____

2. American writing grew more *realistic* after _____

3. Americans sought a *fortune* of gold in _____

Name _____ Date _____

Following-Through Activities

A. CHECK YOUR COMPREHENSION: *Use this chart to complete the Check Your Comprehension activity in the Unit 3 Introduction. In the middle column, fill in two key concepts related to each Essential Question. In the right column, list a major author connected with each concept.*

ESSENTIAL QUESTION	Key Concepts	Major Author
Writer and Society	1. 2.	1. 2.
Place and Literature	1. 2.	1. 2.
American Identity	1. 2.	1. 2.

B. EXTEND YOUR LEARNING: *Use this graphic organizer to help plan your research for the Extend Your Learning activity.*

Speaker	
Speaker's Purpose(s)	
Speaker's Favorite Topics	
Elements of Speaker's Style	

"An Occurrence at Owl Creek Bridge" by Ambrose Bierce
Vocabulary Warm-up Word Lists

Study these words from the selection. Then, complete the activities.

Word List A

assassin [uh SAS in] *n.* murderer, usually of a prominent person
John Wilkes Booth was the <u>assassin</u> who killed President Abraham Lincoln.

assented [uh SENT id] *v.* agreed
When Clara asked her father for permission to visit Tulsa, he readily <u>assented</u>.

audibly [AW duh blee] *adv.* in a manner that can be heard
Tom spoke <u>audibly</u>, so the person in the next row heard every word.

convulsively [kuhn VUL siv lee] *adv.* in a manner marked by spasms and twitches
The dog's tail twitched <u>convulsively</u>, and we immediately called the vet.

intervals [IN ter vuhlz] *n.* spaces between objects or points in time
Gina will record the behavior of her lab mice at 10-minute <u>intervals</u>.

keen [KEEN] *adj.* sharp; vivid; strong
Evelyn's memory is so <u>keen</u> that she can recall what our teacher wore last Tuesday.

matchless [MACH les] *adj.* unequaled; unsurpassed
<u>Matchless</u> musical talent makes Vivian our town's greatest pianist.

rustic [RUS tik] *adj.* of or relating to country life or country people; unrefined
In a <u>rustic</u> cottage, there are few decorations.

Word List B

congestion [kuhn JES chuhn] *n.* crowded condition; excessive build-up
Alice is suffering from lung <u>congestion</u> due to her recent bout of pneumonia.

etiquette [ET i ket] *n.* appropriate behavior; code or system of good manners
Since proper <u>etiquette</u> is important to Lola, she never interrupts when others are talking.

ineffable [in EF uh buhl] *adj.* too overwhelming to be spoken or expressed
After being caught stealing his sister's money, Ian blushed with <u>ineffable</u> shame.

luminous [LOOM in uhs] *adj.* full of light; illuminated
Glowing candlelight makes Jane's face seem <u>luminous</u>.

perilous [PER il uhs] *adj.* dangerous
Traveling through the vast desert can be <u>perilous</u> for children.

sentinel [SEN ti nel] *n.* watchman; guard
Each gate at the military post was guarded day and night by a <u>sentinel</u>.

summarily [sum AYR uh lee] *adv.* promptly and without formality
Kevin was <u>summarily</u> called to the principal's office after being late again.

velocity [vuh LAHS uh tee] *n.* speed; swiftness
The <u>velocity</u> of that high-speed train amazes me.

"An Occurrence at Owl Creek Bridge" by Ambrose Bierce
Vocabulary Warm-up Exercises

Exercise A *Fill in each blank in the paragraph below with the appropriate word from Word List A.*

When Matthew asked me to go bird watching with him last Saturday, I readily
[1] _____. Sunrise is a lovely time of day, and the [2] _____
surroundings outside of town were beautiful. Walking along the nature trail, we could
hear a bird calling [3] _____ and at regular [4] _____.
Knowing what a(n) [5] _____ bird watcher Matthew is, I asked him if he
could identify the call. "Sure," he said, "that's a Northern Shrike. What an elegant little
[6] _____! Shrikes feed on insects, worms, little snakes, and field mice.
You can often see the prey wriggling [7] _____ in a shrike's beak."
Matthew continued, "Shrikes have a(n) [8] _____ ability to plan for the
future. No other birds are quite like them. They store up their food, much the same as
we keep groceries in a fridge or on a kitchen shelf."

Exercise B *Decide whether each statement below is true or false. Circle T or F, and explain your answer.*

1. With *congestion* on the highway, you may not arrive on time at your destination.
   T / F _____

2. People respecting *etiquette* can be expected to behave impolitely.
   T / F _____

3. If an emotion is *ineffable*, it is impossible to put into words.
   T / F _____

4. A *luminous* theory fails to shed light on a scientific issue or problem.
   T / F _____

5. If you undertake a *perilous* mission, you should be prepared for danger.
   T / F _____

6. A person acting as a *sentinel* at night must take good care not to fall asleep.
   T / F _____

7. An action performed *summarily* is carried out slowly and deliberately.
   T / F _____

8. The *velocity* of a vehicle is its total weight.
   T / F _____

"An Occurrence at Owl Creek Bridge" by Ambrose Bierce
Reading Warm-up A

Read the following passage. Pay special attention to the underlined words. Then, read it again, and complete the activities. Use a separate sheet of paper for your written answers.

Because of his pessimistic and sour views of human nature, Ambrose Bierce is often labeled a cynic. Indeed, Bierce's belief that death is meaningless is just as ruthless as the attitude of an <u>assassin</u>.

Today's cynics <u>audibly</u>—sometimes even loudly—raise doubts about the motives of others. Cynics believe that people are selfish and insincere. According to cynics, people strongly pursue personal goals, driven mostly by a <u>keen</u> desire for their own success. There is no such thing as unselfish concern for others. Try to convince a cynic that some people possess the potential for doing good without being rewarded. He or she might laugh <u>convulsively</u> and then gasp spasmodically for breath. Cynics have never <u>assented</u> to the notion that people may act out of a desire to help others. True cynics would vigorously disagree with that idea.

Cynicism can be traced back to the Greek philosopher Diogenes, who lived during the fourth century B.C. The most famous story about Diogenes is that he would roam the streets with a lighted lantern in the daytime, as though he were searching. At <u>intervals</u>—each day at dawn and midday—passersby would stop him to ask what he was doing. "I am looking for an honest man," Diogenes would answer, implying that his unending search really meant that he had little or no hope of finding one. Instead, Diogenes believed that <u>matchless</u> dishonesty is a human trait that overcomes all others.

The Cynics—the philosophical group Diogenes led—stressed self-sufficiency and rejection of luxury. The group led a simple, almost <u>rustic</u> life, even when they did not live in the country. The word *cynic* itself comes from the Greek word for "dog," and one legend has it that because the cynics lived so plainly, they were regarded as dogs, not humans. If you think about it, that is a rather cynical view of Cynics!

1. Underline the phrase in this sentence that gives a clue to the meaning of <u>assassin</u>. What is a synonym for *assassin*?

2. Circle the words in this sentence that add to the meaning of <u>audibly</u>. What are two antonyms for *audibly*?

3. Circle the adverb in this sentence that offers a clue to the meaning of <u>keen</u>. What is a synonym for *keen*?

4. Underline the phrase in this sentence that helps define <u>convulsively</u>. What is a synonym for *convulsively*?

5. Underline the words in the next sentence that are the opposite of <u>assented</u>. Then, rewrite that sentence using a synonym of *assented*.

6. Circle the words in this sentence that give a clue to the meaning of <u>intervals</u>.

7. Circle the words in this sentence that give a clue to the meaning of <u>matchless</u>. What are two synonyms for *matchless*?

8. What clue can you find in this sentence to the meaning of <u>rustic</u>?

Name _____ Date _____

"An Occurrence at Owl Creek Bridge" by Ambrose Bierce
Reading Warm-up B

Read the following passage. Pay special attention to the underlined words. Then, read it again, and complete the activities. Use a separate sheet of paper for your written answers.

In his story, Ambrose Bierce uses all three types of irony: verbal, dramatic, and situational. In verbal irony, a word or phrase is used to suggest the opposite of its usual meaning. Consider, for example, Bierce's statement that death is a "dignitary" who must be greeted politely according to a formal code of <u>etiquette</u>. Bierce describes Peyton Farquhar as "the man who was engaged in being hanged," as if Farquhar was leisurely indulging in a favorite pastime rather than being <u>summarily</u> executed. Both these examples illustrate verbal irony.

The story's unusual structure allows Bierce to create dramatic irony in the flashback in Part II. In this type of irony, there is a striking conflict between what a character thinks and what the reader knows. When Farquhar sets out on his <u>perilous</u> mission to destroy the Owl Creek bridge, we know he has been tricked by a Federal scout.

In Part III, Bierce slows down the <u>velocity</u> of his fast-paced plot so that the story moves at a crawl. Through vivid, <u>luminous</u> images, he sheds light on Farquhar's inner state of consciousness. Slowly, the overcrowding and <u>congestion</u> of thoughts in Farquhar's mind give way to a single goal: to get home to his wife. At length he glimpses her, standing watchfully like a <u>sentinel</u> near the veranda of their home. The joy that seizes Farquhar is <u>ineffable</u>, and he cannot translate his emotions into words. Then, in an almost unbearable stroke of situational irony, Bierce reveals the climax of the story, a surprise ending that violently contradicts our expectations.

1. Underline the words that hint at the meaning of <u>etiquette</u>. Write a sentence using this word.

2. Circle the words that help define <u>summarily</u> through contrast. What is a synonym for *summarily*?

3. Underline the words that hint at the meaning of <u>perilous</u>. What are two antonyms for *perilous*?

4. Underline the words that hint at the meaning of <u>velocity</u>. What is a synonym for *velocity*?

5. Circle the words in this sentence that give a clue to the meaning of <u>luminous</u>. Write two words meaning the opposite of *luminous*.

6. Underline the words in this sentence that help define <u>congestion</u>. What is a synonym for *congestion*?

7. Circle the words in this sentence that hint at the meaning of <u>sentinel</u>. Use the word *sentinel* in an original sentence.

8. Underline the words that give a clear definition of <u>ineffable</u>. What is an antonym for *ineffable*?

Name _____ Date _____

"An Occurrence at Owl Creek Bridge" by Ambrose Bierce
Literary Analysis: Point of View

A writer's purpose helps determine the **point of view** from which a story is told. In "An Occurrence at Owl Creek Bridge," for example, Ambrose Bierce reveals the tragically ironic nature of war through the events surrounding one person—Peyton Farquhar. Limited third-person narration allows Bierce to explore Farquhar's thoughts and feelings while preserving the objective distance needed for the story's ironic ending. As the plot develops in this story, Bierce uses **stream-of-consciousness** writing to help readers see the quick, moment-by-moment working of Farquhar's mind.

DIRECTIONS: *Rewrite the following passages of "An Occurrence at Owl Creek Bridge" from the point of view indicated. Be prepared to explain how each point of view changes the story.*

1. A man stood upon a railroad bridge in northern Alabama, looking down into the swift water twenty feet below. The man's hands were behind his back, the wrists bound with a cord. A rope closely encircled his neck.

First-person point of view, stream of consciousness _____

_____

_____

_____

_____

_____

_____

_____

2. As Peyton Farquhar fell straight downward through the bridge he lost consciousness and was as one already dead. From this state he was awakened—ages later, it seemed to him—by the pain of a sharp pressure upon his throat, followed by a sense of suffocation.

Third-person omniscient point of view _____

_____

_____

_____

_____

_____

_____

_____

_____

"An Occurrence at Owl Creek Bridge" by Ambrose Bierce

Reading Strategy: Identify Chronological Order

To make their stories interesting, writers often begin with an especially dramatic event and then flash backward in time to supply the reader with necessary information. In "An Occurrence at Owl Creek Bridge," the author begins with Peyton Farquhar standing on the railroad bridge about to be hanged. Then he follows with a flashback to tell how Peyton Farquhar got into that situation. In addition, Bierce flashes forward to show events leaping forward in time.

As you read stories like this one, it is a good strategy to keep the **chronological order** clear in your mind.

DIRECTIONS: *In the "mental" flashforward, Ambrose Bierce gives the reader many clues that the events are taking place in an imaginary future rather than in an actual present. Below are excerpts from the story. In the space provided, explain how each excerpt provides a clue to the nature of the flashforward.*

1. He was now in full possession of his physical senses. They were, indeed, preternaturally keen and alert. Something in the awful disturbance of his organic system had so exalted and refined them that they made record of things never before perceived. He felt the ripples upon his face and heard their separate sounds as they struck.

   _____

   _____

   _____

   _____

2. Suddenly he felt himself whirled around and round—spinning like a top. The water, the banks, the forests, the now distant bridge, fort and men—all were commingled and blurred.

   _____

   _____

   _____

   _____

3. At last he found a road which led him in what he knew to be the right direction. It was as wide and straight as a city street, yet it seemed untraveled. No fields bordered it, no dwelling anywhere. Not so much as the barking of a dog suggested human habitation.

   _____

   _____

   _____

   _____

"An Occurrence at Owl Creek Bridge" by Ambrose Bierce
Vocabulary Builder

Using the Latin Root *-dict-*

A. DIRECTIONS: *The word root -dict- is Latin in origin and means "word; saying; expression." On the lines below, explain how each word reflects the meaning of the root -dict-.*

1. contradict (*contra-* means "opposite"): _____

2. dictionary (*-ary* means "thing connected with"): _____

3. predict (*pre-* means "before"): _____

4. *verdict* (*-ver-* means "true"): _____

Using the Word List

   apprised   deference   dictum   etiquette   ineffable   summarily

B. DIRECTIONS: *Replace the underlined word or phrase with a synonym from the Word List.*

1. Any citizen caught . . . will be <u>immediately</u> hanged.

   _____

2. According to military <u>policy</u>, it was necessary to execute the spy.

   _____

3. Farquhar felt <u>unutterable</u> joy.

   _____

4. in the code of military <u>behavior</u>

   _____

5. Silence and fixity are forms of <u>courtesy.</u>

   _____

6. A sharp pain in his wrist <u>informed</u> him.

   _____

"An Occurrence at Owl Creek Bridge" by Ambrose Bierce
Support for Writing

To organize your information to write a **critical essay** about the story you have just read, enter examples of Bierce's stream of consciousness into the chart below.

Stream of Consciousness in "An Occurrence at Owl Creek Bridge"

Example 1 of stream of consciousness from story	How it reveals character's thoughts
_____ _____ _____	_____ _____ _____
Example 2 of stream of consciousness from story	**How it reveals character's thoughts**
_____ _____ _____	_____ _____ _____
Example 3 of stream of consciousness from story	**How it reveals character's thoughts**
_____ _____ _____	_____ _____ _____

On a separate page, write your first draft, showing how each example of stream of consciousness contributes to the dramatic impact of the story. As you revise, add direct quotes from the story to support your opinions.

Name _____ Date _____

Enrichment: The Legal System

Defending Peyton Farquhar

The reader infers from the selection that the hanging of Peyton Farquhar was done without benefit of a formal trial. Would the outcome have been different in a court of law?

DIRECTIONS: *Prepare a legal defense for Peyton Farquhar. You may use anything from the selection, including the map and photographs, to make your case. In the following chart, list at least four issues or facts you will address in Farquhar's defense. You may focus on facts and issues that will help your client, or those the prosecution will probably raise. Conclude with the plea you will enter (innocent or guilty) and the sentence, if any, you will ask for your client. A defense lawyer often considers the following points when preparing a case:*

 A. motive of the client

 B. past offenses of the client

 C. amount and quality of prosecution evidence against the client

 D. extenuating or unusual circumstances affecting the crime

 E. any remorse shown by the client

 F. likelihood of the client's repeating the crime

Fact/Issue	How will you handle this in the trial?

Plea: _____

Sentence: _____

Name _____ Date _____

"An Occurrence at Owl Creek Bridge" by Ambrose Bierce
Open-Book Test

Short Answer *Write your responses to the questions in this section on the lines provided.*

1. "An Occurrence at Owl Creek Bridge" begins with a flat, distant, almost journalistic tone. Given what is about to take place in the story, what is striking or noteworthy about this tone?

   _____

   _____

   _____

2. In "An Occurrence at Owl Creek Bridge," Bierce's description of the planter who is about to be hanged does not portray an evil person. In fact, he even speaks of the planter's "kindly expression." What point about war do you think Bierce is making with this description?

   _____

   _____

   _____

3. "An Occurrence at Owl Creek Bridge" is divided into three main sections. Briefly summarize these three sections in the order in which they occur.

   _____

   _____

   _____

   _____

4. In Part I of "An Occurrence at Owl Creek Bridge" the following passage contains a shift in point of view: "A piece of dancing driftwood caught his attention and his eyes followed it down the current. How slowly it appeared to move!" What is the shift in point of view that takes place in this passage?

   _____

   _____

   _____

5. There are several places in "An Occurrence at Owl Creek Bridge" where there is a change in the time sequence. Identify one of these places and explain the effect it has on the story.

   _____

   _____

   _____

   _____

6. Section II of "An Occurrence at Owl Creek Bridge" reveals a surprising piece of information about the grey-clad horseman. What does this information imply about Farquhar and his responsibility for his deed?

_____

_____

_____

7. In parts of "An Occurrence at Owl Creek Bridge," Bierce uses a literary technique known as stream of consciousness in order to report thoughts and ideas the way the human mind experiences them. What detail in the following passage provides a clue that certain events are occurring in Farquhar's imagination rather than in reality?

    The trees upon the bank were giant garden plants...

_____

_____

_____

8. Find the highlighted word *dictum* in section II of "An Occurrence at Owl Creek Bridge." What example in the context helps you understand the meaning of *dictum*?

_____

_____

9. Bierce uses more than one point of view in "An Occurrence at Owl Creek Bridge." What are the two main points of view that he uses?

_____

_____

10. In "An Occurrence at Owl Creek Bridge," Bierce shifts the time sequence back and forth throughout the story. Use the chart below to place the listed events in the actual sequence in which they happen in the story. Write the number of the event in the column on the right. List the earliest event as 1, and the latest as 4.

Story Event	Numbered Order of Events
Farquhar has a conversation with a Federal scout.	
Farquhar sees his wife waiting for him at home.	
Farquhar dies.	
Farquhar is strung up in preparation for his hanging.	

Essay

Write an extended response to the question of your choice or to the question or questions your teacher assigns you.

11. Based on your reading of "An Occurrence at Owl Creek Bridge," do you think that Bierce would agree with the statement that "all is fair in love and war"? Why or why not? Develop your viewpoint in an essay supported by examples from the story.

12. Ambrose Bierce was known for his cynical, dark view of human life. Is this outlook confirmed or denied by "An Occurrence at Own Creek"? Develop your view in an essay supported by examples from the story.

13. Bierce uses shifting time sequences and points of view in "An Occurrence at Owl Creek Bridge." Do you think the story would have been more or less effective if Bierce had written it from a single point of view and in strict chronological order? Explain your opinion in an essay supported by examples from the story.

14. **Thinking About the Essential Question: What is the relationship between place and literature?** Place becomes charged with danger during times of war. A once benign locale can easily become deadly. Why do you think this might be interesting to a writer of fiction? Use examples from "An Occurrence at Owl Creek Bridge" to support your answer.

Oral Response

15. Go back to questions 2, 6, or 9 or to the question your teacher assigns you. Take a few minutes to expand your answer and prepare an oral response. Find additional details in "An Occurrence at Owl Creek Bridge" that support your points. If necessary, make notes to guide your oral response.

Name _____ Date _____

"An Occurrence at Owl Creek Bridge" by Ambrose Bierce
Selection Test A

Critical Reading *Identify the letter of the choice that best answers the question.*

_____ 1. What activity opens the story "An Occurrence at Owl Creek Bridge"?
   A. A Southern spy is put on trial.
   B. A man is about to be hanged.
   C. Union soldiers are fixing a bridge.
   D. Troops are laying railroad tracks.

_____ 2. What must readers figure out in order to understand "An Occurrence at Owl Creek Bridge"?
   A. how the characters act
   B. the setting and the mood
   C. the order of the events
   D. the reason for the hanging

_____ 3. Which of the following contributes most to the mystery of "An Occurrence at Owl Creek Bridge"?
   A. the breaking of the hangman's noose
   B. the shooting by the Union sentries
   C. Farquhar's underwater struggle
   D. the order in which events occur

_____ 4. In "Occurrence at Owl Creek Bridge," why does Farquhar hear his watch ticking as he dies?
   A. He hopes the watch will start to work.
   B. He wants to know his time of death.
   C. His senses are extra strong before death.
   D. Everything else around him is quiet.

_____ 5. In "An Occurrence at Owl Creek Bridge," which is in third-person limited point of view?
   A. "Peyton Farquhar was a well-to-do planter . . ."
   B. "A man stood upon a railroad bridge in northern Alabama . . ."
   C. "He wore a mustache and a pointed beard . . ."
   D. "He was awakened—ages later, it seemed to him—by . . .a sharp pressure."

Name _____ Date _____

_____ 6. In "Occurrence at Owl Creek Bridge," why does the Federal scout want to burn the bridge?
   A. He wants to help the South win.
   B. He wants to set Farquhar up.
   C. He wants a job building a new bridge.
   D. He wants to disrespect his commandant.

_____ 7. In "Occurrence at Owl Creek Bridge," Farquhar is a gentleman. Why might he be hanged?
   A. for being from the Confederacy
   B. for spying on Union activities
   C. for planning against the enemy
   D. for refusing to feed Union soldiers

_____ 8. Which of these passages from "An Occurrence at Owl Creek Bridge" is written from an omniscient point of view?
   A. "If I could free my hands," he thought, "I might throw off the noose. . ."
   B. "The man who was engaged in being hanged was . . . about thirty-five . . ."
   C. "The thought of his wife and children urged him on."
   D. "To be hanged and drowned . . . that is not so bad; but I do not wish to be shot."

_____ 9. In "Occurrence at Owl Creek Bridge," in which order do the following events occur?
   A. Farquhar imagines reuniting with his wife.
   B. Farquhar is approached by a Federal scout.
   C. Farquhar's board is released and he falls.
   D. Farquhar dies of hanging.
   A. A, B, C, D   B. C, A, B, D   C. A, D, B, C   D. B, C, A, D

_____ 10. Which of these events happens last in the real-time sequence of events in "Occurrence at Owl Creek Bridge"?
   A. Farquhar falls through the bridge.
   B. Farquhar's neck snaps and he dies.
   C. Farquhar imagines greeting his wife.
   D. Farquhar imagines dodging bullets.

Vocabulary

____ 11. In which sentence is the meaning of the word *apprised* suggested?
A. Farquhar was not a soldier but hoped to contribute to the Southern cause.
B. Mrs. Farquhar was informed of her husband's death.
C. The Federal scout encouraged Farquhar to commit sabotage.
D. The authorities went through the proper formalities.

____ 12. When the narrator says that the "pain in his wrist *apprised* him that he was try-ing to free his hands," he means the pain _____ him.
A. overwhelmed
B. deceived
C. informed
D. humored

Essay

13. How is Bierce's dark view reflected in "An Occurrence at Owl Creek Bridge"? Write a brief essay that gives examples of events that reflect a negative view of human experience.

14. What do you think Bierce's view of war is, based on "An Occurrence at Owl Creek Bridge"? Does he find it uplifting or hopeless? Write a brief essay to give your opin-ion about Bierce's viewpoint. Use at least two examples from the story to support your opinion.

15. **Thinking About the Essential Question: What is the relationship between place and literature?** During war, any place can become dangerous, even deadly. Why do you think a writer of fiction would want to write about peaceful places that unex-pectedly become dangerous in wartime? Use examples from "An Occurrence at Owl Creek Bridge" to support your answer.

"An Occurrence at Owl Creek Bridge" by Ambrose Bierce
Selection Test B

Critical Reading *Identify the letter of the choice that best completes the statement or answers the question.*

____ 1. Which of the following quotations from this story reveals an objective point of view?
   A. "He was a captain."
   B. "He closed his eyes in order to fix his last thoughts upon his wife and children."
   C. "His whole body was racked and wrenched with an insupportable anguish!"
   D. "He had not known that he lived in so wild a region."

____ 2. Why does the author describe how Peyton Farquhar reacts to the sound of his watch?
   A. to show that Farquhar's sense perceptions had become very distorted
   B. to illustrate the cruelty of the Union soldiers
   C. to explain why Farquhar had come to the bridge
   D. to draw a parallel between Farquhar and his executioners

____ 3. In order to understand the relationship between the three distinct parts of the story, the reader must clarify
   A. how a civilian like Farquhar became a military prisoner.
   B. shifts in the geographical setting.
   C. the sequence of events.
   D. the story's several conflicting attitudes about the Civil War.

____ 4. Which of the following contributes most to the feeling of suspense in "An Occurrence at Owl Creek Bridge"?
   A. the vivid descriptions of the physical setting
   B. the unexpected sequence in which the events are related
   C. the emotionless description of the procedures used to prepare for the hanging
   D. the sympathetic depiction of Peyton Farquhar's personality

____ 5. When Peyton Farquhar suggests sabotage, the Federal scout suggests that the bridge can be burned down. What does this say about the scout's character?
   A. He is an honest and straightforward man.
   B. He is an arsonist at heart.
   C. He is not above setting up Farquhar.
   D. He dislikes his commandant.

____ 6. What points of view does Bierce use in this story?
   A. objective as well as first person
   B. objective and third-person limited
   C. first person and third person
   D. only third-person limited

____ 7. What is the main function of the flashback in this story?
   A. to describe the effects of the war on women and children
   B. to provide insight into the treacherous nature of the Union soldiers
   C. to generate sympathy for the Southern cause
   D. to explain why Peyton Farquhar is being hanged

Name _____ Date _____

_____ 8. Which message is Bierce trying to convey in this story?
   A. People often get themselves into trouble by taking foolish risks.
   B. Whatever can go wrong, probably will.
   C. Soldiers must follow orders regardless of their personal feelings.
   D. War makes men cruel and indifferent to human life.

_____ 9. Which event happens first in the true sequence of events?
   A. Farquhar stands on the Oak Creek bridge with his neck "in the hemp."
   B. Farquhar's wife brings the soldier water.
   C. The rope breaks, causing Farquhar to fall into the water.
   D. Farquhar runs to greet his wife with open arms.

_____ 10. Which of the following excerpts provides a clue that certain events occur in Peyton Farquhar's imagination rather than in reality?
   A. ". . . he had frequented camps enough to know the dread significance of that deliberate, drawing, aspirated chant . . ."
   B. "The trees upon the bank were giant garden plants; he noted a definite order in their arrangement, inhaled the fragrance of their blooms."
   C. "Suddenly he heard a sharp report and something struck the water smartly within a few inches of his head, spattering his face with spray."
   D. "At last he found a road which led him in what he knew to be the right direction."

_____ 11. Why is the narrator surprised to find Peyton Farquhar about to hanged?
   A. Farquhar looks kindly and is a gentleman.
   B. Hanging has been outlawed in Alabama.
   C. Farquhar is already dead.
   D. Only gentlemen are hanged in Alabama.

_____ 12. Which of the following excerpts shows a limited third-person point of view?
   A. "Peyton Farquhar was a well-to-do planter, of an old and highly respected Alabama family."
   B. "The company faced the bridge, staring stonily, motionless."
   C. "The power of thought was restored; he knew that the rope had broken and he had fallen into the stream."
   D. "The man's hands were behind his back, the wrists bound with a cord."

Vocabulary

_____ 13. What are the meanings of the italicized words in the following sentence? "In the code of military *etiquette*, silence and fixity are forms of *deference*."
   A. training, soldiering
   B. manners, disrespect
   C. hangings, bravery
   D. behavior, courtesy

____ 14. Which word is closest in meaning to the italicized word in the phrase ". . . will be *summarily* hanged"?
   A. quietly
   B. promptly
   C. justifiably
   D. brutally

____ 15. Which of these could most clearly be called a *dictum?*
   A. a biography of Ambrose Bierce
   B. "An occurrence at owl Creek Bridge"
   C. a politician's statement on an issue
   D. a restaurant menu

____ 16. Farquhar describes his wife's smile as expressing "*ineffable* joy." What does he mean?
   A. Her joy was fixed and permanent.
   B. Her joy was too overwhelming to be spoken.
   C. Her joy was artificial.
   D. Her joy was mixed with sadness.

Essay

17. Do you think Bierce agreed that "all is fair in love and war"? Answer this question in a short essay, using examples from "An Occurrence at Owl Creek Bridge" to support your position.

18. In "An Occurrence at Owl Creek Bridge," the reader is surprised to learn that the man with whom Farquhar discusses Owl Creek bridge is not a Confederate soldier but a Federal, or Union, scout. What is the true significance of their brief conversation, and how does the incident set the tone for the rest of the story? In an essay, relate this flashback to the events of the story and explore how this initial deception might be said to foreshadow the story's ending.

19. Ambrose Bierce uses both a flashback and different points of view to tell "An Occurrence at Owl Creek Bridge." Imagine that Bierce had written the story in the true sequence of events and from an objective point of view. Do you think the story would have been as effective? State your opinion in a brief essay, supporting your opinion with examples from the story.

20. **Thinking About the Essential Question: What is the relationship between place and literature?** A once peaceful place can quickly become the scene of deadly events during war. Why do you think this might be interesting to a fiction writer? Use examples from "An Occurrence at Owl Creek Bridge" to support your answer.·

Name _____ Date _____

from **Mary Chesnut's Civil War** by Mary Chesnut
"Recollections of a Private" by Warren Lee Goss
"A Confederate Account of the Battle of Gettysburg" by Randolph McKim
Primary Sources: War Correspondence

A. DIRECTIONS: *Read each passage from one of the selections. Then, generate two questions that arise from the quotation.*

Today at dinner there was no allusion to things as they stand in Charleston Harbor. There was an undercurrent of intense excitement. There could not have been a more brilliant circle. . . . These men all talked so delightfully. For once in my life I listened.

—*Mary Chesnut's Civil War*

1. _____

2. _____

"Cold chills" ran up and down my back as I got out of bed after the sleepless night, and shaved preparatory to other desperate deeds of valor. I was twenty years of age, and when anything unusual was to be done, like fighting or courting, I shaved.

—*"Recollections of a Private"*

3. _____

4. _____

The first day I went out to drill, getting tired of doing the same things over and over, I said to the drill sergeant: "Let's stop this fooling and go over to the grocery." His only reply was addressed to a corporal: "Corporal, take this man out and drill him"; and the corporal did! I found that suggestions were not so well appreciated in the army as in private life, and that no wisdom was equal to a drillmaster's "Right face," "Left wheel," and "Right, oblique, march."

—*"Recollections of a Private"*

5. _____

6. _____

Then came General Ewell's order to assume the offensive and assail the crest of Culp's Hill, on our right. . . . The works to be stormed ran almost at right angles to those we occupied. Moreover, there was a double line of entrenchments, one above the other, and each filled with troops. In moving to the attack we were exposed to enfilading fire from the woods on our left flank, besides the double line of fire which we had to face in front, and a battery of artillery posted on a hill to our left rear opened upon us at short range. . . .

—*"A Confederate Account of the Battle of Gettysburg"*

7. _____

8. _____

from **Mary Chesnut's Civil War** by Mary Chesnut
"Recollections of a Private" by Warren Lee Goss
"A Confederate Account of the Battle of Gettysburg" by Randolph McKim
Vocabulary Builder

Using the Word List

adjourned	brigade	convention	entrenchments	fluctuation
intercepted	obstinate	offensive	recruits	spectator

DIRECTIONS: *Rewrite each sentence below, replacing the italicized word or phrase with an appropriate word from the Word List.*

1. The *newly drafted soldiers* did not know how to march.

   _____

2. The enemy *seized* a letter that was being sent to headquarters.

   _____

3. The officers failed to make a decision, so they *closed for a time* the meeting.

   _____

4. The soldiers stayed in *long deep holes with steep sides* in order to avoid being shot.

   _____

5. The *unit of soldiers* prepared for battle.

   _____

6. The general was *stubborn* and wouldn't give up the fight.

   _____

7. A *person watching who wasn't involved in the fight* stood on the distant hill.

   _____

8. Citizens held a *meeting* to talk about ways they could help the wounded.

   _____

9. The battle showed a marked *change in intensity* throughout the day.

   _____

10. The commander told the officers to plan a *position of attack*.

   _____

Name _____ Date _____

from Mary Chesnut's Civil War by Mary Chesnut
"Recollections of a Private" by Warren Lee Goss
"A Confederate Account of the Battle of Gettysburg" by Randolph McKim
Selection Test

MULTIPLE CHOICE

Critical Reading *Identify the letter of the choice that best completes the statement or answers the question.*

____ 1. What kind of primary document is *Mary Chesnut's Civil War*?
   A. newspaper account
   B. diary
   C. journal
   D. letters

____ 2. In *Mary Chesnut's Civil War*, Mary Chesnut's husband
   A. participates in negotiations with the commander of Fort Sumter.
   B. is commander of Fort Sumter.
   C. is commander of the forces attacking Fort Sumter.
   D. is a reporter covering the conflict over Fort Sumter.

____ 3. In the excerpt from *Mary Chesnut's Civil War*, Mary Chesnut hosts numerous merry, witty dinners. Why do the guests enjoy themselves so much when war seems to be so near?
   A. They are sure their side will win.
   B. They think war and battle are exciting.
   C. They are not personally involved.
   D. They are convinced there will not be a war.

____ 4. Which of the following passages from *Mary Chesnut's Civil War* is an opinion?
   A. "My husband has been made an aide-de-camp of General Beauregard."
   B. "Now he tells me the attack upon Fort Sumter may begin tonight."
   C. "Lincoln or Seward have made such silly advances. . . ."
   D. "Today Miles and Manning, colonels now . . . dine with us."

____ 5. The final words of journal entry in "Recollections of a Private" are "on to Washington!" What do these words mean?
   A. The recruits can go home.
   B. The recruits are assigned to General George Washington.
   C. The recruits are ready to join in the war.
   D. The recruits have been ordered to Washington for more training.

____ **6.** In "Recollections of a Private," Goss says he stood before the recruiting office
and reread the recruiting advertisement. He says, "I thought I might have made
a mistake in considering war so serious after all." What he means is that the
advertisement made the war sound like

    A. a boring job.

    B. an unrewarding experience.

    C. a deadly business.

    D. a good opportunity.

____ **7.** What do you learn from Goss's journal, "Recollections of a Private," that you
would not usually learn from a history book's account of the Civil War?

    A. how a soldier feels as events happen

    B. the time and date of events

    C. the military strategy for each side in the conflict

    D. the names of important figures in the events

____ **8.** What is the result of the attack described in the entry "A Confederate Account
of the Battle of Gettysburg"?

    A. After a loss of many lives, the Confederate soldiers retreated.

    B. The Confederate soldiers surrendered.

    C. After a loss of many lives, the Union soldiers retreated.

    D. The Union soldiers surrendered.

____ **9.** Based on the excerpt from "A Confederate Account of the Battle of Gettysburg,"
McKim's brigade lost the skirmish because the

    A. soldiers were poorly equipped.

    B. soldiers lacked the courage to finish the charge.

    C. opposing army was much larger.

    D. attack was poorly planned.

____ **10.** Which word best describes the picture of war painted by Randolph McKim in "A
Confederate Account of the Battle of Gettysburg"?

    A. honorable

    B. exciting

    C. dreadful

    D. necessary

Vocabulary Warm-up Word Lists

Study these words from the selections. Then, complete the activities.

Word List A

bugler [BYOO gler] *n.* person who plays a bugle or trumpet
The <u>bugler</u> played "Taps" slowly and beautifully, and the entire crowd was moved.

comrades [KAHM radz] *n.* members of the same group; friends
Because we all want the same freedoms in life, we should consider ourselves <u>comrades</u>.

infantry [IN fuhn tree] *n.* branch of an army trained to fight on foot
Troops in the <u>infantry</u> can't move as quickly as sailors or air force personnel.

lieutenant [loo TEN uhnt] *n.* a rank of a commissioned military officer
After serving as a <u>lieutenant</u> for two years, Steve was promoted to the rank of captain.

reverberated [ri VER buh ray ted] *v.* echoed repeatedly; sounded over and over
The sound of the sirens <u>reverberated</u> through the air.

spectators [SPEK tayt erz] *n.* onlookers; witnesses; observers
When the game went into overtime, the <u>spectators</u> became very excited.

stragglers [STRAG lerz] *n.* those who have strayed or fallen behind
Every marathon has a few <u>stragglers</u> who are happy just to finish the race.

sympathetically [sym puh THET ik uhl ee] *adv.* in a manner showing feeling and care
To show us that he understood, Larry nodded his head <u>sympathetically</u>.

Word List B

aggregation [ag ruh GAY shuhn] *n.* cluster; group of individuals or objects
The art dealer is interested in Betsy's <u>aggregation</u> of antique vases.

appropriated [uh PROH pree ayt ed] *v.* took possession of
Before our exam, Professor Wright <u>appropriated</u> all the students' textbooks.

astoundingly [uh STOWN ding lee] *adv.* very surprisingly; astonishingly
Oscar is <u>astoundingly</u> tall for a boy his age.

berating [bi RAYT ing] *v.* scolding severely
We could hear the father <u>berating</u> his son for breaking the rules.

catastrophe [kuh TAS truh fee] *n.* complete failure; disaster
No one showed up, so the surprise party was a <u>catastrophe</u>.

endowed [en DOWD] *v.* equipped with; provided with
We were lucky because our team was <u>endowed</u> with new helmets and ice-hockey sticks.

interminable [in TER mi nuh buhl] *adj.* stretching so far or lasting so long as to seem endless
The line moved so slowly that the wait seemed <u>interminable</u>.

singular [SIN gyoo ler] *adj.* unusual; remarkable
The critic was positive, asserting that Gladys gave a <u>singular</u> performance last night.

Name _____ Date _____

"An Episode of War" by Stephen Crane
Vocabulary Warm-up Exercises

Exercise A *Fill in each blank below using the appropriate word from Word List A.*

Kyle was an exceptionally talented student and very popular among his

[1] _____. His grades were excellent, and he had impressive athletic abil-

ity, especially in football and baseball. Kyle was also the best [2] _____ in

the high school band. Everyone paused to listen as his melodies

[3] _____ across the field. Kyle thought actively about his future and

often talked about his ideas with his grandfather, who listened [4] _____.

Kyle didn't want to be counted among the [5] _____ in getting started

with a career. His philosophy was that you had to be a doer in life and not sit back in

the ranks of [6] _____, passively looking on. His grandfather had been in

the [7] _____ during the Vietnam War and had become a commissioned

officer with the rank of [8] _____. Impressed by how much the military

had helped his grandfather, Kyle thought that military service might give him focus.

Exercise B *Revise each sentence so that the underlined vocabulary word is used in a logical way. Be sure to keep the vocabulary word in your revision.*

Example: Because the task was so <u>fatiguing</u>, we didn't feel any need to rest.
Because the task was so <u>fatiguing</u>, we had to stop often for a rest.

1. On the beach, we saw an <u>aggregation</u> of one or two seagulls.

   _____

2. Ollie <u>appropriated</u> Mike's bicycle, allowing Mike to ride it for the rest of the day.

   _____

3. We were not surprised at the <u>astoundingly</u> large number of concertgoers.

   _____

4. <u>Berating</u> me soundly, Dad warmly praised my report card.

   _____

5. The game was a <u>catastrophe</u> for our football team, which won by a score of 35-0.

   _____

6. That school was very well <u>endowed</u>, with barely adequate facilities for athletics.

   _____

7. The time passed so quickly that the play seemed <u>interminable</u>.

   _____

8. The art exhibit was <u>singular</u>, resembling lots of other shows that had been held before.

   _____

Name _____ Date _____

"An Episode of War" by Stephen Crane
Reading Warm-up A

Read the following passage. Then, complete the activities.

Almost everyone knows "Taps," the haunting melody played by a military <u>bugler</u> at military and memorial services. This tune has twenty-four solemn notes, one for each hour of the day, and all the notes are part of a single chord.

"Taps" had its beginnings in Europe. It is a revision of a French bugle tune played in the evening. A <u>lieutenant</u> or another officer in charge of a regiment in the <u>infantry</u>—soldiers on foot—would order the tune played to notify everyone it was time to return to their barracks. "Taps" thus functioned as a kind of curfew call. It warned late <u>stragglers</u>, still wandering around, that they had only a short time to return to base. Troops who were roaming at liberty needed to report to their officers, or they would be disciplined.

The tune spread to the United States. One evening during the Civil War, General Daniel Butterfield, a Union officer, fondly recalled hearing the French tune. Butterfield made a request to his soldiers, asking them to play "Taps" each evening at sundown instead of a bugle call named "Extinguish the Lights." The tune soon spread to the Confederate army. It was even played while mourners listened <u>sympathetically</u>, in caring remembrance, at the funeral of Confederate General Stonewall Jackson.

These days, "Taps" no longer symbolizes a curfew call. Instead, it functions as a solemn farewell. When its twenty-four notes ring out at a state occasion, mellow and true, they often bring tears to the eyes of the <u>spectators</u> in attendance. They remember those from their group, fallen <u>comrades,</u> and think of other times when these same notes have <u>reverberated</u> through the air, echoing solemnly.

1. Underline the words in this sentence that give a clue to the meaning of <u>bugler</u>. Use the word *bugler* in an original sentence.

2. Circle the words in this sentence that give a clue to the meaning of <u>lieutenant</u>. Use *lieutenant* in a sentence of your own.

3. Circle the phrase that means nearly the same as <u>infantry</u>. In an army, where does the *infantry* fight: on land, at sea, or in the air?

4. Underline the words in this sentence that give a clue to the meaning of <u>stragglers</u>. Where would the *stragglers* be among the runners in a marathon?

5. Circle the word that gives a clue to the meaning of <u>sympathetically</u>. Name a noun, verb, and adjective related to *sympathetically*.

6. Underline the words that give a clue to the meaning of <u>spectators</u>. What is a synonym for *spectators*?

7. Underline the words in this sentence that mean nearly the same as <u>comrades</u>. Use *comrades* in a sentence of your own.

8. Circle the words that tell what <u>reverberated</u>. Name something that you have heard *reverberate*.

"An Episode of War" by Stephen Crane
Reading Warm-up B

Read the following passage. Then, complete the activities.

When Mason McClane played his first concert in high school, he was still a shy kid whose face could hardly be seen behind his long hair. The audience was an <u>aggregation</u> of high school students and local music fans, none of them expecting too much from a timid singer of acoustic ballads. Mason had no money for equipment, so he had <u>appropriated</u> a microphone and P.A. from his high school's theater department.

It took Mason almost five minutes to tune his guitar, and soon a group of boys started shouting criticisms, <u>berating</u> him for taking so much time. He appeared disastrously nervous, unable to begin singing, and everyone in the crowd expected a <u>catastrophe</u>. Then he began, strumming three simple chords, but with such vigor that the strings seemed in danger of breaking. He closed his eyes and then opened them, turning to the audience with an <u>astoundingly</u> fierce and surprisingly confident expression, as if he had turned into another person.

It turned out that Mason was <u>endowed</u> with a powerful voice that provided warmth and clarity to his songs. His folk ballads were fascinating stories about people that everyone in the audience could understand. There were songs about parents and children, work and politics. They were sophisticated, especially for a teenager, but Mason used simple, everyday language in his lyrics. No one had ever heard anything like his songs—they were utterly <u>singular</u>. When he stopped singing, people sat in stunned silence before they burst into applause, which lasted so long that it seemed <u>interminable</u>. Mason had been an outcast before the concert, but now he had instantly become a kind of star in the school. Achieving that kind of attention made him uncomfortable. Such is the price of stardom!

1. Underline the words in this sentence that give a clue to the meaning of the word <u>aggregation</u>. What is a synonym for *aggregation*?

2. Circle the phrase in this sentence that gives a clue to the meaning of <u>appropriated</u>. Use *appropriated* in an original sentence.

3. Underline the words in this sentence that give a clue to the meaning of <u>berating</u>. What is the opposite of *berating*?

4. Circle the word that gives a clue to the meaning of <u>catastrophe</u>. Why might a hurricane be considered a *catastrophe*?

5. Circle the word in this sentence that means nearly the same as <u>astoundingly</u>. What is an antonym for *astoundingly*?

6. Circle the words in this sentence that tell what Mason was <u>endowed</u> with. Use *endowed* in an original sentence.

7. Underline the phrase in this sentence that gives a clue to the meaning of <u>singular</u>. What are two synonyms for *singular*?

8. What lasted so long that it seemed <u>interminable</u>? Tell something that has seemed *interminable* to you.

Name _____ Date _____

"**An Episode of War**" by Stephen Crane
Literary Analysis: Realism and Naturalism

Realism is a type of literature that tries to show people and their lives as realistically as possible. Authors who write material within this literary movement focus on ordinary people rather than on exaggerated models of idealistic behavior. Often such writers emphasize the harsh realities of ordinary daily life, even though their characters are fictional.

Naturalism expands on the base begun by realism. Writers who create naturalistic literature follow the traits of realism, but they add the ideas that people and their lives are often deeply affected by natural forces such as heredity, environment, or even chance. People cannot control such forces, yet they must carry on the best way they can.

The main difference between the two movements is that naturalism emphasizes the lack of control its realistic characters have over the changes taking place in their lives. The influence of both literary movements can often be seen in the same piece of literature, such as "An Episode of War" by Stephen Crane.

DIRECTIONS: *Read the following passages from "An Episode of War." Tell whether you think each one reflects realism, naturalism, or both. Explain your answer.*

1. He was on the verge of a great triumph in mathematics, and the corporals were thronging forward, each to reap a little square [of coffee], when suddenly the lieutenant cried out and looked quickly at a man near him as if he suspected it was a case of personal assault. The others cried out also when they saw blood upon the lieutenant's sleeve.

   Realism, Naturalism, or both: _____

   Explain: _____

   _____

   _____

2. When he reached home, his sisters, his mother, his wife, sobbed for a long time at the sight of the flat sleeve. "Oh, well," he said, standing shamefaced amid these tears. "I don't suppose it matters so much as all that."

   Realism, Naturalism, or both: _____

   Explain: _____

   _____

Name _____ Date _____

"**An Episode of War**" by Stephen Crane
Reading Strategy: Clarify Historical Details

Your knowledge of the historical time period of a selection can help you make the most of a reading experience. Consider the historical, social, and political climate surrounding a piece of writing as part of its setting and context. For example, in "An Episode of War," the author writes, "His lips pursed as he drew with his sword various crevices in the heap. . . ." The detail about the sword helps you realize that the story did not happen recently—it happened in a time when swords were weapons of war.

Pay careful attention to **historical details** that make the story more vivid and meaningful.

DIRECTIONS: *Record some of your historical knowledge about the following issues during the American Civil War. Then write how the details affect your reading of the selections.*

Issues	Historical Knowledge	Effect on Reading
1. War tactics		
2. Medicine		
3. Communication		
4. Transportation		

"An Episode of War" by Stephen Crane
Vocabulary Builder

Using the Root -greg-

A. DIRECTIONS: *The word root -greg- means "herd or flock." On the line, write a word from the list that is suggested by the bracketed word or phrase.*

aggregation   congregation   egregious   gregarious

1. Marc is so [sociable] _____ that he always has a crowd of friends around him.

2. His mistake was so [conspiciously bad] _____, Eli asked if he could begin his audition again.

3. Lourdes' family has belonged to the same [church group] _____ for generations.

4. The students at Hoffman School are a(n) [collection] _____ of the city's diverse population.

Using the Word List

commotion   disdainfully   precipitate   sinister

B. DIRECTIONS: *On the line, write the letter of the word or phrase that has the same meaning as the word in CAPITAL letters.*

____ 1. COMMOTION:
    A. bustle   B. action   C. delivery   D. restriction

____ 2. PRECIPITATE:
    A. prevent   B. dissuade   C. cause   D. expect

____ 3. DISDAINFULLY:
    A. loudly   B. contemptuously   C. gladly   D. beautifully

____ 4. SINISTER:
    A. joyful   B. puzzling   C. righteous   D. threatening

C. DIRECTIONS: *Write the letter of the word or phrase that best completes each sentence.*

1. Laurel looked upon her brother disdainfully when he _____.
    A. spilled syrup on her skirt   C. helped her fix her car
    B. won the race   D. gave her the CD she'd wanted

2. Amelie was afraid that her grandmother's pneumonia might precipitate her _____.
    A. recovery   B. cough   C. death   D. lungs

3. The moving van was stuffed with an _____ of furniture, tools, and automobile parts.
    A. extravaganza   B. aggregation   C. imbalance   D. offload

Name _____ Date _____

"An Episode of War" by Stephen Crane
Support for Writing

Use the chart to gather details for your **response to criticism.** List your responses to "An Episode of War" in the left column. In the right column, list quotations, incidents, examples, and other details that develop and support each response.

Main Idea	Quotations, examples, other details

On a separate page, write a draft of your **response to criticism,** using the details you have collected in the chart. When you revise your work, make sure you have supported each main idea with details. Recheck quotations to ensure that you have quoted the words accurately and enclosed them in quotation marks.

"An Episode of War" by Stephen Crane
Enrichment: Photography

The Words a Picture Speaks

DIRECTIONS: *Look at the Civil War photographs of wounded soldiers that accompany "An Episode of War." Fill in the following chart with quotations that you think fit the photographs.*

Photograph	Quotation
1.	
2.	
3.	

4. Stephen Crane thought that "a wound gives strange dignity to him who bears it." How do these photographs support that idea? Or don't they? Explain your reasoning.

_____

_____

_____

_____

_____

_____

_____

_____

Name _____ Date _____

"**An Episode of War**" by Stephen Crane
Open-Book Test

Short Answer *Write your responses to the questions in this section on the lines provided.*

1. Naturalism was a literary movement that sought to portray realistic details of ordinary people's lives. How do the first two paragraphs of "An Episode of War" establish a naturalistic feeling for this story?

   _____

   _____

   _____

   _____

2. In "An Episode of War," how does Crane's account of the lieutenant's wound underscore the naturalistic style of the story?

   _____

   _____

   _____

   _____

3. The details of a story can provide important clues about its historical setting. What detail of the opening paragraphs of "An Episode of War" most clearly provides a clue that the story takes place more than a hundred years ago?

   _____

   _____

   _____

4. In "An Episode of War," Crane seldom directly reveals the lieutenant's thoughts or feelings. Why do you think Crane adopted this strategy in writing the story?

   _____

   _____

   _____

   _____

5. In "An Episode of War," as the lieutenant drifts toward the field hospital, he seems detached from all the furious activities of the battle that swirl around him. What key element of naturalism is emphasized by the wounded lieutenant's distance from these activities of war?

   _____

   _____

   _____

   _____

6. Naturalism is a literary movement that suggests that ordinary people's lives are governed by forces outside their understanding and control. Use the chart below to provide three details from "An Episode of War" that illustrate this philosophy. In each case, explain how the detail exemplifies this outlook. Then, on the lines below, state whether you think the lieutenant is in control of his own fate in this story, and briefly explain your answer.

Details from the Story	How Detail Exemplifies Philosophy of Naturalism
Detail 1:	
Detail 2:	
Detail 3:	

_____

_____

7. In "An Episode of War," Crane's describes the field hospital as a scene of commotion and chaos. What does this description suggest about the fate that lies ahead for the lieutenant when he undergoes treatment there?

_____

_____

_____

8. In "An Episode of War," Crane chose not to describe the amputation procedure. Why do you think he made this choice?

_____

_____

_____

9. What is the primary method of transportation in "An Episode of War," and what does this method tell the reader about the historical context of the story?

_____

_____

_____

10. If someone commented disdainfully on your new sweater, would that comment be a favorable or unfavorable one? Base your answer on the definition of *disdainfully* as it is used in "An Episode of War."

_____

_____

Essay

Write an extended response to the question of your choice or to the question or questions your teacher assigns you.

11. After the officer is wounded in "An Episode of War," several comments are made that refer to his condition. In an essay, choose some of those comments, and discuss their meaning and how these comments made the lieutenant feel.

12. Reread the first two pages of "An Episode of War." What do these pages imply about the relationship between the lieutenant and his men? In a few paragraphs, discuss how they feel about one another. Use details from the story to support your opinion.

13. "An Episode of War" can be read as a commentary on the Civil War in particular or war in general. What kind of comment do you think Crane is making about war in this story? Explain your answer in an essay supported by examples from the story.

14. **Thinking About the Essential Question: How does literature shape or reflect society?** Crane reveals the stark emotional realities of war without adding ideas of glory and honor. Should fiction writers inspire readers to reconsider their own preconceptions? Discuss this question in an essay, using examples from "An Episode of War" to support your answer.

Oral Response

15. Go back to questions 3, 4, or 6 or to the question your teacher assigns you. Take a few minutes to expand your answer and prepare an oral response. Find additional details in "An Episode of War" that support your points. If necessary, make notes to guide your oral response.

Name _____ Date _____

"An Episode of War" by Stephen Crane
Selection Test A

Critical Reading *Identify the letter of the choice that best answers the question.*

____ 1. What is the setting of "An Episode of War," based on the use of horses?
   A. the First World War
   B. the Second World War
   C. the Vietnam War
   D. the Civil War

____ 2. In "An Episode of War," which element shows that soldiers become friends during wartime?
   A. how the lieutenant makes coffee
   B. how the men treat the wounded lieutenant
   C. how the doctors talk to the soldiers
   D. how the hospital is set up

____ 3. Which element of "An Episode of War" helps identify the historical setting of the story?
   A. the division of men into military ranks
   B. the fear of the lieutenant over his wound
   C. the grief of the lieutenant's family
   D. the use of swords as a weapon of war

____ 4. Which of these statements describes why "An Episode of War" is a naturalistic story?
   A. The events take place outdoors.
   B. The characters cannot control events.
   C. The events romanticize war.
   D. The characters act as symbols for ideas.

____ 5. In "An Episode of War," which historical description helps you predict what will happen to the lieutenant's arm?
   A. the description of the camp layout
   B. the description of the medical facilities
   C. the description of the battle
   D. the description of the cavalry

____ 6. Which element of "An Episode of War" shows it to be an example of naturalism?
   A. It is set in the Civil War.
   B. It shows lives controlled by outside forces.
   C. It shows people who control their lives.
   D. It uses formal language.

____ 7. Why does the lieutenant stare at the wood after he has been wounded?
   A. The enemy that shot him is hiding in the wood.
   B. The wood make him think of home.
   C. He knows he will be safe if he can reach the wood.
   D. The hospital is located in the wood.

____ 8. How does the doctor's attitude toward the lieutenant change when he notices that the lieutenant is wounded?
   A. He becomes more considerate.
   B. He becomes respectful.
   C. He becomes disdainful.
   D. He becomes professional.

____ 9. What serves as a hospital in "An Episode of War"?
   A. an old horse barn
   B. a group of ambulances
   C. an old schoolhouse
   D. a former jailhouse

____ 10. In "An Episode of War," what happens before the lieutenant is reunited with his family?
   A. He has been wounded several more times.
   B. He has deserted the army and made his way home.
   C. He has lost his wounded arm through amputation.
   D. He has refused to let the doctor treat his wounded arm.

Vocabulary

____ 11. In which sentence is the meaning of the word *disdainfully* suggested?
   A. The men looked upon their wounded lieutenant with shock.
   B. A surgeon speaks scornfully about the lieutenant's wound.
   C. Some men helpfully showed the lieutenant to the hospital.
   D. The lieutenant was embarrassed at his family's grief.

___ **12.** When the narrator speaks of something that may "precipitate the tragedy," he means that it may _____.

    A. cause the tragedy

    B. prevent the tragedy

    C. overshadow the tragedy

    D. counteract the tragedy

Essay

13. Naturalism is a literary movement that suggests that what happens to people is out of their control. Write a brief essay to show how "An Episode of War" illustrates naturalism. Use examples from the story to support your ideas.

14. Thinking About the Essential Question: How does literature shape or reflect society? Crane paints an unadorned picture of war in "An Episode of War." He shows its brutality and human cost; he doesn't make it seem glorious or romantic. Is it the job of fiction writers to challenge readers to see things as they are rather than disguised by some romantic viewpoint? Discuss this question in an essay, using examples from "An Episode of War" to support your answer.

"**An Episode of War**" by Stephen Crane
Selection Test B

Critical Reading *Identify the letter of the choice that best completes the statement or answers the question.*

____ 1. "An Episode of War" is the story of
   A. a young soldier named Willie.
   B. how a lieutenant lost his arm.
   C. the Battle at Gettysburg.
   D. the conflict between a soldier and a doctor.

____ 2. Which statement best explains why "An Episode of War" may be viewed as a naturalistic story?
   A. It takes place outdoors.
   B. In this tale an ordinary man's life is shaped by a force he cannot control, but he endures this life-changing event with strength and dignity.
   C. It shows the harsh realities of everyday life rather than an optimistic view of the world.
   D. It shows the sentimental side of war.

____ 3. In "An Episode of War," Crane seldom directly reveals the lieutenant's thoughts or feelings. He may have chosen to do this to show
   A. that a good soldier has no feelings.
   B. how fascinated the lieutenant has become with the war.
   C. that the lieutenant likes to observe events around him.
   D. how his injury has stunned or shocked the lieutenant.

____ 4. Why does the lieutenant seem so surprised when he notices he is bleeding?
   A. There was no fighting going on.
   B. He thought the war was over.
   C. His men were protecting him.
   D. He was not part of a battle.

____ 5. The fact that the lieutenant can now "see many things which as a participant in the fight were unknown to him" helps emphasize that
   A. war is a waste of human life
   B. his injury has changed his role in the war and his perspective on the world
   C. wounded men are often treated as "non-people."
   D. the complex machinery of war is an "aggregation of wheels, levers, and motors."

____ 6. As you read "An Episode of War," thinking about the grave injuries inflicted during the Civil War makes you
   A. better able to envision the setting.
   B. more likely to think the lieutenant is going to have complications with his wound.
   C. better able to laugh at the humorous parts.
   D. more likely to notice details about the lieutenant's wife, mother, and sisters.

____ 7. By describing a battery of men engaged in battle as an "aggregation of wheels, levers, motors," with "a beautiful unity," what does Crane emphasize about the wounded lieutenant?
A. He is alone.
B. He is an outsider now who has no place in the machinery of war.
C. He has become more observant.
D. He is witnessing something noble and patriotic.

____ 8. If you make predictions about the fate of the lieutenant's arm in "An Episode of War," you must
A. believe that the story will end happily.
B. recognize the story's witty tone.
C. consider the medical situation in its historical context.
D. assume the doctor is telling the truth.

____ 9. In "An Episode of War," details such as the rubber blanket, neat squares of coffee, breast-work, puffs of white smoke in the woods, and even an ashen-looking man smoking a corncob pipe all serve to heighten the _____ of the story.
A. naturalism
B. sentimentalism
C. romanticism
D. realism

____ 10. Which element of "An Episode of War" reveals the influence of *naturalism* in this story?
A. the calm, peaceful day and the leisurely and ordinary activity of dividing the coffee
B. the lieutenant's inability to sheath his sword
C. the kindness of the soldier who bandages the lieutenant's wounded arm
D. the large crowd of wounded, bandaged men that surrounded the hospital tents

____ 11. In "An Episode of War," why do you suppose Crane chose not to depict the amputation procedure?
A. It was too gruesome.
B. He couldn't find out what such an experience was like.
C. He didn't want to shock his readers.
D. He wanted to focus the story on the lieutenant's changing perspective on life.

____ 12. To better understand the lieutenant's battlefield experiences in "An Episode of War," you must consider your knowledge of
A. the 1990 Persian Gulf War.
B. the terrible conditions facing injured Civil War soldiers.
C. the lieutenant's military training.
D. the lieutenant's relationship with his soldiers.

Vocabulary

___ 13. "An Episode of War" focuses on a wounded _____, rather than on an *aggregation* of wounded soldiers.
- A. individual
- B. platoon
- C. congregation
- D. army

___ 14. The lieutenant looks *disdainfully,* or _____, toward the woods.
- A. scornfully
- B. harshly
- C. sympathetically
- D. considerately

___ 15. The men hesitate to help their wounded lieutenant because they fear even a slight touch might *precipitate,* or _____ , the tragedy.
- A. remove any doubt about
- B. involve them all in
- C. make real
- D. cause to happen sooner than necessary

___ 16. Which of these is the most *sinister?*
- A. a kind fairy godmother
- B. an evil villain
- C. a brave hero
- D. a boring storyteller

Essay

17. How does "An Episode of War" move readers to identify with the main characters? Answer the question in a short essay supported with examples from the text.

18. "An Episode of War" is characteristic of two literary movements that were popular at the time Crane was writing: Realism and Naturalism. In an essay, define Realism as a literary movement. Then, use details from "An Episode of War" to show the ways in which the story can be seen as a product of this movement.

19. **Essential Question: How does literature shape or reflect society?** Crane reveals the stark emotional realities of war without adding ideas of glory and honor. Should fiction writers inspire readers to reconsider their own preconceptions? Discuss this question in an essay, using examples from "An Episode of War" to support your answer.

Vocabulary Warm-up Word Lists

Study these words from the selection. Then, complete the activities.

Word List A

apt [APT] *adj.* capable; quick to learn or understand
An <u>apt</u> student will usually do well on exams.

congenial [kuhn JEE nee uhl] *adj.* agreeable
Sue is <u>congenial</u>, so it is very easy to get along with her.

consternation [kahn ster NAY shuhn] *n.* shock or fear causing bewilderment
When Gary saw how steeply the mountain descends, he was struck with <u>consternation</u>.

domestic [doh MES tik] *adj.* typical of home life
I enjoy <u>domestic</u> activities, such as cooking, gardening, and knitting.

incompatible [in kuhm PAT uh buhl] *adj.* incapable of blending with one another
They were <u>incompatible</u> roommates because their interests were so different.

overthrow [oh ver THROH] *v.* to overturn or throw over
The angry crowd at the rock concert threatened to <u>overthrow</u> the stage.

variable [VER ree uh buhl] *adj.* likely to change or vary
The interest Janice earns from her savings account is <u>variable</u>, so she can't depend on it.

victorious [vik TOR ee uhs] *adj.* winning a contest or struggle
The <u>victorious</u> team celebrated their win in the championship game.

Word List B

chafed [CHAYFD] *v.* wore away; annoyed
The tight dress <u>chafed</u> Nancy's skin, and she felt extremely uncomfortable.

consenting [kuhn SENT ing] *adj.* agreeing
<u>Consenting</u> to drive us into town, Lori went to fetch her car keys.

depravity [dee PRAV it ee] *n.* corruption; wickedness
The violence and <u>depravity</u> depicted in the movie caused people to stay away.

destitute [DES ti toot] *adj.* utterly lacking; very poor
These <u>destitute</u> orphans live in appalling conditions.

mirth [MERTH] *n.* gladness; amusement; merriment
The audience's <u>mirth</u> rewarded the actors' efforts at comedy.

opposition [op uh ZISH uhn] *n.* resistance
Despite <u>opposition</u> from his boss, Fred went ahead and ordered more office supplies.

prudence [PROOD uhns] *n.* caution; careful management
A wise and cautious person exhibits <u>prudence</u> at all times.

riveted [RIV uh tid] *v.* fastened; fixed firmly
The movie was intriguing, and Jack was <u>riveted</u> to the screen.

from **My Bondage and My Freedom** by Frederick Douglass
Vocabulary Warm-up Exercises

Exercise A *Fill in each blank in the paragraph below with the appropriate word from Word List A. Use each word only one.*

Twelve-year-old Kelsey badly wanted a dog. She had set her sights on a golden retriever puppy she'd seen in a pet store window. To her [1] _____, though, her parents thought a large dog would be [2] _____ with their crowded living conditions in a small apartment. Kelsey, though, who sometimes felt lonely, thought a dog would be a[n] [3] _____ companion. She didn't want to provoke a(n) [4] _____ crisis, and she wondered how to convince her parents that she would be a(n) [5] _____ pet owner. Finally, she had the idea of drawing up a formal contract. She included all the promises she would make, such as walking the dog, supervising its food and water, and grooming it. She had to persuade her parents that her attention to the dog would be constant, rather than [6] _____. When her parents saw the contract, they knew it was time to [7] _____ their misgivings. The whole family signed the agreement, and Kelsey was [8] _____ in her campaign.

Exercise B *Revise each sentence so that the underlined vocabulary word is logical. Be sure to keep the vocabulary word in your revision.*

Example: The horror movie's plot included scenes of depravity and wickedness, so it earned a "G" rating.
> *The horror movie's plot included scenes of* <u>*depravity*</u> *and wickedness, so only adults went to see it.*

1. The T-shirt label <u>chafed</u> the back of my neck and made my skin feel comfortable.

_____

2. <u>Consenting</u> to our proposal, Rose denied us permission to begin the plan's first phase.

_____

3. Ken was so <u>destitute</u> that he had to make do with a large suburban house and two cars.

_____

4. When she heard that comment, Yolanda expressed her <u>mirth</u> with a stern frown.

_____

Name _____ Date _____

from **My Bondage and My Freedom** by Frederick Douglass
Reading Warm-up A

Read the following passage. Pay special attention to the underlined words. Then, read it again, and complete the activities. Use a separate sheet of paper for your written answers.

One afternoon, Debbie discovered her new foster brother, Nate, struggling to read a comic book that he'd found in a chest. Since his arrival at their house the week before, Nate's shyness had kept them from talking very much. When Debbie came into the room, Nate looked up at her and tried to hide the comic book in consternation, as if she might be angry. Everything about domestic life—the family meals, the after-dinner TV sessions—made him anxious.

"Don't get upset," said Debbie in a congenial voice, trying to make friends. "Why don't you show me what you're reading?"

Unfortunately, it turned out that Nate didn't know how to read; he was simply looking at the pictures. This startled Debbie, because at the age of nine, Nate was surely old enough to know how to read. The fact that he couldn't seemed incompatible with the intelligence she could see in his eyes.

Although Debbie had never taught anyone how to read, Nate wanted so desperately to learn that she couldn't refuse. She taught him the alphabet, how to sound out words, and how to guess a word's meaning from the other words surrounding it in the sentence. At first, his success was variable—sometimes he understood, sometimes he didn't. However, he turned out to be an apt student, eventually grasping everything she explained to him. They worked their way gradually through the comic book, and Nate improved immensely. The comic book concerned a gang of villains who tried to overthrow the government and rule the country. Debbie found the story tedious, but Nate's progress fascinated her. When he got to the end—the moment when the superhero defeats the villains—Nate turned to her with a victorious smile, having conquered his first book.

1. Underline the words in this sentence that give a clue to the meaning of consternation. Use this word in a sentence.

2. Circle the words in this sentence that hint at the meaning of domestic.

3. Underline the words in this sentence that give a clue to the meaning of congenial. Write two words meaning the opposite of *congenial.*

4. Underline the words in this and the previous sentence that hint at the meaning of incompatible. What is an antonym for *incompatible*?

5. Circle the words that offer a clue to the meaning of variable. What is a synonym for *variable*?

6. Underline the words that hint at the meaning of apt. Write two antonyms of *apt*.

7. Circle the words that hint at the meaning of overthrow. What is a synonym for this word?

8. Underline the word in this sentence that hints at the meaning of victorious. What are two synonyms for *victorious*?

from **My Bondage and My Freedom** by Frederick Doulass
Reading Warm-up B

Read the following passage. Pay special attention to the underlined words. Then, read it again, and complete the activities. Use a separate sheet of paper for your written answers.

Frederick Douglass once predicted that, if an African American were allowed to serve in the U.S. Army, "there is no power on earth which can deny that he has earned the right to citizenship in the United States."

During the first year of the Civil War, many people supported military service by African Americans in the Union army. There was some underline{opposition} to the idea, however. Such a plan underline{chafed} against the preconceived notions of some white soldiers and officers, who believed that African Americans lacked the courage to fight well. Some critics of the plan reacted with disbelief, even with amusement or underline{mirth}, at what they considered a ridiculous risk for the army to take.

In July 1862, Congress passed two acts underline{consenting} to the enlistment of African Americans. Official underline{prudence} prevailed, however, and actual enrollment of black soldiers was cautiously delayed until the issuance of the Emancipation Proclamation in September. Frederick Douglass's two sons, in fact, were among the first to serve in the Union forces. Both free Americans and runaways from the moral underline{depravity} of slavery joined the fight.

It was soon clear that the critics were drastically mistaken. Far from being underline{destitute} of courage and skill, black regiments underline{riveted} the attention of all Americans with their heroic deeds. At engagements in Missouri, Louisiana, and the Indian Territory (now Oklahoma), African American soldiers distinguished themselves for courage and fighting ability. General James Blunt said of them, "I never saw such fighting . . . they make better soldiers in every respect than any troops I have ever had under my command."

In all, some 180,000 African Americans served in the Union army during the Civil War. Of these, about 38,000 gave their lives for the cause of freedom.

1. Underline the words in this and the previous sentence that hint at the meaning of opposition. What is a synonym for *opposition*?

2. Circle the words in this sentence that hint at the meaning of the word chafed. What is a synonym for this word?

3. Underline the word that hints at the meaning of mirth. Use *mirth* in a sentence.

4. Underline the words that hint at the meaning of consenting. What is an antonym for *consenting*?

5. Circle the words that hint at the meaning of prudence. Use *prudence* in a sentence.

6. Circle the words that are clues to the meaning of depravity. What is a synonym for *depravity*?

7. Underline the words that hint at the meaning of destitute. Write an antonym of *destitute*.

8. Underline the words that hint at the meaning of riveted. What is a synonym for *riveted*?

from **My Bondage and My Freedom** by Frederick Douglass
Literary Analysis: Autobiography and Tone

In his autobiography, Frederick Douglass provides his readers with a unique view of what it was like to be a slave. Douglass could have chosen to write a fictional work instead of an autobiography, but his purpose was to give readers a sense of the brutality of slavery, a goal that he could best convey through the power of real experiences. Notice how the tone of Douglass's autobiography complements his purpose and makes the experiences even more powerful.

DIRECTIONS: *Read the following passages from the selection. Describe the effect of each passage and tell how Douglass's tone and use of autobiography strengthens that effect.*

It was no easy matter to induce her to think and to feel that the curly-headed boy, . . . who was loved by little Tommy, and who loved little Tommy in turn; sustained to her only the relation of a chattel. I was *more* than that, and she felt me to be more than that. I could talk and sing; I could laugh and weep; I could reason and remember; I could love and hate.

_____

_____

_____

I was no longer the light-hearted, gleesome boy, full of mirth and play, as when I landed first at Baltimore. Knowledge had come . . . This knowledge opened my eyes to the horrible pit, and revealed the teeth of the frightful dragon that was ready to pounce upon me, but it opened no way for my escape.

_____

_____

_____

It was slavery—not its mere *incidents*—that I hated. I had been cheated. I saw through the attempt to keep me in ignorance . . . The feeding and clothing me well, could not atone for taking my liberty from me. The smiles of my mistress could not remove the deep sorrow that dwelt in my young bosom. Indeed, these, in time, came only to deepen my sorrow. She had changed; and the reader will see that I had changed, too. We were both victims to the same overshadowing evil—*she* as mistress, *I* as slave.

_____

_____

_____

_____

Name _____ Date _____

from **My Bondage and My Freedom** by Frederick Douglass
Reading Strategy: Establish a Purpose

Establishing a purpose for reading gives you an idea to focus on as you read. In reading the excerpt from *My Bondage and My Freedom*, one possible purpose is to evaluate the ethical influences of the period that shaped the characters and events of this period. As you read the selection, use this chart to record your conclusions.

Incident or character's behavior	Ethical influence of period

Name _____ Date _____

from **My Bondage and My Freedom** by Frederick Douglass
Vocabulary Builder

Using the Root *-bene-*

A. DIRECTIONS: *The root -bene- means "well" or "good" and is part of many words relating to goodness. Complete each sentence with one of these words:* beneficent, beneficial, beneficiary, benign.

1. As a _____, my mother received some money and jewelry after her aunt's death.

2. The petitioners were fortunate to have a judge with a _____ temperament.

3. Her work with the sick in Calcutta made Mother Teresa one of the most _____ people of our time.

4. The labor reforms of the nineteenth century were _____ to factory workers struggling for better working conditions.

Using the Word List

benevolent   consternation   deficient   fervent   intolerable   opposition

B. DIRECTIONS: *Match each word in the left column with its definition in the right column. Write the letter of the definition on the line next to the word it defines.*

___ 1. benevolent   A. passionate; zealous
___ 2. opposition   B. unbearable; unendurable
___ 3. consternation   C. kindly; charitable
___ 4. fervent   D. dismay; alarm
___ 5. intolerable   E. lacking; incomplete
___ 6. deficient   F. hostility; objection

Name _____ Date _____

from **My Bondage and My Freedom** by Frederick Douglass

Support for Writing

As you prepare to write a **college admission essay,** think about one experience that has shaped your life, just as Douglass describes how knowledge led to his freedom. Think about events that have made a difference in how you think or act today. Use the graphic organizer below to collect your information.

An Experience That Has Shaped My Life

My Experience (title): _____

_____

What happened first—How I felt or what kind of action I took	What happened next—How I felt or what kind of action I took	What happened finally—How I felt or what kind of action I took

On a separate page, write a first draft of the experience that helped shaped who you are today. Put your events in chronological order. When you revise your work, be sure to make it clear to readers how this experience affected you.

Name _____ Date _____

from My Bondage and My Freedom by Frederick Douglass
Enrichment: Career as a Teacher

Teacher Training

Frederick Douglass wrote about both teaching and learning in his autobiography. In addition to teaching basic skills, successful teachers motivate students and inspire them to learn.

DIRECTIONS *Find passages in which Frederick Douglass describes the process and the excitement of learning to read. Identify each passage and make a note of the lesson you think a teacher could learn from it. In particular, describe how a teacher could use Douglass's experiences to teach and encourage others to read.*

Lessons for Teachers From Frederick Douglass	
Passage	**Lesson**
1.	
2.	
3.	

from **My Bondage and My Freedom** by Frederick Douglass
Open-Book Test

Short Answer *Write your responses to the questions in this section on the lines provided.*

1. In *My Bondage and My Freedom*, which clues immediately tell the reader that he or she is reading both an autobiography and the story of a person who had been enslaved? Reread the first paragraph, and cite examples that provide this information.

   _____

   _____

   _____

2. In *My Bondage and My Freedom*, Douglass states, "Nature has done almost nothing to prepare men and women to be either slaves or slaveholders." Briefly summarize the attitude toward slavery that the reader can infer from this remark.

   _____

   _____

   _____

3. In *My Bondage and My Freedom*, Douglass writes that, when he was growing up, he "was more than that [a slave]." Is Douglass's self-assessment accurate? Briefly explain why or why not.

   _____

   _____

   _____

   _____

4. If a reader of *My Bondage and My Freedom* was mostly interested in finding out more about the Aulds, he or she would probably have what main purpose in reading the selection?

   _____

   _____

   _____

5. If your purpose in reading *My Bondage and My Freedom* is to understand slavery's effect on people, what conclusion would you draw from Mrs. Auld's opposition to Douglass's learning to read?

   _____

   _____

   _____

6. In the course of *My Bondage and My Freedom*, Douglass recount's Mrs. Auld's evolution from a kindhearted Christian to a typically stern slaveholder. Briefly explain this change in Mrs. Auld's behavior, citing examples from the text.

_____

_____

_____

_____

7. In the middle section of *My Bondage and My Freedom*, Douglass recounts how he learned to read on the sly from young white boys of his age. What does this part of Douglass's autobiography say about race relations during that era?

_____

_____

_____

8. In *My Bondage and My Freedom*, Mr. Auld was especially firm in his opposition to teaching Douglass how to read. Why do you think Mr. Auld believed it was so dangerous to teach a slave to read?

_____

_____

_____

9. If the king of a country was benevolent toward his subjects, would he be likely to treat them kindly or cruelly? Base your answer on the meaning of *benevolent* as it is used in *My Bondage and My Freedom*.

_____

_____

_____

10. In *My Bondage and My Freedom*, Douglas describes Mrs. Auld's behavior during both his early childhood and his later childhood. Use the following chart to offer several details that contrast Mrs. Auld's early and later behavior toward Douglass.

Mrs. Auld's Early Behavior	Mrs. Auld's Later Behavior

Essay

Write an extended response to the question of your choice or to the question or questions your teacher assigns you.

11. *My Bondage and My Freedom* shows how Douglass grew as a human being from learning how to read. It also shows how he learned to cherish the ideas he encountered in books. Does this selection make an effective case for the value of education for all people? Why or why not? Explain your views in a brief essay supported by examples from the selection.

12. In *My Bondage and My Freedom*, Douglass argues that slavery runs counter to the natural instincts and tendencies of human nature: "Nature has done almost nothing to prepare men and women to be either slaves or slaveholders." Do you agree with Douglass? Why or why not? Explain your opinion in an essay supported by details from the selection.

13. The radical shift in Mrs. Auld's behavior toward him is a central concern of Douglass's in *My Bondage and My Freedom*. He writes:

    Conscience cannot stand much violence. Once thoroughly broken down, who is he that can repair the damage? . . . It must stand entire, or it does not stand at all.

    Do you agree with Douglass's explanation for Mrs. Auld's change from kind, maternal figure to harsh slaveholder? Why or why not? Develop your views in an essay supported by examples from the selection.

14. **Thinking About the Essential Question: How does literature shape or reflect society?** Douglass used his brilliance as a writer and orator to champion the causes of freedom and equality in *My Bondage and My Freedom* as well as in his other work. His career embodied the idea that the pen can be mightier than the sword. What quality do you think plays a role in writing that makes a difference? Is it skill, personality, passion, truth, or some combination of these? Discuss your answer in an essay, using examples from the story to support your opinions.

Oral Response

15. Go back to questions 1, 4, or 6 or to the question your teacher assigns you. Take a few minutes to expand your answer and prepare an oral response. Find additional details in *My Bondage and My Freedom* to support your points. If necessary, make notes to guide your oral response.

Name _____ Date _____

from **My Bondage and My Freedom** by Frederick Douglass
Selection Test A

Critical Reading *Identify the letter of the choice that best answers the question.*

____ 1. What does Douglass like most about Baltimore life in *My Bondage and My Freedom*?
   A. changes in the weather
   B. learning to read and write
   C. playing with the boys in the street
   D. working for Mr. and Mrs. Auld

____ 2. Based on *My Bondage and My Freedom*, which statements express Douglass's beliefs?
   I.   People should be trained to be both slaves and slaveowners.
   II. Slavery can be endured as long as the slaveowner is kind.
   III. Slavery destroys both the slave and the slaveowners.
   IV. Slavery makes enemies out of people who should be friends.
   A. I, II, III
   B. II, III, IV
   C. III, IV
   D. I, II, IV

____ 3. What made *My Bondage and My Freedom* an important work in 1855, a few years before the Civil War?
   A. It led the North eventually to declare war on the South.
   B. It presented a scathing portrait of a slaveowning family.
   C. It was one of few books written from a former slave's viewpoint.
   D. It revealed the forbidden practice of teaching slaves to read.

____ 4. What common attitudes did *My Bondage and My Freedom* challenge?
   I.   Slaves were incapable of reading and writing.
   II. Slaves were not the equal of their whites.
   III. Slaves wished to escape their enslavement.
   IV. Slaves were comfortable with their position in life.
   A. I, II, III
   B. I, II, IV
   C. I, III, IV
   D. II, III, IV

____ 5. If your purpose for reading is to understand slavery's effect on people, what conclusion can you draw about Mrs. Auld's opposition to Douglass's learning to read in *My Bondage and My Freedom*?

A. Mrs. Auld should have fought to resist slavery.

B. Mrs. Auld did not possess a strong conscience.

C. Mrs. Auld's conscience was destroyed by slavery.

D. Mrs. Auld should have fed and clothed more slaves.

____ 6. Given what Douglass endures as a slave, what element of *My Bondage and My Freedom* surprises you?

A. He trades reading lessons for biscuits.

B. He feels real affection for Mrs. Auld.

C. His learning makes him unhappier.

D. The Aulds try to keep him ignorant.

____ 7. In *My Bondage and My Freedom*, what does Douglass suggest will probably happen to the white boys in the future, when they are older and dealing with "the cares of life"?

A. They will one day help him escape from his slaveowners.

B. They will likely accept slavery when they become adults.

C. They will grow up to be abolitionists and resist slavery.

D. They will be overwhelmed by business concerns.

____ 8. If your purpose in reading *My Bondage and My Freedom* was to find out how a former slave wrote world-famous books, which question might you ask before reading?

A. How did Douglass escape slavery?

B. How did Douglass end up in Baltimore?

C. How did Douglass learn to write?

D. How did Douglass meet Mrs. Auld?

____ 9. What is Douglass's final judgment of Mrs. Auld in *My Bondage and My Freedom*?

A. She should not have taught him to read.

B. She should have helped him to escape.

C. She was not well-suited to slavery.

D. She could not run a household well.

___ **10.** What is an important message in *My Bondage and My Freedom*?
   A. Slaveowners and slaves should be friends.
   B. The wish for freedom can be rooted out of one's soul.
   C. Slaves have a generally good life in Baltimore.
   D. A kind owner cannot relieve the injustice of slavery.

Vocabulary

___ **11.** At first, Douglass says, his mistress acted in a *benevolent* manner. He means that she acted _____ toward him.
   A. indifferently
   B. selfishly
   C. kindly
   D. brutally

___ **12.** When Mrs. Auld caught Douglass reading, she would sometimes rush at him in *consternation*, or _____, and grab it from him.
   A. elation
   B. fear
   C. confusion
   D. anger

Essay

13. How do you think you might have handled the changes Douglass discusses in *My Bondage and My Freedom*? In a brief essay, offer a response that describes how you might have reacted to events if you had been in Douglass's position.

14. How does *My Bondage and My Freedom* make a case for the education of all people? How does it relate to education in today's world? In a brief essay, describe why you think education is important. Use examples from Douglass's writing to support your viewpoint.

15. Essential Question: How does literature shape or reflect society? Douglass supported the causes of freedom and equality in *My Bondage and My Freedom*. During his career he regularly used his writing to support causes he believed in. Do you think writers can make a real difference when they support causes? How and why? Discuss your answer in an essay, using examples from the story to support your opinions.

from My Bondage and My Freedom by Frederick Douglass
Selection Test B

Critical Reading *Identify the letter of the choice that best completes the statement or answers the question.*

_____ 1. Which of the following statements best expresses Douglass's attitude toward slavery?
   A. Under the care of a decent master, slavery can be a tolerable situation.
   B. What makes slavery evil is how comfortable it becomes.
   C. Slavery is only possible for children to endure.
   D. Slavery goes against the nature of both slaves and slaveholders.

_____ 2. One of the most successful strategies Douglass used for learning to read was
   A. having Mrs. Auld teach him.
   B. memorizing books read by Mrs. Auld.
   C. buying books from Mr. Knight on Thames street.
   D. getting his young white playmates to teach him in exchange for biscuits.

_____ 3. In what way are Douglass's efforts to educate himself paradoxical?
   A. The more he learns, the more unhappy he becomes.
   B. Even as he accumulates more facts, he is more uncertain of his principles.
   C. The faster he reads, the more books he enjoys.
   D. Forbidden to read as a child, he grows up to be an important writer.

_____ 4. *My Bondage and My Freedom* reveals that in the South of its time slaves and women were both
   A. enemies of slavery.
   B. against Christian teaching.
   C. emotional rather than reasonable.
   D. subject to white male authority.

_____ 5. What additional information would be most appropriate to Douglass's autobiography?
   A. Mrs. Auld's feelings about her husband
   B. a description of Douglass's views about Baltimore during the 1830s
   C. the bookseller's rationale for allowing Douglass to purchase a schoolbook
   D. what Mrs. Auld would have done if she had known of Douglass's unhappiness

_____ 6. If your reading purpose is to learn from a slave about his life, what overall conclusion can you draw about Frederick Douglass from this excerpt?

   My feelings were not the result of any marked cruelty in the treatment I received; they sprung from the consideration of my being a slave at all. It was *slavery*—not its mere *incidents*—that I hated.

   A. Douglass was not treated badly by his owners.
   B. Douglass did not object to the day-to-day aspects of his life as a slave.
   C. Douglass thought slavery often inspired slaveholders to commit acts of cruelty.
   D. Douglass was a proud man who believed himself entitled to freedom.

____ 7. What does Douglass mean by saying "Conscience cannot stand much violence"?
  A. Conscience and violence often work together.
  B. Most people have no conscience.
  C. Compromise one belief and the conscience is easily broken down.
  D. Anyone with a strong conscience hates violence.

____ 8. What is the most important message of *My Bondage and My Freedom*?
  A. Slavery harms both master and slave.
  B. A little learning is a dangerous thing.
  C. Human nature cannot be changed.
  D. Knowledge makes slaves better workers.

____ 9. Why is it helpful to set a purpose for reading?
  A. It helps you understand concepts such as slavery.
  B. You can debate the author's purpose for writing.
  C. It helps you focus on ideas and information as you read.
  D. You can learn about the writer's personal experiences and attitudes.

____ 10. What might you have learned had this account been written by Master Hugh?
  A. Douglass's thoughts and feelings about Mrs. Auld
  B. why Master Hugh believed that educating slaves was a bad thing to do
  C. how Douglass learned to read and write
  D. what caused Mrs. Auld to realize that she should stop trying to educate Douglass

____ 11. How do you know that Douglass is writing about his childhood from the point of view of an adult?
  A. He cannot imagine any view other than his own.
  B. He uses a very simple vocabulary.
  C. He idealizes his memories of his childhood with the Aulds.
  D. He interprets his childhood experiences with an adult's insight.

____ 12. Which of the following details would help you achieve your reading purpose of understanding slavery from a slave's point of view?
  A. Mrs. Auld often gave bread to the hungry.
  B. Little Tommy loved Mrs. Auld.
  C. Frederick had to sneak reading lessons from his white friends.
  D. Frederick's friends studied from the *Columbian Orator.*

Vocabulary

____ 13. The word most nearly opposite in meaning to *consternation* is _____.
  A. thoughtfulness
  C. fear
  B. confidence
  D. despair

____ 14. At first, Mrs. Auld was *deficient,* or _____, in the skills and attitude necessary to be a brutal slave owner.
  A. lacking
  B. highly skilled
  C. practiced
  D. experienced

_____ 15. The word that is most nearly the same in meaning as *fervent* is _____.
A. useful
B. quick
C. indifferent
D. eager

_____ 16. Because she was so _____ when he first arrived there, Douglass says that Mrs. Auld was a model of affection and tenderness.
A. intolerable
B. benevolent
C. fervent
D. deficient

Essay

17. Mrs. Auld's character changed dramatically after her husband persuaded her not to teach young Frederick to read and write. Write a comparison-contrast essay in which you describe the character of Mrs. Auld before and after this turning point. Use incidents and examples from the text to show the changes in her.

18. Douglass says that

> Nature has done almost nothing to prepare men and women to be either slaves or slave-holders. Nothing but rigid training, long persisted in, can perfect the character of the one or the other. One cannot easily forget to love freedom; and it is as hard to cease to respect that natural love in our fellow creatures.

Write an essay in which you argue for or against this statement. Use examples from Douglass's autobiography to support your position.

19. To explain Mrs. Auld's change in behavior toward him, Douglass says,

> Conscience cannot stand much violence. Once thoroughly broken down, who is he that can repair the damage? . . . It must stand entire, or it does not stand at all.

Write an essay in which you support this explanation for Mrs. Auld's behavior or present an alternative explanation.

20. **Essential Question: How does literature shape or reflect society?** Douglass used his brilliance as a writer and orator to champion the causes of freedom and equality in *My Bondage and My Freedom* as well as in his other work. His career embodied the idea that the pen can be mightier than the sword. What quality do you think plays a role in writing that makes a difference? Is it skill, personality, passion, truth, or some combination of these? Discuss your answer in an essay, using examples from the story to support your opinions.

Spirituals
Vocabulary Warm-up Word Lists

Study these words from the selections. Then, complete the activities.

Word List A

band [BAND] *n.* group
   In Charles Dickens's famous novel, Oliver Twist was forced to join a <u>band</u> of pickpockets.

banned [BAND] *v.* forbidden; outlawed
   In many restaurants and other public places, smoking has now been <u>banned</u>.

captivity [cap TIV uh tee] *n.* state of being imprisoned, enslaved, or held captive
   Some slaves wrote interesting narratives describing their <u>captivity</u>.

deprived [dee PRYVD] *v.* kept from having
   When the plants were <u>deprived</u> of water, they wilted.

fugitives [FYOO ji tivz] *n.* runaways; exiles
   The police successfully hunted down those <u>fugitives</u> from justice.

legal [LEE guhl] *adj.* lawful
   Driving under the age of sixteen is not <u>legal</u> in this state.

rebellions [ree BEL yuhnz] *n.* uprisings; revolts
   Several <u>rebellions</u> against the king's rule signaled that his subjects were not happy.

spiritual [SPIR i choo uhl] *n.* folk song that originated among enslaved African Americans
   "Swing Low, Sweet Chariot" is a famous <u>spiritual</u> that is still often sung.

Word List B

activists [AK tiv ists] *n.* energetic workers for a cause
   Thousands of <u>activists</u> took part in the civil rights movement, fighting for social justice.

chariot [CHAR ee uht] *n.* ornamental wagon-like carriage, usually drawn by horses
   In the parade, the ancient Roman general rode at the head of his troops in a splendid <u>chariot</u>.

enacted [en AK tid] *v.* passed or put into effect
   The legislature <u>enacted</u> a new law to restrict smoking in public places.

eventually [ee VEN choo uhl ee] *adv.* after the passage of some time
   With practice, Sam <u>eventually</u> will become fluent in Spanish.

network [NET werk] *n.* group of connected or linked members
   That news service has an extensive <u>network</u> of reporters spread across several continents.

oppressed [oh PRESD] *v.* treated harshly; put down
   <u>Oppressed</u> by his misfortunes, Josh was in a constantly sullen, disagreeable mood.

pharaoh [FAR oh] *n.* supreme ruler in ancient Egypt
   Tutankhamen ruled as <u>pharaoh</u> in ancient Egypt in the late fourteenth century B.C.

smite [SMYT] *v.* to strike forcefully; to hit hard
   Muscular and strong, the blacksmith prepared to <u>smite</u> the anvil with a gigantic hammer.

Name _____ Date _____

Spirituals
Vocabulary Warm-up Exercises

Exercise A *Fill in each blank in the paragraph below with the appropriate word from Word List A. Use each word only once.*

Everyone agreed that Althea had one of the most beautiful singing voices. Every time she sang gospel music or a(n) [1] _____, her listeners were on the verge of tears. She was able to put such feeling in her music because she visualized the scenes behind the words. As she sang "Go Down, Moses," for example, Althea could see a(n) [2] _____ of [3] _____, released at last from [4] _____ in ancient Egypt. They had suffered so much, just like enslaved African Americans in later times, when the [5] _____ authorities [6] _____ rights for them or put down their [7] _____. Althea experienced the slaves' anguish when masters [8] _____ them of their chance to learn to read and write. Such were the feelings that lay behind Althea's passionate singing.

Exercise B *Decide whether each statement below is true or false. Circle T or F, and explain your answer.*

1. <u>Activists</u> are generally reluctant to get involved in political issues or social causes.
   T / F _____

2. In ancient times, a horse-drawn <u>chariot</u> was a luxurious form of transportation.
   T / F _____

3. If a state legislature has <u>enacted</u> a law, it has considered the measure and rejected it.
   T / F _____

4. Events that occur <u>eventually</u> are separated from the present by a significant time span.
   T / F _____

5. A <u>network</u> of broadcasting stations is linked in an association.
   T / F _____

6. When people are <u>oppressed</u>, they feel generally happy and content.
   T / F _____

7. The ruler of modern Egypt is called the <u>pharaoh</u>.
   T / F _____

8. When you <u>smite</u> an object, you give it a gentle nudge.
   T / F _____

Name _____ Date _____

Spirituals
Reading Warm-up A

Read the following passage. Pay special attention to the underlined words. Then, read it again, and complete the activities. Use a separate sheet of paper for your written answers.

For two years, Mary had been making songs with a drum machine, two turntables, and a computer. Her friends were excited when she played a new piece that included a sample of a man's voice. When asked where she had gotten it, she explained that it was from an old spiritual, a song sung by African American slaves.

She decided to put together a songbook of the old spirituals, along with their history. It amazed her that such beautiful music had been made by people who had had so many rights taken away from them; they had been cruelly deprived of education or training. Held in captivity like hostages without freedom, they managed to rise above their situation through music. At a time when slaves had no rights, their songs were like little rebellions against the system that enchained them. Any song that spoke out too strongly against slavery would have been banned; no one could have sung about forbidden topics for fear of punishment. However, the singers found a way to talk about slavery by using Bible stories. It was perfectly legal and lawful to sing about the Israelites who were slaves in Egypt. In this way, slaves disguised their dangerous but empowering messages within spirituals.

Mary's songbook included many spirituals that deserved to be remembered. Her favorite one remained the first song she had sampled on her computer. It told the story of a band of escaped slaves—a group making their way north to freedom. Although Mary had never been a slave, she understood how it felt to be trapped, unhappy, and forced to do things she didn't want to do. When she listened to the song, she could imagine herself as one of the fugitives, running from the law, heading toward a better life.

1. Circle the word in this sentence that means nearly the same as spiritual. Use the word *spiritual* in an original sentence.

2. Underline the words in this sentence that give a clue to the meaning of deprived. What would happen to a tree that is *deprived* of sunlight?

3. Underline the words that give a clue to the meaning of captivity. What is an antonym for *captivity*?

4. Circle the word that gives a clue to the meaning of rebellions. What is a synonym for *rebellions*?

5. Circle the word in this sentence that means nearly the same as banned. What is the opposite of *banned*?

6. Underline the word in this sentence that means nearly the same as legal. What are two antonyms for *legal*?

7. Circle the word in this sentence that gives a clue to the meaning of band. Use the word *band* in an original sentence.

8. Underline the words in this sentence that give a clue to the meaning of fugitives. Use *fugitives* in a sentence of your own.

Spirituals
Reading Warm-up B

Read the following passage. Pay special attention to the underlined words. Then, read it again, and complete the activities. Use a separate sheet of paper for your written answers.

One of the great movie classics tells the story of Moses. Released in 1956, this film, *The Ten Commandments,* was directed by Cecil B. DeMille and starred Charlton Heston, Yul Brynner, and Anne Baxter. The film had a huge cast and won an Oscar for special effects.

Before he became a prophet, teacher, and leader of the Hebrew people, Moses was brought up as an Egyptian. The Egyptians had <u>enacted</u> a law ordering the death of all newborn Hebrew boys. According to the biblical story, Moses's parents saved their baby by hiding him for three months and then setting him adrift in a reed basket on the river Nile. The child was found by the daughter of the <u>pharaoh</u>, and so Moses was brought up in the ruler's house as a prince at the royal court. He learned martial arts and, like other high-ranking Egyptian nobles, was privileged to ride in his own beautifully decorated <u>chariot</u>.

After some time, Moses <u>eventually</u> discovered his Hebrew origins. Shocked and saddened by the <u>oppressed</u> condition of his people, he gave his support to a <u>network</u> of <u>activists</u>—groups of like-minded Hebrews who were intent on the cause of throwing off the yoke of slavery and escaping from Egypt to freedom.

Moses's beliefs soon led to an open confrontation with the pharaoh. In some of the most dramatic scenes of the film, Moses warns the ruler to let the Hebrew people go. At first, the pharaoh firmly refuses. However, plagues of locusts and serpents <u>smite</u> the Egyptians, hitting hard and causing great suffering. Finally, the pharaoh's own son is stricken and dies. Reluctantly, the ruler allows Moses to lead the Hebrews out of Egypt to the Promised Land.

1. Underline the word in this sentence that gives a clue to the meaning of <u>enacted</u>. Use the word *enacted* in an
1. original sentence.

2. Circle the words in this sentence that give a clue to the meaning of <u>pharaoh</u>. Where and when was the word *pharaoh* a term for "king" or "ruler"?

3. Underline the words that give a clue to the meaning of <u>chariot</u>. Give an example of a modern-day *chariot*.

4. Underline the words that give a clue to the meaning of <u>eventually</u>. What is the opposite of *eventually*?

5. Circle the words in this sentence that give a clue to the meaning of <u>oppressed</u>. What is an antonym for *oppressed*?

6. Underline the words in this sentence that mean nearly the same as <u>network</u>. Use *network* in an original sentence.

7. Underline the words that give a clue to the meaning of <u>activists</u>. What might pollution *activists* support?

8. Circle the words that give a clue to the meaning of <u>smite</u>. Use *smite* in a sentence.

"Swing Low, Sweet Chariot" and "Go Down, Moses" Spirituals
Literary Analysis: Refrain, Allusion, and Allegory

A **refrain** is a word, phrase, line, or group of lines repeated at regular intervals. In spirituals, one of the main things a refrain does is emphasize the most important ideas. In "Go Down, Moses," for example, the refrain "Let my people go" is repeated seven times. The constant repetition serves to turn the cry for freedom into a demand for freedom.

These spirituals also rely upon **biblical allusions,** which are references to people, places, or events in the Bible. The allusion to Moses in "Go Down, Moses" refers to the biblical leader Moses, who led the Israelites out of Egypt.

Both spirituals include allegories. An **allegory** is a story that has two levels of meaning—one literal, the other symbolic. The symbolic meaning of "Swing Low, Sweet Chariot" refers to crossing the Ohio River to freedom for slaves.

DIRECTIONS: *Answering the following questions will help you understand how the use of refrains, biblical allusions, and allegory in "Go Down, Moses" and "Swing Low, Sweet Chariot" function to enrich the spirituals' meanings.*

1. Identify a refrain in "Swing Low, Sweet Chariot." _____
   _____
   _____

2. Identify and explain the allegory in "Go Down, Moses."
   _____
   _____
   _____

3. What is the significance of the allusion to Jordan in "Swing Low, Sweet Chariot"?
   _____
   _____

4. In "Go Down, Moses," what emotional effect does the continual repetition of the refrains have? _____
   _____
   _____

5. Compare the refrains of "Go Down, Moses" and "Swing Low, Sweet Chariot." How are they alike and different? In your answer, consider what the refrains ask for or hope for and how those desires are conveyed in the two spirituals. _____
   _____
   _____
   _____
   _____
   _____

Name _____ Date _____

Reading Strategy: Listen

DIRECTIONS: *Listen carefully to the sounds and rhythms of "Swing Low, Sweet Chariot" and "Go Down, Moses" as the two spirituals are read aloud. Pay particular attention to the rhymes and the sounds or phrases that are repeated. Often rhythm and repetition suggest a certain mood or attitude and contribute to the intensity of feeling generated by the song and its message. Fill in the two charts below to help you focus on your listening skills and identify the message presented in each spiritual.*

"Swing Low, Sweet Chariot"
Words that rhyme
Words or phrases that are repeated
Mood or attitude suggested by rhyme and repetition
Overall message of spiritual

"Go Down, Moses"
Words that rhyme
Words or phrases that are repeated
Mood or attitude suggested by rhyme and repetition
Overall message of spiritual

"Swing Low, Sweet Chariot" and "Go Down, Moses" Spirituals
Vocabulary Builder

Using the Root -press-

A. DIRECTIONS: *The root -press- means "push." In addition to being a complete word itself in English, press is also combined with many different prefixes and suffixes to form other words. Choose one of the words in the box to complete each sentence.*

depression	express	impression	press	pressurize	suppress

1. Barry tried hard to control himself, but he could not _____ his laughter.
2. In order to communicate with others, you must _____ your ideas clearly.
3. It is necessary to _____ an airplane's cabin so people can breathe at higher altitudes.
4. The dry cleaners will _____ the suit so it looks neat.
5. Anyone going on a job interview wants to make a good _____.
6. A person who feels sad all the time may be suffering from _____.

Using the Word List

oppressed   smite

B. DIRECTIONS: *Match each word in the left column with its definition in the right column. Write the letter of the definition on the line next to the word it defines.*

___ 1. oppressed   A. kill with a powerful blow
___ 2. smite   B. kept down by a cruel power or authority

C. DIRECTIONS: *On the line, write the letter of the pair of words that best expresses a relationship similar to that expressed in the pair in CAPITAL LETTERS.*

___ 1. SMITE : SLAP ::
    A. language : French
    B. seek : discover
    C. costume : clothing
    D. happy : miserable
    E. laugh : smile

___ 2. OPPRESSED : FREE ::
    A. myth : legend
    B. waiter : restaurant
    C. temporary : permanent
    D. computer : monitor
    E. scuff : scrape

"Swing Low, Sweet Chariot" and "Go Down, Moses" Spirituals
Support for Writing

Use the chart to gather background details for your **electronic slide presentation.** List the spirituals you will use in your presentation in the left column. In the right column, list three details about each spiritual. Details should focus on the historic context that influenced the writing of the spiritual and where, when, and why it was sung.

Spirituals	Background Notes
	1. _____ 2. _____ 3. _____
	1. _____ 2. _____ 3. _____
	1. _____ 2. _____ 3. _____
	1. _____ 2. _____ 3. _____

On a separate page, write a draft of the introductions you will use in your **electronic slide presentation,** using the background details you have recorded in the chart. When you revise your work, make sure that you have supported each main idea with details.

"**Swing Low, Sweet Chariot**" and "**Go Down, Moses**" Spirituals
Enrichment: Social Studies

The Message in Spirituals

Some spirituals contained disguised messages concerning escape from slavery. Spirituals such as "Follow the Drinking Gourd," for example, advised slaves to follow the north-pointing Big Dipper star constellation. Other verses were altered to give specific directions for slaves to locate Underground Railroad routes. "Go Down, Moses" also has a freedom-related message.

DIRECTIONS: *Answer the series of questions below to help you decode the message of the spiritual "Go Down, Moses."*

1. What is a pharaoh, and what kind of power does a pharaoh have?

   _____

   _____

2. In a southern plantation, who might hold a position similar to that of a pharaoh?

   _____

3. What was the condition of the people of Israel when they were in Egypt?

   _____

4. How was the situation of the slaves in the American South similar to that of the people of Israel?

   _____

5. What demand did Moses make of the pharaoh?

   _____

   _____

6. What demand does "Go Down, Moses" convey, and to whom is the demand directed?

   _____

   _____

Name _____ Date _____

"Swing Low, Sweet Chariot" and "Go Down, Moses"
Open-Book Test

Short Answer *Write your responses to the questions in this section on the lines provided.*

1. Many spirituals had double meanings. They spoke of characters and incidents from the Bible as a way of commenting on current conditions of life. Briefly summarize both the surface meaning and hidden meaning of "Swing Low, Sweet Chariot."

   _____

   _____

   _____

2. Line 7 of "Swing Low, Sweet Chariot" refers to a "band of angels." What does the term "band of angels" imply in this spiritual? Is there just a surface meaning or is there a deeper meaning implied?

   _____

   _____

   _____

3. The repetition of the word *home* in "Swing Low, Sweet Chariot" signals to the reader that this word has special meaning. Think of several possible meanings that the word *home* would have had for the enslaved people who lived on plantations. Use the diagram below to list those meanings.

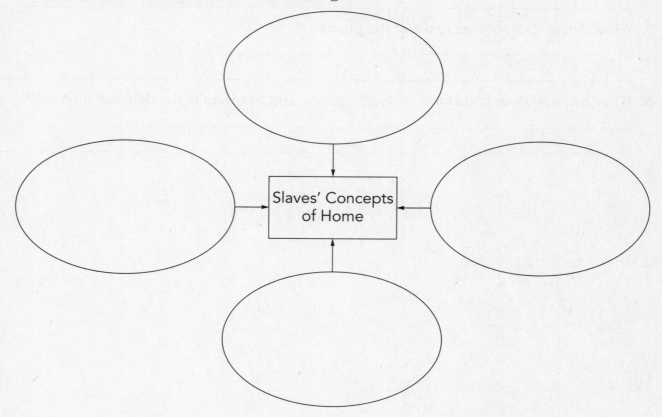

Name _____ Date _____

4. In a spiritual such as "Swing Low, Sweet Chariot," what purpose does the refrain serve for the listener or reader?

_____

_____

5. What mood and feelings are suggested by the rhythm and repetition of key phrases in "Swing Low, Sweet Chariot"?

_____

_____

6. Spirituals often made reference to biblical figures and stories. For enslaved African Americans, why was Moses an especially meaningful figure in "Go Down, Moses"?

_____

_____

7. The phrase "let my people go" is repeated several times in "Go Down, Moses." Why might the creator or creators of this spiritual have wanted to repeat this particular line? Whom might they have been addressing? What effect were they aiming for in the listener?

_____

_____

_____

_____

8. The phrase "Egypt land" is used several times in "Go Down, Moses." What is the likely effect on the listener of the repetition of the phrase "way down in Egypt land"?

_____

_____

_____

9. Spirituals were often disguised pleas for freedom and indirect commentaries on the conditions of the enslaved African Americans of the South. Which line of "Go Down, Moses" most clearly refers to the harsh conditions endured by the slaves on Southern plantations?

_____

_____

10. If a group of people spoke of being oppressed, would they be protesting or celebrating their situation? Base your answer on the meaning of the word *oppressed* as it is used in "Go Down, Moses."

_____

_____

Essay

Write an extended response to the question of your choice or to the question or questions your teacher assigns you.

11. Both "Swing Low, Sweet Chariot" and "Go Down, Moses" make liberal use of repetition. For each spiritual, give examples of repeated words or phrases that seem the most significant. Then, in an essay, explain why they are significant and how they help convey the song's message.

12. In both "Swing Low, Sweet Chariot" and "Go Down, Moses," there are several references to stories and figures from the Bible. In an essay, discuss how religion or God is used in each spiritual, and which one you think uses religion more effectively to get its message across. Support your answer with examples from the spirituals.

13. Spirituals often had different levels of meaning. On the surface, they could seem to be just religious songs. On another level, the slaves might understand them as coded pleas for freedom and/or protests against the injustices of slavery. Select at least two key words or phrases from "Swing Low, Sweet Chariot." In an essay, explain how those words or phrases convey a coded message about freedom or how to get freedom for the enslaved people of the South.

14. **Thinking About the Essential Question: What is the relationship between place and literature?** The "place "of spirituals is often an imagined promised land. Explore the idea of the power of a place in heart and mind, and how it can give hope, comfort, and even escape from a harsh world. Use details from "Swing Low, Sweet Chariot" and/or "Go Down, Moses" to support your essay.

Oral Response

15. Go back to question 2, 4, or 7 or to the question your teacher assigns you. Take a few minutes to expand your answer and prepare an oral response. Find additional details in "Swing Low, Sweet Chariot" and/or "Go Down, Moses" that support your points. If necessary, make notes to guide your oral response.

"Swing Low, Sweet Chariot" and **"Go Down, Moses"** Spirituals
Selection Test A

Critical Reading *Identify the letter of the choice that best answers the question.*

_____ 1. "Swing Low, Sweet Chariot" is a spiritual with a coded meaning related to slaves escaping the South. Given this fact, what is surprising about the mood of the refrain?
A. It is scary and suspenseful.
B. It is lyrical and relaxed.
C. It is demanding and rude.
D. It is fearful and timid.

_____ 2. How does the chariot in "Swing Low, Sweet Chariot" represent an escape from slavery?
A. It is a wagon with very fast horses.
B. It is a wagon driven by slaveowners.
C. It is a chariot sent from heaven.
D. It is part of the Underground Railroad.

_____ 3. In a spiritual such as "Swing Low, Sweet Chariot," what does the refrain establish for the reader?
A. a rhyme scheme
B. the setting of the song
C. the rhythm and mood
D. the singer's identity

_____ 4. In "Swing Low, Sweet Chariot," what emotion is communicated as you listen to the refrain?
A. anger
B. boredom
C. longing
D. fear

_____ 5. In "Swing Low, Sweet Chariot," to whom does the singer refer in the following: "If you get there before I do . . . Tell all my friends I'm coming too"?
A. relatives who have abandoned her
B. slaves who have already escaped
C. blacks who were born in the North
D. whites on the Underground Railroad

_____ 6. As you listen to the three stressed syllables at the beginning of the refrain of "Go down, Moses," what do you hear?
A. a command
B. a question
C. a statement
D. a plea

_____ 7. Which element of "Go down, Moses" is characteristic of many spirituals?
A. references to biblical places
B. references to Moses
C. warnings of punishment
D. demands upon leaders

_____ 8. In "Go down, Moses," what do Pharaoh and the people of Israel stand for?
A. Egypt and Moses
B. the U.S. and Egypt
C. the president and U.S. citizens
D. slaveowners and slaves

_____ 9. Why were spirituals such as "Go down, Moses" a threat to slaveowners?
A. They made fun of slaveowners.
B. They carried coded messages.
C. They called for work strikes.
D. They ignored white culture.

_____ 10. In "Go down, Moses," what effect does repeating "Let my people go" have on the listener?
A. It shows confusion.
B. It shows determination.
C. It shows disgust.
D. It shows secrecy.

Vocabulary

_____ 11. In which sentence is the meaning of the word *oppressed* suggested?
A. The company treated the workers badly.
B. The workers decided to strike.
C. Protesters supported workers' rights.
D. The company raised workers' pay.

____ **12.** Moses said the Lord threatened to *smite*, or _____, your first-born.
   A. starve
   B. bless
   C. strike
   D. enrich

Essay

13. "Swing Low, Sweet Chariot" refers to a chariot "Coming for to carry me home." However, "Go down, Moses" announces: "Tell old Pharaoh," / "Let my people go!" Both refrains express the wish for freedom, but they have different moods. Write a brief essay to compare the two refrains in terms of their mood and message.

14. Spirituals were often coded messages among slaves, as well as being spiritually uplifting. Select at least two of these words or phrases from "Swing Low, Sweet Chariot": *chariot, home, Jordan, band of angels, get there,* and *tell my friends.* Write a brief essay to discuss the messages they contain about freedom or how to get to freedom.

15. Essential Question: What is the relationship between place and literature?
Spirituals often describe a promised land. This is the "place" of spirituals. How does this place provide hope, comfort, and escape? Use details from "Swing Low, Sweet Chariot" and/or "Go Down, Moses" to support your essay.

"Swing Low, Sweet Chariot" and "Go Down, Moses" Spirituals
Selection Test B

Critical Reading *Identify the letter of the choice that best completes the statement or answers the question.*

____ 1. "Swing Low, Sweet Chariot" is about the
    A. importance of community.
    B. need for equality.
    C. desire for freedom.
    D. uncertainty of religious faith.

____ 2. In what literary element of a spiritual will you most likely find its key ideas?
    A. refrain
    B. opening line
    C. solo lyrics
    D. title

____ 3. How does the sound of the repetition of the word *home* in "Swing Low, Sweet Chariot" convey the mood of the spiritual?
    A. It lulls the listener into a sense of contentment.
    B. It reminds the listener that the singer is at home.
    C. It tells the listener of the hominess of plantation life.
    D. It builds on the listener's feelings about home to emphasize the message of longing.

____ 4. In "Swing Low, Sweet Chariot," what is home a metaphor for?
    A. the South
    B. Africa
    C. Heaven
    D. Jordan

____ 5. Which of the following phrases is part of the refrain of "Swing Low, Sweet Chariot"?
    A. "If you get there before I do"
    B. "A band of angels coming after me"
    C. "Tell all my friends I'm coming too"
    D. "Coming for to carry me home"

____ 6. What is the most important function of the refrain in "Swing Low, Sweet Chariot"?
    A. The refrain introduces a biblical context for the spiritual.
    B. The refrain separates the soloist and chorus.
    C. The refrain reinforces the idea of deliverance.
    D. The refrain ends the spiritual on a happy tone.

____ 7. What mood is suggested by listening to the rhythm and repetition of "Swing Low, Sweet Chariot"?
    A. longing, patience, and hope
    B. rebellion
    C. secrecy
    D. fear and resignation

____ **8.** What makes "Go Down, Moses" typical of spirituals?
  A. quotations from Moses
  B. lack of a refrain or chorus
  C. warnings of rebellion
  D. references to biblical figures

____ **9.** Moses is an appropriate figure for a spiritual because he
  A. received the Ten Commandments.
  B. owned slaves in Egypt.
  C. brought plagues to Egypt.
  D. led his people to freedom.

____ **10.** The spiritual is most closely related to which of the following literary traditions?
  A. call-and-response
  B. narrative poetry
  C. autobiography
  D. sermon

____ **11.** Enslaved African Americans experienced which of the following circumstances described in "Go Down, Moses"?
  I. oppression
  II. having lived in Egypt
  III. captivity
  IV. resisting an unjust authority with force
  A. I and II
  B. III and IV
  C. I and III
  D. I and IV

____ **12.** From the point of view of the slaveholder, what made spirituals most dangerous?
  A. They were insulting to white people.
  B. They carried hidden messages.
  C. They rejected organized Christianity.
  D. They kept alive African musical traditions.

____ **13.** How does listening to a repeated phrase such as "Let my people go" in "Go Down, Moses" help convey the spiritual's mood and message?
  A. The repetition dulls listeners' ears to key messages of the spiritual.
  B. The phrase reminds listeners that the slaves' plight is similar to that of the Israelites.
  C. The phrase is a demand and helps convey a mood of determination.
  D. The repetition of such phrases could be decoded to reveal hidden messages.

____ **14.** In a spiritual, the part sung by the chorus seldom changed because the chorus
  A. was an African tradition.
  B. sang the refrain.
  C. played the role of the Lord.
  D. let everyone take part.

Vocabulary

_____ 15. A word or phrase that means about the same as *smite* is
A. hit with a powerful blow
B. reassure
C. strengthen with faith
D. renew

_____ 16. Choose the word that could best substitute for the underlined word in the following line from "Go Down, Moses".

   <u>Oppressed</u> so hard they could not stand.

A. starved
B. rewarded
C. exhausted
D. abused

Essay

17. Which of the two spirituals, "Swing Low, Sweet Chariot" or "Go Down, Moses," do you think would have been considered more "dangerous" by a slave owner who paid careful attention to the words of the spirituals? Use examples from each of the spirituals to support your ideas.

18. "Swing Low, Sweet Chariot" and "Go Down, Moses" are both about the hope for release from hardship. However, the spirituals express very different views in regard to *when* release might come about. In an essay, identify for each spiritual when release is expected and how this affects the overall mood of each spiritual.

19. Make a case for the Moses of "Go Down, Moses" as a symbol for the activities of the abolitionist Harriet Tubman. Use what you have learned about her to interpret the spiritual in this light.

20. **Essential Question: What is the relationship between place and literature?** The "place" of spirituals is often an imagined promised land. Explore the idea of the power of a place in heart and mind, and how it can give hope, comfort, and even escape from a harsh world. Use details from "Swing Low, Sweet Chariot" and/or "Go Down, Moses" to support your essay.

Name _____ Date _____

Unit 3: Division, Reconciliation, and Expansion
Benchmark Test 4

MULTIPLE CHOICE

Literary Analysis and Reading Skills

Read the poem. Then, answer the questions that follow.

Dead Men Tell No Tales

THEY say that dead men tell no tales!

Except of barges with red sails
And sailors mad for nightingales;

Except of jongleurs stretched at ease
Beside old highways through the trees;   5

Except of dying moons that break
The hearts of lads who lie awake;

Except of fortresses in shade,
And heroes crumbled and betrayed.

But dead men tell no tales, they say!   10

Except old tales that burn away
The stifling tapestries of day:

Old tales of life, of love and hate,
Of time and space, and will, and fate.

                    —Haniel Long

1. What kind of rhyme did the poet, Haniel Long, use in this poem?
   A. exact   C. internal
   B. slant   D. blank verse

2. What is the author's main purpose for writing this poem?
   A. to persuade the reader to honor the dead
   B. to entertain with an old tale
   C. to describe a sailor's life
   D. to convey a message about the dead

Answer the following questions.

3. What type of rhyme does the word pair *good* and *food* demonstrate?
   A. exact   C. end
   B. slant   D. internal

Unit 3 Resources: Division, Reconciliation, and Expansion

4. The title of an Emily Dickinson poem, "Much Madness Is Divinest Sense," is a contradiction. This title illustrates which figure of speech?

   A. metaphor   C. allusion

   B. paradox   D. simile

5. Which of the following is true of poetry written in free verse?

   A. The first, second, and fifth lines rhyme.

   B. It is written in unrhymed iambic pentameter.

   C. The first and third lines each have five syllables.

   D. It is not written in a regular pattern of meter or rhyme.

6. What structure is evident in the following wisdom?

> To err is human, to repent divine; to persist devilish
>
> —from *Poor Richard's Almanac* (1742)

   A. parallelism   C. onomatopoeia

   B. restatement   D. analogy

7. What figure of speech is evident in the following line?

> This blessed plot, this earth, this realm, this England . . .
>
> —from *Richard II* by William Shakespeare

   A. hyperbole   C. anaphora

   B. oxymoron   D. consonance

8. Which part of a song or poem is most likely to recur and emphasize a particular idea?

   A. the introduction

   B. the middle verses

   C. the coda

   D. the refrain

9. Arthur Miller's play, *The Crucible*, was written in the early 1950s. It contains a reference to the New Jerusalem, a well-known term for the holy city of heaven. The reference is an example of which of the following?

   A. an anecdote

   B. irony

   C. a biblical allusion

   D. local color

10. Which is always true of an allegory?

   A. It is a story in which literal elements are also symbols for idea and qualities.

   B. It is told in dramatic form through dialogue.

   C. It arises from the oral traditions of peoples around the globe.

   D. It focuses on the writer's involvement in historically significant events.

11. What is the point of view in this sentence?

> While Janis dreamed of nothing more than fame and Marla was obsessed by her looks, Kayley wanted more than anything merely to blend in.

   A. limited first person   C. omniscient first person

   B. limited third person   D. omniscient third person

12. In which point of view is the narrator a participant and not an objective observer?

    A. third person omniscient point of view

    B. limited third person limited point of view

    C. first person point of view

    D. limited second person

13. What does stream-of-consciousness writing try to capture?

    A. the natural flow of characters' thoughts

    B. the natural rhythm of everyday speech

    C. the experiences and outlook of childhood

    D. the social concerns important to the author

Read the passage. Then, answer the question that follows.

    Soon after they left Chicago, the land grew flat as a pancake. The suburbs faded away, and they passed cornfield after cornfield. "We could buy an old farm and move out here," Jonathan told her. "It would be a nice, peaceful place for you to write."

    Deb stared at the passing landscape. She remembered the same flat land from her own childhood in Colorado. Her father had loved ranch life. She remembered how he used to sing as he worked in the fields.

    Yes, this part of Illinois had the same look. Didn't Abe Lincoln grow up around here? Was it here that he had made his long walks to school? She remembered waiting for the school bus back in Colorado. The land was so flat you could see the bus for miles. She turned to Jonathan. "Of course we can live here, darling. It would be a lovely change."

14. Where in the selection does Deb's stream of consciousness start?

    A. at the sentence beginning, "The suburbs faded away. . ."

    B. at the sentence, "Deb stared at the passing landscape."

    C. at the sentence beginning, "She remembered the same flat land. . ."

    D. at the sentence beginning, "She remembered waiting for the school bus. . ."

Read the passage. Then, answer the questions that follow.

    I was born in Tuckahow, near Hillsborough, and about twelve miles from Easton, in Talbot County, Maryland. I have no accurate knowledge of my age, never having seen any authentic record containing it. By far the larger part of the slaves know as little of their ages as horses know of theirs, and it is the wish of most masters within my knowledge to keep their slaves thus ignorant.

    –from *Narrative of the Life of Frederick Douglass: An American Slave, written by Himself*

15. What genre is the selection?

    A. biography   **C.** science fiction

    B. autobiography   **D.** historical fiction

16. Which of the following has the greatest influence on the excerpt from this narrative?

    A. religious beliefs of the time   **C.** ethical issues involving slavery

    B. advances in industry at the time   **D.** the geography of the deep South

Name _____ Date _____

Read the passage. Then, answer the question that follows.

   Grinner toothpaste contains helpful herbal compounds designed to help you say goodbye to tooth decay, breath odor, and unsightly yellow teeth. Use it three or four times a day for a healthy, friend-winning smile. Our competitors may promise the same results that we do, but don't be fooled by their empty promises. Brush with GRINNER and be a WINNER!

17. What is the main purpose of this selection?
    A. to persuade readers to take better care of their teeth
    B. to persuade readers to buy Grinner toothpaste
    C. to persuade readers that herbal compounds are safe and practical
    D. to help readers gain new friends in a safe and practical way

Answer the following questions.

18. Besides religious faith, which of the following is an important theme of spiritual songs?
    A. desire for earthly freedom   C. responsibility to others
    B. importance of culture   D. the value of work

19. Which strategy will best help you understand text that contains elliptical phrasing?
    A. pay special attention to the beginning of each paragraph
    B. say the words aloud
    C. skim the text instead of reading all the words
    D. mentally fill in words that could be missing

Read the passage. Then, answer the questions that follow.

A Letter to John Adams, 1796
   Dear Sir—The public and the public papers have been much occupied lately in placing us in a point of opposition to each other. I trust with confidence that less of it has been felt by ourselves personally. . . I knew it impossible you should lose a vote North of the Delaware, and even if that of Pennsylvania should be against you in the mass, yet that you would get enough South of that to place your succession out of danger. . .

20. How might recognizing historical details help the reader's comprehension of this selection?
    A. The reader might learn personal information about the life of the writer.
    B. The reader might learn outmoded vocabulary.
    C. The reader might learn about the selection's social and political context.
    D. The reader might learn about contemporary ideas and beliefs.

21. Which is the most important factor that will cause you to adjust your reading rate for this passage?
    A. its complexity of style   C. its many interesting details
    B. the length of the passage   D. the letter format

22. Which would you need to know to effectively evaluate the letter?
    A. its purpose
    B. personal information about Jefferson's life
    C. how the letter was received by Adams
    D. how long it took Jefferson to write it

Answer the following questions.

23. Chronological order is associated with which of the following?
    A. space
    B. distance
    C. position
    D. time

24. Why is listening a particularly important skill in appreciating song lyrics and poetry?
    A. They are particularly difficult to understand.
    B. They are intended to be heard.
    C. They are filled with interesting words.
    D. They have various types of rhyme and rhythm.

Vocabulary

25. Based on your knowledge of the root *-greg-*, choose the phrase that is a congregation.
    A. an injured farm animal
    B. a group of children crowding around a painting
    C. a couple taking a stroll around the lake
    D. a man watching a large fire on the mountains

26. Based on your knowledge of the root *-bene-*, choose the word with the same meaning as *beneficial.*
    A. knowledgeable
    B. confident
    C. merciful
    D. advantageous

27. Based on your knowledge of the root *-fin-*, choose the action you would do after the finale of a play.
    A. watch the curtain go up
    B. go to the lobby for the intermission
    C. leave the theater
    D. follow the usher to your seat

28. What is the meaning of the root word that is shared by *dictionary* and *verdict?*
    A. word
    B. order
    C. flow
    D. climb

29. Based on your knowledge of the root *-dict-*, choose the occupation that has the greatest need for clear diction.
    A. an accountant
    B. a radio newscaster
    C. a scientist
    D. a carpenter

Unit 3 Resources: Division, Reconciliation, and Expansion
87

30. What is the meaning of the word *tension* in the following sentence?

The <u>tension</u> of the bow gives speed to the arrow.

A. stretched condition

B. mental or nervous strain

C. electric force

D. device to control the pull on something

31. What is the meaning of the word *descend* in the following sentence?

The countdown before a rocket lift-off consists of numbers that <u>descend</u> from ten to zero.

A. make a sudden attack

B. come down from an earlier to a later time

C. slope downward

D. go from larger to smaller numbers

ESSAY

32. Suppose that you have written a research report that was well received by your teacher and classmates, all of whom want to know more about the subject. You have decided to expand the report by creating a multimedia presentation on the subject. Write a plan for your presentation. Begin with the topic of your report. Then, list at least three media that you intend to use. Briefly explain how each medium will contribute to the report.

33. Think of a time when you changed your mind about something or someone. What was the situation? Why did you change you mind? What did the experience teach you? Write a reflective essay in which you reveal your thoughts about the experience, and explain why the situation had an impact on you.

34. Write a review of a movie or television program you have seen recently. Begin by giving general information, such as the title, the actors, and the director. Then describe the setting and characters and summarize the plot. End your review by giving your opinion about the movie or program. For example, you might evaluate the quality of the writing and/or the actors' performances. Back up your opinion with relevant details.

Name _____ Date _____

Vocabulary in Context

Identify the answer choice that best completes the statement.

1. The rocket curved across the sky in a(n) _____ before exploding.
   A. arc
   B. noose
   C. pendulum
   D. provision

2. The noisy crowd in the street kept me awake with all their _____.
   A. commotion
   B. distinction
   C. qualification
   D. significance

3. The sun outside shone brightly, making the visitor a dark _____ in the doorway.
   A. lieutenant
   B. picket
   C. recruit
   D. silhouette

4. After scrubbing the floor on my knees, I knew I had cleaned it _____ .
   A. accordingly
   B. ceremoniously
   C. delightfully
   D. sufficiently

5. The winner of the contest was asked how it felt to be _____ .
   A. distressed
   B. victorious
   C. violent
   D. wretched

6. No one will believe what you say if you continue to _____ .
   A. compel
   B. exaggerate
   C. persist
   D. render

7. Do good to others is my father's personal _____ .
   A. almanac
   B. dialogue
   C. mirth
   D. philosophy

8. Bala expected his plans to fail because he had a strong sense of _____ .
   A. demonstration
   B. discrimination
   C. foreboding
   D. racism

9. Priti acted like a queen with a(n) _____ manner.
   A. frenzied
   B. imperious
   C. matchless
   D. witty

10. Gretel did not like Hans because she thought his insults were _____ .
    A. calico
    B. offensive
    C. variable
    D. virtuous

11. Before the operation, the doctor made sure to clean her _____ instruments.
    A. almighty
    B. encased
    C. feuding
    D. surgical

12. The award-winning idea came to Frank in a sudden _____ .
    A. astoundingly
    B. revelation
    C. singular
    D. sinister

13. For his speeches against slavery, Frederick Douglass gained fame as a(n) _____ .
    A. Christian
    B. orator
    C. prophet
    D. slaveholder

14. To match the country surroundings, Gabi decorated her house in a _____ style.
    A. grotesque
    B. monotonous
    C. perilous
    D. rustic

15. The attacking enemy troops _____ the fort.
    A. assented
    B. encompassed
    C. excluded
    D. smitten

16. The spy who wanted to enter the base had to sneak past the _____ .
    A. civilian
    B. politician
    C. sentinel
    D. veranda

17. At the funeral, the widow's friends tried to offer her _____ .
    A. emancipation
    B. multitude
    C. solace
    D. valor

18. For safety in the war zone, several trucks traveled together in a _____ .
    A. convoy
    B. dictator
    C. directive
    D. stench

19. Lara is determined to win the prize, so she will _____ for it strongly.
    A. calamity
    B. contend
    C. discontented
    D. strife

20. Manny looks forward to Thanksgiving, and he _____ a delicious feast.
    A. anticipates
    B. attains
    C. leases
    D. strives

Vocabulary Warm-up Word Lists

Study these words from the selections. Then, complete the activities.

Word List A

arrayed [uh RAYD] *v.* arranged as to be ready for use; organized
   Both sides were <u>arrayed</u> against each other, desperately looking for a way out.

conceived [kuhn SEEVD] *v.* thought up; created
   The architect had <u>conceived</u> a wonderful plan for the whole area.

establishment [uh STAB lish muhnt] *n.* the act or condition of being founded or set up
   His <u>establishment</u> here as a doctor has helped the town.

patient [PAY shuhnt] *adj.* able to endure waiting without becoming annoyed or upset
   My dog very <u>patient</u> when I get busy and can't take him for a walk.

prosperity [prahs PER uh tee] *n.* the condition of having good fortune or financial success
   The family is experiencing a happy time of peace and <u>prosperity</u>.

resolve [ri ZAHLV] *v.* make your mind up to; decide
   People often <u>resolve</u> to go on a diet, but it is difficult to follow through.

retard [ri TAHRD] *v.* slow down, delay; hold back
   Placing bread in the refrigerator helps <u>retard</u> the growth of mold.

virtuous [VER choo us] *adj.* leading a good life; obeying rules of right and wrong
   Mr. Green always led a <u>virtuous</u> life.

Word List B

anticipate [an TIS uh payt] *v.* expect; foresee
   People often <u>anticipate</u> stormy weather when they see dark clouds approach.

avert [uh VERT] *v.* to turn away
   Sometimes the dog will <u>avert</u> his eyes from his owner in order to hide his guilt.

contend [kuhn TEND] *v.* to argue or claim that something is true; assert
   Susan continued to <u>contend</u> that she was innocent.

engaged [en GAYJD] *adj.* actively doing something; occupied; busy
   Bob was <u>engaged</u> in building a car for the soapbox derby.

miseries [MIZ er eez] *n.* sufferings; deprivations
   The drought and crop failure caused untold <u>miseries</u>.

perusal [puh ROO zuhl] *n.* a read-through; examination
   She enjoyed spending hours in a bookstore, engaging in the <u>perusal</u> of books and magazines.

restraint [ri STRAYNT] *n.* the act of holding back
   When the family came to America, they were free to live without <u>restraint</u>.

strife [STRYF] *n.* bitter conflict
   The <u>strife</u> between them went on for years.

Name _____ Date _____

"The Gettysburg Address" by Abraham Lincoln
"Letter to His Son" by Robert E. Lee
Vocabulary Warm-up Exercises

Exercise A *Fill in the blanks, using each word from Word List A only once.*

The battle troops were [1] _____ on the field in their colorful uni-
forms. The night before, they had been stopped by enemy troops whose leaders
[2] _____ an unusual plan. As part of their offensive strategy, the enemy
troops had backed the opposition into the wilderness in order to
[3] _____ their mobility. Despite the setback of being poorly situated, the
assembled troops would [4] _____ to win the next round. They planned
on charging the enemy troops for the [5] _____ as victors of the day. Their
[6] _____ leader inspired great courage among the men as he informed
them of the long battle ahead. He explained the priorities and told them they must be
[7] _____. The goal was to achieve victory so that peace and
[8] _____ could be returned to the town that they were defending.

Exercise B *Decide whether each statement is true or false. Circle* T *or* F, *and explain your
answers.*

1. While telling the truth, it is common for people to <u>avert</u> their eyes.
   T / F _____

2. No matter how much we disagreed, he continued to <u>contend</u> that he was right.
   T / F _____

3. To <u>anticipate</u> the arrival of a long, lost friend could be exciting.
   T / F _____

4. Showing <u>restraint</u> is necessary when trying to remain objective about a situation.
   T / F _____

5. If you are deeply <u>engaged</u> in a project, you are easily distracted.
   T / F _____

6. Most people enjoy being engaged in <u>strife</u> with friends and family.
   T / F _____

7. After a careful <u>perusal</u> of the article, she had no idea what it said.
   T / F _____

8. The hurricane inflicted <u>miseries</u> on thousands of people.
   T / F _____

"The Gettysburg Address" by Abraham Lincoln
"Letter to His Son" by Robert E. Lee
Reading Warm-up A

Read the following passage. Then, complete the activities.

The so-called "Rebel Yell" became famous on the battlefields of the Civil War. The now-famous battle cry was <u>conceived</u> for the Southern soldiers, created to <u>retard</u> their stress before a fight. A good yell could totally release their stress, not just slow it down. The reputation of such shouting earned the "Rebel Yell" its <u>establishment</u> in our vocabulary, setting it up for use by future generations.

The yell was often used to scare Northern forces, the Yankees. Often the Rebels would <u>resolve</u> to holler for the duration of their charge, deciding to yell for minutes at a time. Sometimes the Yankees thought that they were outnumbered based solely on the amount of noise coming from their enemy.

The yell was also used a lot when fighting occurred under the cover of trees or the night sky. Out of nowhere, the Northern soldiers would hear the eerie and frightening "Rebel Yell." It was also effective on fields set for large-scale battles. Cannons would be <u>arrayed</u> in long, neat lines in front of troops standing shoulder to shoulder. The generals, whom soldiers admired and thought of as <u>virtuous</u> leaders, were mounted on <u>patient</u> steeds, waiting calmly for the battle. However, the yell could even spook them.

While the "Rebel Yell" became famous during the Civil War, its origins can be traced to an earlier time. Some people believe that the shout was used for hunting. Other research discusses the Southern Appalachian region, where there used to be quite some distance between neighbors. People often climbed the hilltops and shouted in order to talk with one another. Today's greater <u>prosperity</u> and technical advances have changed that. Now, most people can afford to use phones and computers to communicate across distances. They no longer need to yell!

1. What does the use of <u>conceived</u> tell you about the yell? Use *conceived* in a sentence.

2. How might yelling <u>retard</u> a soldier's stress? Give a word with a meaning opposite to that of *retard*.

3. Underline the phrase that provides additional information about the <u>establishment</u> of the term "Rebel Yell" into our vocabulary. Use *establishment* in an original sentence.

4. Underline the words that tell what the Rebels would <u>resolve</u> to do. Name something that people often *resolve* to do.

5. Describe how the cannons were <u>arrayed</u>. Name something in the classroom that is *arrayed* alphabetically.

6. Who thought of the generals as <u>virtuous</u> men? Name a famous American who is considered by many to be *virtuous*, and explain your response.

7. Underline what was <u>patient</u>. Name a time when you had to be *patient*.

8. Why has today's <u>prosperity</u> made it unnecessary to shout a message? Generally, tell why people want *prosperity*.

Name _____   Date _____

"The Gettysburg Address" by Abraham Lincoln
"Letter to His Son" by Robert E. Lee
Reading Warm-up B

Read the following passage. Then, complete the activities.

Once the union fell apart and the <u>miseries</u> of the Civil War began, men became soldiers. They left the security of their homes for the deprivations of makeshift, temporary campsites. Such drastic changes to their lifestyles were in addition to the effects of <u>strife</u> that both Northern and Southern soldiers felt. Despite the hardships from the bitter war, soldiers had no choice but to make themselves and their campsites as comfortable as possible.

Contrary to what some people think, many Civil War soldiers spent weeks, sometimes months, without being <u>engaged</u> in a battle. There are many reports from both sides of the conflict that boredom was a common occurrence. Soldiers were better off if they held back and showed <u>restraint</u> by trying not to worry about what would happen next. Instead, they stopped trying to <u>anticipate</u> when battles would happen and focused more on making the campsite comfortable and livable.

The conditions at these campsites varied depending on many factors, but most were undesirable. Since both sides continued to <u>contend</u> that they were right, these assertions extended the war, and the soldiers were apt to spend a long time in camp. Most soldiers attempted to <u>avert</u> their attention from the bad conditions by focusing on more positive and entertaining aspects of "tenting" with fellow soldiers. Common forms of diversion included playing cards, the <u>perusal</u> of newspapers to read up on the latest events, and simply talking about family and home. These activities were popular on both sides of the Mason-Dixon line. They brought relief to the soldiers when camp conditions were bad. Although they filled their days and nights with things to pass the time, the soldiers found the campsite a far cry from the comfort and security of their homes.

1. Why is the word <u>miseries</u> appropriate to categorize the Civil War experience? Give another word with the same meaning as *miseries*.

2. Why did soldiers on both sides feel the effects of <u>strife</u>? Use *strife* in a sentence.

3. Were the Civil War soldiers <u>engaged</u> in battle at all times? What did they feel during the periods when they were not *engaged* in battle?

4. Underline the words in the sentence that help define <u>restraint</u>. Why is the quality of *restraint* a beneficial one in this situation?

5. Circle what the soldiers should not have tried to <u>anticipate</u>. What is something that you *anticipate* with pleasure?

6. Underline the words that hint at the meaning of <u>contend</u>. Use *contend* in an original sentence.

7. If soldiers were able to <u>avert</u> their attention from bad camp situations, where did they refocus it? Use *avert* in an original sentence.

8. Underline the words that give a clue to the meaning of <u>perusal</u>. Name some other things that might undergo *perusal*.

"The Gettysburg Address" by Abraham Lincoln
"Letter to His Son" by Robert E. Lee
Literary Analysis: Diction

Diction, or word choice, gives the writer's voice its unique quality. The writer's diction reflects the audience and purpose of the work. Consider how Lincoln, in "The Gettysburg Address," chooses words and constructs sentences to reflect the formal, austere occasion at which he spoke and to evoke feelings of dedication and patriotism in his audience. Lee's "Letter to His Son," in contrast, is more conversational, reflecting his familial relationship with his son, the informal occasion of a letter, and his desire to express his anguish over the impending war.

DIRECTIONS: *Read each question, and then circle the letter of the best answer.*

1. What was Lincoln's purpose in speaking at Gettysburg?
   A. to honor the dead and inspire listeners
   B. to display his oratorical powers

2. What was Lee's purpose in writing his letter to his son?
   A. to encourage his son to act with honor and to support the South
   B. to explain his position on the political situation and the actions he would take

3. Which sentence is better suited for a letter?
   A. As an American citizen, I take great pride in my country. . . .
   B. As a citizen of this great country, I take great pride in my nation. . . .

4. Which sentence is better suited for a speech?
   A. People will quickly forget what we have said here.
   B. The world will little note, nor long remember what we say here, . . .

5. Which phrase is better suited for a letter?
   A. Four score and seven years ago . . .
   B. Eighty-seven years ago . . .

6. Which phrase is better suited for a letter?
   A. . . . we are stuck between chaos and war.
   B. . . . we find ourselves entrapped between anarchy and civil war.

7. Which phrase is better suited for a letter?
   A. No one will remember or pay attention to today's speeches, . . .
   B. The world will little note, nor long remember what we say here, . . .

8. Which sentence is better suited for a public speech?
   A. We are met on a great battlefield of that war.
   B. Here we are at this great battlefield.

Name _____   Date _____

Reading Strategy: Use Background Knowledge

Background knowledge may include information about the author, about the characters or subjects of the selection, or about the times and events discussed in the selection. Background knowledge can often include personal experiences of people and experiences similar to those in the selection. You learned that Robert E. Lee believed in the Union but opposed both slavery and secession. In this activity, you will learn more about Robert E. Lee to understand further the personal conflict he felt.

DIRECTIONS: *Read the information below. Then use the facts to explain your understanding of each excerpt from Lee's letter to his son.*

- Lee attended the United States Military Academy at West Point in 1825, graduating in 1829.
- In the late 1840s, Lee served in the Mexican War, where he was recognized for his skill and courage.
- Lee's family was a well-established, important family of Virginia. His father was a cavalry commander in the Revolutionary War and a friend of George Washington. Lee admired the first president and named one of his sons George Washington Custis Lee.
- Lee was an honorable and respected man who displayed kindness and humor, and who did not smoke, drink alcohol, or swear.
- Lee did not believe in slavery. Long before the Civil War broke out, he freed the slaves he had inherited.
- Lee felt that Virginia stood for George Washington's principles. He considered the Civil War as a second "Revolutionary War" for independence.

1. How [Washington's] spirit would be grieved could he see the wreck of his mighty labors!

   _____

   _____

2. I feel the aggression [of acts of the North] and am willing to take every proper step for redress. It is the principle I contend for, not individual or private benefit.

   _____

   _____

3. As an American citizen, I take great pride in my country, her prosperity and institutions, and would defend any state if her rights were invaded.

   _____

   _____

"The Gettysburg Address" by Abraham Lincoln
"Letter to His Son" by Robert E. Lee
Vocabulary Builder

Using the Word List

anarchy   consecrate   hallow   redress

A. DIRECTIONS: *Circle the synonym for the underlined word in each sentence or phrase.*

1. . . . we cannot <u>consecrate</u> (bless, profane)

2. . . . we cannot <u>hallow</u> (honor, haunt)

3. As far as I can judge by the papers, we are between a state of <u>anarchy</u> and civil war. (progress, chaos)

4. I feel the aggression and am willing to take every proper step for <u>redress</u>. (armament, atonement)

B. DIRECTIONS: *For each item, choose the word pair that best expresses a relationship similar to that expressed in the numbered pair. Circle the letter of your choice.*

___ 1. REDRESS : GRIEVANCE ::
A. define : rectify
B. survive : privilege
C. prepare : examination
D. revive : suspension

___ 2. HALLOW : SACRED ::
A. forget : remember
B. defy : injustice
C. revive : rejuvenation
D. discover : learn

___ 3. ANARCHY : GOVERNMENT ::
A. warfare : peace
B. solution : answer
C. commitment : promise
D. excellence : success

___ 4. CONSECRATE : SANCTIFY ::
A. initiate : commence
B. identify : conceal
C. fascinate : mystify
D. innovate : perish

Name _____ Date _____

Support for Writing

Use the chart to gather and organize ideas for your Compare-and-Contrast essay. Use the graphic organizer to compare and contrast the writers' historical perspective, affection for America, grief over the nation's crisis, and hopes for the future. In the right column, list quotations, incidents, examples, and other details that develop and support each response.

Abraham Lincoln	Robert E. Lee
Different:	Different:
Alike:	

On a separate page, write your Compare-and-Contrast essay about Lincoln's and Lee's historical perspective, affection for America, grief over the nation's crisis, and hopes for the future.

"**The Gettysburg Address**" by Abraham Lincoln
"**Letter to His Son**" by Robert E. Lee
Enrichment: Music

Songs of Peace

The desire for peace, similar to the ideas in Lincoln's "Gettysburg Address" and Lee's "Letter to His Son," has often been portrayed as a theme in music.

DIRECTIONS: *Find a song that you think portrays the desire for peace. Write the name of the song, the author or performer (if you know it), and the lyrics that display the desire for peace. Tell how you think it compares with the desire for peace expressed in either Lincoln's "Gettysburg Address" or Lee's "Letter to His Son."*

Song (and author or performer): _____

Lyrics that display the desire for peace: _____

_____

_____

_____

_____

_____

_____

_____

_____

How the song compares to either Lincoln's or Lee's desire: _____

_____

_____

_____

_____

_____

_____

_____

_____

_____

Name _____ Date _____

"The Gettysburg Address" by Abraham Lincoln; **"Letter to His Son"** by Robert E. Lee
Open-Book Test

Short Answer *Write your responses to the questions in this section on the lines provided.*

1. Reread the first paragraph of "The Gettysburg Address." How are the beginning phrase "Four score and seven years ago" and the ending word "equal" designed to impact the audience?

   _____

   _____

   _____

2. In "The Gettysburg Address," if Lincoln had chosen to begin his speech with the words "Eighty-seven years ago," how would that have affected the diction of his speech? Would it have been more or less formal? Why do you think he chose to phrase it the way he did?

   _____

   _____

   _____

   _____

3. In the third paragraph of "The Gettysburg Address," why does Lincoln say that he and the observers "cannot consecrate this ground"? What is he trying to imply about both himself and his audience?

   _____

   _____

   _____

   _____

4. Read this sentence from "The Gettysburg Address":

   The world will little note, nor long remember, what we say here, but it can never forget what they did here.

   On the lines below, restate this passage in your own words, using more informal diction.

   _____

   _____

5. Having background knowledge can often deepen a reader's appreciation of a historical document. In what way would background knowledge of the Battle of Gettysburg enhance a reader's appreciation of "The Gettysburg Address"?

   _____

   _____

   _____

   _____

6. Lincoln ends "The Gettysburg Address" with the words "that government of the people, by the people, for the people, shall not perish from the earth." What does this ending tell you about Lincoln's purpose in giving the speech? What does it tell you about the effect he hoped to have on his audience?

_____

_____

_____

_____

7. Reread the first two sentences of "Letter to His Son." Is the diction of these sentences more or less formal than that of a typical letter from a father to a son? Why do you think Lee chose the kind of diction that is evident in these lines?

_____

_____

_____

_____

8. In "Letter to His Son," why does Lee write that he will "draw my sword on none"? How does this statement express his feelings about "strife and civil war"? What is the one exception to this statement?

_____

_____

_____

_____

9. In "Letter to His Son," Lee shows conflicting feelings about the impending Civil War between North and South. Some of his remarks sound pro-Union, others anti-Union. Use the chart below to quote at least two examples of each kind of argument advanced by Lee in his letter.

Pro-Union Arguments	Anti-Union Arguments

10. If your teacher declared, "Anarchy prevails in this classroom," would there most likely be an orderly atmosphere in the classroom? Why or why not? Base your answer on the definition of *anarchy* as it is used in "Letter to His Son."

_____

_____

_____

_____

Name _____ Date _____

Essay

Write an extended response to the question of your choice or to the question or questions your teacher assigns you.

11. In "The Gettysburg Address," Lincoln reminds his audience that the Union soldiers died at Gettysburg so that the nation might live. In what way was Lincoln trying to inspire his audience? Explain your thoughts in an essay supported by details from the speech.

12. Although they were foes during the Civil War, Lincoln and Lee express many points of agreement about the fate of the Union in "The Gettysburg Address" and "Letter to His Son." In what ways do Lincoln and Lee agree with each other? In what ways to they differ? Explain these points of agreement and disagreement in an essay supported by details from the selections.

13. Both "The Gettysburg Address" and "Letter to His Son" convey a great deal about the character and beliefs of the two authors. Choose either Lincoln or Lee as your subject, and then write an essay in which you discuss the author's character, citing details from the selection to support your impressions.

14. **Thinking About the Essential Question: What makes American literature American?** Patriotism runs through both "The Gettysburg Address" and "Letter to His Son." Both Lincoln and Lee are dedicated to what they believe to be the best interests of their country. In an essay, explore the idea that people can disagree but be equally patriotic.

Oral Response

15. Go to question 1, 5, or 7 or to the question your teacher assigns you. Take a few minutes to expand your answer and prepare an oral response. Find additional details in "The Gettysburg Address" or "Letter to His Son" that support your points. If necessary, make notes to guide your oral response.

"The Gettysburg Address" by Abraham Lincoln
"Letter to His Son" by Robert E. Lee
Selection Test A

Critical Reading *Identify the letter of the choice that best answers the question.*

____ 1. Why does Lincoln deliver "The Gettysburg Address"?
A. to make a formal declaration of war
B. to dedicate ground for a cemetery
C. to end the Civil War
D. to make plans for the Civil War

____ 2. In "The Gettysburg Address," what kind of diction does Lincoln use in the phrase "Four score and seven years ago"?
A. abstract
B. informal
C. private
D. formal

____ 3. What event does Lincoln refer to when he says that "our fathers brought forth on this continent a new nation, conceived in Liberty" in "The Gettysburg Address"?
A. the end of the Civil War
B. the beginning of the Civil War in 1861
C. the signing of the Declaration of Independence in 1776
D. the exploration of the New World by Columbus

____ 4. What is another way to state the following from "The Gettysburg Address"?
"The brave men, living and dead, who struggled here, have consecrated it [made it holy], far above our poor power to add or detract"
A. Those who forget history are doomed to repeat it.
B. Actions speak louder than words.
C. Keep your friends close and your enemies closer.
D. The pen is mightier than the sword.

____ 5. What is the "great task remaining before us" that Lincoln says Americans should dedicate themselves to?
A. freeing the slaves
B. preserving the United States
C. establishing a new nation
D. remembering the dead

____ 6. What great event took place at Gettysburg?

  A. A Revolutionary War battle was won that gave the United States its independence.

  B. The peace treaty ending the Civil War was signed.

  C. A major Civil War battle was won by the Union.

  D. The first National Cemetery was established.

____ 7. Which of these elements in Lee's "Letter to His Son" gives historical background?

  A. his reference to receiving a book as a gift from his son

  B. his reference to his pride as a citizen of his country

  C. his reference to the four states that have left the union

  D. his reference to feeling helpless in the face of events

____ 8. What element in "Letter to His Son" makes it surprising that Lee became the military leader of the Confederate armies?

  A. He says he will fight only to defend his or some other state.

  B. He says the South has been badly treated by the North.

  C. He says that George Washington would be unhappy with a civil war.

  D. He hopes God will keep the nation from falling apart.

____ 9. What does Lee refer to when he says he "can anticipate no greater calamity for the country"?

  A. its breakup

  B. a civil war

  C. financial ruin

  D. loss of independence

____ 10. In "Letter to His Son," Lee says he would be willing to sacrifice everything—except one—in order to avoid the separation of the Union. What is the one thing?

  A. his sword

  B. honor

  C. evil

  D. progress

Vocabulary

____ 11. In which sentence is the meaning of the word *hallow* expressed?

  A. Lincoln spoke of the nation in his speech.

  B. Lee disapproved of a civil war.

  C. Lincoln advised that wrongs be forgiven.

  D. The dead made the ground holy.

_____ **12.** Which word means most nearly the *same* as the underlined word in this line from Lee's "Letter to His Son"?

"As far as I can see by the papers, we are between a state of <u>anarchy</u> and civil war."

A. restoration

B. disorder

C. failure

D. forgiveness

Essay

13. In "The Gettysburg Address," Lincoln states that the soldiers who died at Gettysburg died so that the nation might live. What was Lincoln encouraging his listeners to do? In a brief essay, express your thoughts about what Lincoln was trying to accomplish in this speech.

14. In his "Letter to His Son," Lee refers to the founders of the nation and its constitution. He hates the possibility of secession and civil war. Yet, he finally led the armies of the Confederacy. Write a brief essay to explain his decision. Include how his letter to his son might explain why he led the Southern armies against the Union.

15. Essential Question: What makes American literature American? Patriotism is a major theme of "The Gettysburg Address" and "Letter to His Son." Both Lincoln and Lee believed in their country, and each fought for it in his own way. In an essay, explain how people can still be patriotic even though they disagree about what is best for the country.

"The Gettysburg Address" by Abraham Lincoln
"Letter to His Son" by Robert E. Lee
Selection Test B

Critical Reading *Identify the letter of the choice that best completes the statement or answers the question.*

____ 1. In "The Gettysburg Address" Lincoln explains that the stated purpose for meeting on this battlefield is to _____.
A. dedicate the nation to the Southern cause
B. dedicate themselves to revenging the Gettysburg dead
C. dedicate a portion of the field as a final resting place for fallen soldiers
D. dedicate themselves to God

____ 2. Lincoln's main purpose in "The Gettysburg Address" is to _____.
A. argue why the Union will win the war
B. explain the importance of the war and inspire people to support the Union
C. seek money for the families of those who died
D. identify the soldiers who died in battle

____ 3. Considering the diction of "The Gettysburg Address," describe Lincoln's view of himself and his audience.
A. powerless and defeated
B. humble and dedicated
C. cowardly and fearful
D. noble and proud

____ 4. Lincoln's references to birth at the beginning and the end of "The Gettysburg Address" suggest that he
A. recognizes the need for humor at a sad time.
B. is concerned with population losses due to battlefield casualties.
C. is aware of the nation's short history.
D. wishes to relate complex ideas to a common experience.

____ 5. The main idea of Lee's "Letter to His Son" could be expressed best as
A. belief that the integrity of the Union must be preserved at all costs.
B. determination that the South will not be subdued.
C. despair over a Union that can only be maintained by force.
D. an argument in favor of secession.

____ 6. In his letter, Lee reflects an attitude toward impending events that is
A. fatalistic about the prospects of war.
B. confident in the South's military strength.
C. hateful toward the North.
D. opposed to the principles of the Constitution.

____ 7. One of Lee's main reasons for opposing secession is his
A. pride as a Virginian.
B. belief in the importance of the Union.
C. commitment to states' rights.
D. position as an officer in the army.

Unit 3 Resources: Division, Reconciliation, and Expansion

____ 8. Lee's letter seeks to persuade by
   A. appealing to emotion.
   B. invoking the authority of great writers.
   C. making an irrational argument.
   D. analyzing events within historical context.

____ 9. Prior knowledge in which of the following areas would best help you understand the ideas Lee expresses in his letter?
   A. the principles of the United States Constitution
   B. Lee's military experience
   C. the economy of the pre-Civil War South
   D. the relationship between Lee and his son

____ 10. Lee's diction in "A Letter to His Son" is somewhat informal because he is
   A. delivering a public speech.
   B. writing to his son.
   C. discussing a trivial subject.
   D. speaking in code to avoid suspicion.

____ 11. From what you know of the causes of the Civil War, by what "acts of the North" might Southerners, including Lee, have been aggrieved?
   A. the Union's policy regarding which states shall be slaveholding states
   B. the Union's policy regulating how much slaves should cost
   C. Lincoln's Emancipation Proclamation
   D. the Union's granting to African Americans the right to vote

____ 12. From what you know of United States history, which document was Lincoln quoting when he said in "The Gettysburg Address" that the nation was dedicated to the proposition "that all men are created equal"?
   A. the Emancipation Proclamation
   B. the Declaration of Independence
   C. the Equal Rights Amendment
   D. the Missouri Compromise

____ 13. In "Letter to His Son," what does Lee say he plans to do if the Union dissolves?
   A. lead the South in war against the North
   B. return home and live in peace, if possible
   C. surrender to the invading Union army
   D. try to reunite the country

Vocabulary

____ 14. The word or phrase closest in meaning to *consecrate* is _____.
   A. sanctify
   B. violate
   C. remember
   D. eliminate

_____ 15. When Lee referred to a "state of *anarchy*," he meant America was almost in
a condition of _____.
A. overbearing government power
B. civil war
C. losing its liberty
D. having no government

_____ 16. The word most opposite in meaning to *hallow* is _____.
A. sanctify
B. justify
C. defile
D. restrict

_____ 17. Which phrase means almost the same as the underlined word in this line from Lee's
"Letter to His Son"?
"I will not, however, permit myself to believe, until all ground of hope is gone, that
the fruit of his noble deeds will be destroyed, and that his. . . <u>virtuous</u> example will
so soon be forgotten by his countrymen."
A. moral
B. immoral
C. memorable
D. forgotten

Essay

18. Both Lincoln and Lee placed a great deal of importance on preserving the Union. Write an
essay in which you discuss either Lincoln's or Lee's ideas about the Union. Use examples
from the text of Lincoln's speech or Lee's letter to support your points.

19. Lincoln's speech conveys a great deal about his beliefs and his character in general. Likewise, Lee's letter reveals a good deal about the nature of its author. Choose either Lincoln or
Lee as your subject. Then write an essay in which you describe the man's character, using
details from his writing to support your impressions.

20. **Thinking About the Essential Question: What makes American literature American?**
Patriotism runs through both "The Gettysburg Address" and "Letter to His Son." Both Lincoln and Lee are dedicated to what they believe to be the best interests of their country. In
an essay, explore the idea that people can disagree but be equally patriotic.

Name _____ Date _____

Nell Irvin Painter Introduces "An Account of an Experience with Discrimination" by Sojourner Truth

DIRECTIONS: *Use the space provided to answer the questions.*

1. According to Nell Irvin Painter, what kind of volunteer work did Sojourner Truth carry out in Washington, D.C., during the Civil War?

   _____

   _____

2. What were the events that Sojourner Truth dictated for publication in the antislavery press?

   _____

   _____

3. According to Painter, what are the "two American histories" to which Truth's experience of discrimination belongs?

   _____

   _____

   _____

   _____

4. Why was the war between black people and American railroads "national in scope"?

   _____

   _____

5. Identify three of the well-known African Americans named by Painter, and briefly describe how they suffered discrimination on railroad trains.

   _____

   _____

   _____

   _____

6. If you had a chance to interview Nell Irvin Painter, what are two questions you might ask her about how she performs historical research?

   _____

   _____

   _____

   _____

Name _____ Date _____

Nell Irvin Painter
Listening and Viewing

Segment 1: Meet Nell Irvin Painter
- How did Nell Irvin Painter first become interested in studying history?
- Why do you think historical writing is so important to society?

_____

_____

_____

_____

Segment 2: Nell Irvin Painter Introduces Sojourner Truth
- Who was Sojourner Truth, and why was she an important historical figure during the Civil War?
- What two facts, which are often unknown, does Nell Irvin Painter want students to know?

_____

_____

_____

_____

Segment 3: The Writing Process
- What is a primary source, and why are primary sources important to Nell Irvin Painter's historical narratives?

_____

_____

_____

_____

Segment 4: The Rewards of Writing
- According to Nell Irvin Painter, why is it important that students view history critically?
- What do you think you can learn by reading historical narratives about people like Sojourner Truth?

_____

_____

_____

_____

Vocabulary Warm-up Word Lists

Study these words from the selections. Then, complete the activities.

Word List A

ascended [uh SEN did] *v.* climbed
  She kept talking as she <u>ascended</u> the stairs.

clenching [KLENCH ing] *v.* gripping tightly; clutching
  He was <u>clenching</u> the quarter tightly in his hand so he wouldn't lose it.

company [KUM puh nee] *n.* association with another
  I usually travel in <u>company</u> with friends.

conductor [kuhn DUK ter] *n.* a person who collects fares on a public conveyance
  The <u>conductor</u> walked down the train car, punching the tickets of all the passengers.

dragged [DRAGD] *v.* pulled along, usually unwillingly
  Although he had to be <u>dragged</u> to the concert, he actually enjoyed it.

platform [PLAT fawrm] *n.* an open step at the rear of a bus or streetcar for passengers to stand on as they enter or leave the vehicle
  The bus driver didn't see me about to step on the <u>platform</u> as he began to drive away.

streetcar [STREET kahr] *n.* a vehicle somewhat like a bus that runs on rails on city streets, providing public transportation
  I traveled to San Francisco especially to ride a <u>streetcar</u>.

succeeded [suhk SEE ded] *v.* achieved a goal; was successful
  Mary <u>succeeded</u> in graduating from college, which had been her goal.

Word List B

arrested [uh REST ed] *v.* detained by law enforcement
  The thieves were <u>arrested</u> quickly once they were identified.

assault and battery [uh SAWLT and BAT er ee] *n.* the crime of physically attacking somebody; an unlawful beating
  He was convicted of <u>assault and battery</u> for beating the student.

furiously [FYOOR ee uhs lee] *adv.* very angrily; heatedly
  She responded <u>furiously</u> when she was falsely accused of cheating.

humanity [hyoo MAN uh tee] *n.* the human race; mankind
  Her kindness to the elderly in the neighborhood restored my faith in <u>humanity</u>.

lame [LAYM] *adj.* sore or injured, especially a leg
  His leg was <u>lame</u> after he fell down the stairs.

mistreated [mis TREET ed] *v.* badly treated; injured
  Because the dog had been <u>mistreated</u>, he was afraid of strangers.

necessities [nuh SES uh teez] *n.* supplies; requirements for life
  After the flood, many people were left without life's <u>necessities</u>.

violence [VY uh lens] *n.* physical force used to injure or damage
  He had a history of <u>violence</u>, so he was a likely suspect.

112

Name _____ Date _____

"An Account of an Experience with Discrimination" by Sojourner Truth
Vocabulary Warm-up Exercises

Exercise A *Fill in the blanks, using each word from Word List A only once.*

Maria went to San Francisco especially to ride the [1] _____. Ever
since she was a young girl and saw a commercial featuring the cars, she was determined to visit someday. Finally, she had [2] _____. She felt better in the
[3] _____ of her friend Queenie and talked her into coming on the trip.
The minute they checked into their hotel, Maria [4] _____ Queenie out
the door. They [5] _____ one of the steep hills to the stop. Soon one
arrived! [6] _____ her friend's hand, Mary stepped onto the
[7] _____ and climbed aboard. The [8] _____ took their
tickets and they grabbed a handhold and began the trip. The view was everything that
Maria had expected!

Exercise B *Decide whether each statement is true or false. Circle T or F, and explain your*
answers.

1. They were caught on video robbing the store and quickly <u>arrested</u>.
   T / F _____

2. An act of <u>violence</u> does not hurt anyone.
   T / F _____

3. Food and water are <u>necessities</u> of life.
   T / F _____

4. A victim of <u>assault and battery</u> may have to go to the hospital.
   T / F _____

5. If you react <u>furiously</u> to an insult, it doesn't really bother you.
   T / F _____

6. He was angry because he felt that he had been <u>mistreated</u>.
   T / F _____

7. The dog was <u>lame</u> because he had been hit by a car.
   T / F _____

8. If you have faith in <u>humanity</u>, you believe that people are basically evil.
   T / F _____

"An Account of an Experience with Discrimination" by Sojourner Truth
Reading Warm-up A

Read the following passage. Then, complete the activities.

When Aaron was a little boy, his grandfather was a railroad engineer. Aaron didn't really know what that meant, but he did know that he had to be very quiet after dinner so his grandfather could sleep. This was hard, but he usually <u>succeeded</u> thanks to the large supply of books that his grandmother would read to him. If he burst out laughing at something she read, he would stop himself by <u>clenching</u> his hands tightly over his mouth.

Aaron knew that his grandfather went to bed so early because he had to get up at 3:30 almost every morning to go drive a train. One night when it was still dark, Aaron's grandmother woke him up and told him they were taking him for a ride on the train! Aaron was so excited that he could hardly stand it.

First, they had to take a <u>streetcar</u> to the train station because it was too far to walk. They were in <u>company</u> with only a few other early riders when they stepped on the <u>platform</u> of the waiting car and climbed in. Before he knew it, they were at the train station. Aaron waved to his grandfather, who went to take over for the current engineer. Aaron and his grandmother climbed the stairs and <u>ascended</u> into a train car, where the train <u>conductor</u> took their tickets and greeted them as if they were royalty.

They rode for several hours in the observation car, where they had a wonderful view of the sunrise as well as the country through which they passed. Aaron couldn't see his grandfather, but it gave him a great feeling of pride to know that he was driving the powerful locomotive that <u>dragged</u> all the cars in the long train. Now he understood why it was so important to let grand-father get his sleep!

1. Tell what Aaron <u>succeeded</u> in doing. What is a word with the opposite meaning of *succeeded*?

2. Circle the words that tell what Aaron was <u>clenching</u>. Give some words that mean the same as *clenching*.

3. Underline the words that tell where they were taking the <u>streetcar</u>. Are there *streetcars* where you live?

4. Circle the words that help explain the meaning of <u>company</u>. Tell some people with whom you have been in *company*.

5. Underline the words in the passage that give a clue to the meaning of <u>platform</u>. Give your own definition of *platform*.

6. Circle the words that are a clue to the meaning of <u>ascended</u>. Use *ascended* in an original sentence.

7. Circle the words in the sentence that tell what a train <u>conductor</u> does. What other means of transportation have a *conductor*?

8. Underline the words that tell what was <u>dragged</u>. Write your own sentence using the word *dragged*.

Name _____ Date _____

"An Account of an Experience with Discrimination" by Sojourner Truth
Reading Warm-up B

Read the following passage. Then, complete the activities.

In the American South before the Civil War, under the law a slave depended on his owner for everything. Slaves generally owned nothing, not even such basics as life's <u>necessities</u>. Rather, slaves were regarded as property. For example, it was the owner's responsibility to recover damages if a third party caused either his cow or his slave to be <u>lame</u>, or disabled. An owner was also required to control his "property" and was held responsible for any <u>violence</u> or other crimes committed by his slaves.

There were penalties for crimes against a slave by a stranger. Laws made in ancient Rome had introduced the concept that a slave was a person, a member of <u>humanity</u>. Thus injuring a slave could be a crime. Of course, a slave could be <u>mistreated</u> by his owner and the owner would incur no penalty for any harm or injury he caused.

In the American South, laws explicitly stated that slaves could have no honor, personal status, or prestige. South Carolina law noted that the slave was not "within the peace of the state, and therefore the peace of the state [was] not broken by an <u>assault and battery</u> on him." In other words, beating a slave was legal. On the other hand, if a slave angrily and <u>furiously</u> assaulted a free-man, the freeman could recover damages from the slave's owner. Elsewhere, when the state <u>arrested</u> and punished a slave, the penalty typically was more severe than for a free person.

Overall, the deprivation of a slave's rights was expressed in the Alabama case Creswell's Executor v. Walter in 1860. The slave, said the court, had "no legal mind, no will which the law can recognize. . . . Because they are slaves, they are incapable of performing civil acts."

1. Underline the words that tell who would be made <u>lame</u>. Give another word that means the same as *lame*.

2. Underline the word that helps tell what <u>violence</u> is similar to. Name a type of crime that is referred to as *violence*.

3. What is meant by life's <u>necessities</u>? Name some things that are true *necessities*.

4. Underline the words that give clues to the meaning of <u>humanity</u>. Give another word that means the same as *humanity*.

5. Underline the word that tells who was <u>mistreated</u>. Use *mistreated* in a sentence.

6. In your own words, tell what <u>assault and battery</u> means.

7. Circle the word that provides a clue to the meaning of <u>furiously</u>. Give another word that means the same as *furiously*.

8. Why are people normally <u>arrested</u>? Use *arrested* in an original sentence.

Name _____ Date _____

Literary Analysis: Author's Purpose and Tone

An **author's purpose** is his or her reason for writing. For example, an author might write a letter to stay in touch with friends. Someone might write a journal entry to record feelings and details about an event in his or her life. An author's purpose helps shape his or her **tone,** which is the author's attitude toward the subject and audience. You may detect a tone of compassion, sorrow, anger, or pride, for example.

DIRECTIONS: *Complete each item using information from the selection and what you know about an author's purpose and tone.*

1. What is the author's purpose in these opening lines from "An Account of an Experience with Discrimination"? Explain your response.

   A few weeks ago I was in company with my friend Josephine S. Griffing, when the conductor of a streetcar refused to stop his car for me, although [I was] closely following Josephine and holding on to the iron rail.

   _____

   _____

   _____

2. What is Sojourner Truth's tone in these lines? How do you know?

   As I ascended the platform of the car, the conductor pushed me, saying "Go back—get off here." I told him I was not going off, then "I'll put you off" said he furiously, clenching my right arm with both hands, using such violence that he seemed about to succeed, when Mrs. Haviland told him he was not going to put me off.

   _____

   _____

   _____

3. Does the author's purpose or tone change in the course of this account? Explain.

   _____

   _____

   _____

Name _____ Date _____

"An Account of an Experience with Discrimination" by Sojourner Truth
Reading Strategy: Identify Relevant Details and Facts

To determine the **essential message** of a piece of writing, learn to **identify relevant facts and details.** Details and facts that are most relevant, or important, are those that are essential to understanding the main idea, characters, and setting. As you read, look for these relevant facts and details and how they are related.

DIRECTIONS: *Read the following excerpts from "An Account of an Experience with Discrimination."* *Each statement includes details and facts. Identify the two most relevant details and facts that will help you understand the selection.*

1. A few weeks ago I was in company with my friend Josephine S. Griffing, when the conductor of a streetcar refused to stop his car for me, although [I was] closely following Josephine and holding on to the iron rail.

   _____

   _____

2. She reported the conductor to the president of the City Railway, who dismissed him at once, and told me to take the number of the car whenever I was mistreated by a conductor or driver.

   _____

   _____

3. On the 13th I had occasion to go for necessities for the patients to the Freedmen's hospital where I have been doing and advising for a number of months. I thought now I would get a ride without trouble as I was in company with another friend, Laura S. Haviland of Michigan.

   _____

   _____

4. As I ascended the platform of the car, the conductor pushed me, saying "Go back—get off here."

   _____

   _____

5. "Does she belong to you?" said he in a hurried angry tone. "She replied, 'She does not belong to me, but she belongs to humanity.'

   _____

   _____

6. My shoulder was very lame and swollen, but is better. It is hard for the old slaveholding spirit to die. But die it must.

   _____

   _____

Name _____   Date _____

"An Account of an Experience with Discrimination" by Sojourner Truth
Vocabulary Builder

Using the Word List

 ascended   assault

A. DIRECTIONS: *Rewrite each sentence, substituting a word from the Word List for each underlined word or phrase.*

1. Sojourner Truth <u>climbed up</u> the steps to enter the streetcar.

   _____

2. The conductor denied that he had made a <u>violent attack</u> against Truth.

   _____

B. DIRECTIONS: *For each item, choose the word pair that best expresses a relationship similar to that expressed in the numbered pair. Circle the letter of your choice.*

1. ASCENDED : MOUNTAIN ::
   A. swam : sea
   B. survived : continued
   C. enjoyed : responded
   D. relaxed : preference

2. ASSAULT : DEFEND ::
   A. souvenir : remember
   B. apology : forgive
   C. restraint : chain
   D. injustice : reform

Name _____ Date _____

"An Account of an Experience with Discrimination" by Sojourner Truth
Support for Writing

A newspaper reporter tries to answer the questions Who? What? When? Where? Why? and How? The most important information appears in the first paragraph so a reader can scan it and get an idea of what the story is about. Details to fill in the story are given in the following paragraphs.

Use the chart to gather and organize ideas for your **newspaper article** reporting on Sojourner Truth's experience with discrimination.

Questions	Answers (quotations, relevant facts, and details)
Who?	
What?	
When?	
Where?	
Why?	
How?	

On a separate page, write your newspaper article. Begin with a summary of the important facts of the incidents. Develop the story in the following paragraphs.

Name _____ Date _____

"An Account of an Experience with Discrimination" by Sojourner Truth
Enrichment: Personal Account Versus Dramatic Account

Sojourner Truth's personal account of her experience with discrimination tells exactly what happened from Truth's point of view. She gives the hard facts. Now consider how a filmmaker would present this episode. How would the story change? What would be gained by dramatizing the episode? What would be lost? How would the audience's response change?

DIRECTIONS: *Use the chart below to compare and contrast the effects of "An Account of an Experience with Discrimination" as it appears in Truth's account and as it might appear if dramatized in a film or on stage. Consider how the audience's response would change depending upon the genre. What conclusions can you draw?*

	Personal Account	**Dramatic Account**
Gained		
Lost		
Audience's reaction		
Conclusion		

Name _____ Date _____

"An Account of an Experience With Discrimination" by Sojourner Truth
Open-Book Test

Short Answer *Write your responses to the questions in this section on the lines provided.*

1. The title of this selection, "An Account of an Experience with Discrimination," would likely lead the reader to expect a completely objective report about the facts of the experience. Is this expectation borne out by the end of the piece? Why or why not?

   _____

   _____

   _____

2. In the first sentence of "An Account of an Experience with Discrimination," Truth writes that she was not allowed on a streetcar "although [I was] closely following Josephine." The fact that Truth expected that her being with Josephine would make it easier for her to board the streetcar allows the reader to infer what about Josephine?

   _____

   _____

3. Based on Josephine's actions following the streetcar incident in "An Account of an Experience with Discrimination," what can the reader infer about her character?

   _____

   _____

   _____

4. What do you think is the primary purpose of "An Account of an Experience with Discrimination"?

   _____

   _____

   _____

5. In "An Account of an Experience with Discrimination," Truth reports the following:

   > On the 13th I had occasion to go for necessities for the patients in the Freedman's hospital where I have been doing and advising for a number of months.

   From these details and facts, what conclusions can you draw about the overall concerns and activities of Sojourner Truth?

   _____

   _____

   _____

   _____

6. In "An Account of an Experience with Discrimination," during the second reported attempt to board a streetcar, how does Truth respond when the conductor tries to push her off the platform? What does this response tell you about her character?

_____

_____

_____

7. During her second attempt to board a streetcar in "An Account of an Experience with Discrimination," the angry conductor asks Truth's friend, Mrs. Haviland, "Does she belong to you?" What does this question show about racial attitudes of that era?

_____

_____

_____

8. What do the two streetcar incidents reported in "An Account of an Experience with Discrimination" reveal about Truth's methods of fighting discrimination and injustice?

_____

_____

_____

9. At what point in "An Account of an Experience with Discrimination" does Truth's tone shift clearly from reporting facts to advocating a strong viewpoint?

_____

_____

_____

10. If you ascended to the second floor of a department store on an escalator, would you have come from the first floor or the third floor? Explain your answer, basing it on the definition of *ascended* as it is used in "An Account of an Experience with Discrimination."

_____

_____

_____

Essay

Write an extended response to the question of your choice or to the question or questions your teacher assigns you.

11. In "An Account of an Experience with Discrimination," Sojourner Truth relates a number of interactions she had with white people of that era: her friends Josephine Griffing and Laura Haviland, the two streetcar conductors, and the president of the streetcar company. In an essay, describe the state of race relations of that era as revealed by Sojourner Truth's encounters with these whites. Support your answer with details from the text.

12. "An Account of an Experience with Discrimination" reveals many sides of the personality and character of Sojourner Truth. In an essay, explain the key elements of her character that emerge from this selection. Support your answer with details from the text.

13. In "An Account of an Experience with Discrimination," Sojourner Truth recounts two episodes of discrimination against an African American in 1865. Do you think that the racist attitudes and practices that she exposes in this selection have been completely overcome in the United States today? Or are there still examples of unequal treatment of African Americans in the United States? Develop your opinion in an essay supported by examples from the selection, news reports, and your own personal experience.

14. **Thinking About the Essential Question: What makes American literature American?** Courage is a key ingredient in Sojourner Truth's work. Can you think of a more recent writer and/or activist who has displayed the kind of courage needed to speak truth to power, to call attention to injustices, or to touch the conscience of a nation?

Oral Response

15. Go back to question 1, 3, or 7 or to the question your teacher assigns you. Take a few minutes to expand your answer and prepare an oral response. Find additional details in "An Account of an Experience with Discrimination" that support your points. If necessary, make notes to guide your oral response.

"An Account of an Experience with Discrimination" by Sojourner Truth
Selection Test A

MULTIPLE CHOICE

Critical Reading *Identify the letter of the choice that best answers the question.*

_____ 1. When did the events that Truth describes in "An Account of an Experience with Discrimination" occur?
   A. before the Civil War
   B. during the period of slavery
   C. during the civil rights marches in the 1950s
   D. immediately after the Civil War

_____ 2. What does "An Account of an Experience with Discrimination" reveal about Sojourner Truth?
   A. She was easily made afraid of white people.
   B. She was capable of defending herself.
   C. She disliked streetcar conductors.
   D. She avoided standing up for her rights.

_____ 3. Sojourner Truth was a
   A. former slave
   B. former slave owner
   C. streetcar conductor
   D. white abolitionist

_____ 4. During the first incident with the streetcars that Truth describes, what does the conductor do when Truth tries to follow her friend, Josephine Griffing, onto the streetcar?
   A. He tries to overcharge Truth because she is black.
   B. He starts up the streetcar and drags her several yards.
   C. He pauses long enough for her to get on board.
   D. He closes the door in her face.

_____ 5. What is the response of the president of the streetcar company when he learns of the first incident with the streetcar?
   A. He supports the conductor's actions.
   B. He refuses to take sides.
   C. He fires the conductor.
   D. He refunds the price of Truth's ticket.

____ 6. Why did Truth think she would not have trouble riding the streetcars when she was going for supplies for patients in the hospital?

A. Streetcar conductors always treated people from the hospitals fairly.

B. The hospital was in a better part of town and people were rarely mistreated there.

C. She was accompanied by Laura Haviland of Michigan.

D. Many black people rode the streetcar in that part of town.

____ 7. During the second incident with streetcars, what does the conductor mean when he asks Mrs. Haviland, "Does she belong to you?"

A. Is she your slave?

B. Is she your friend?

C. Is she with you?

D. Is she working for the hospital?

____ 8. What happens when Truth reports the incident to the streetcar company's president?

A. Truth is told she cannot ride the streetcars any more.

B. The conductor is dismissed.

C. Truth is blamed for causing the incident.

D. The conductor is arrested.

____ 9. What is Truth's tone as she tells about her experience?

A. humorous and agreeable

B. violently angry

C. sad and despairing

D. measured and calm

____ 10. "An Account of an Experience with Discrimination" was written as a

A. letter

B. newspaper report

C. court document

D. speech

Vocabulary

____ **11.** In which sentence is the meaning of the word *assault* suggested?

    A. The conductor grabbed Truth and hurt her as he pushed her from the streetcar.

    B. Mrs. Haviland tried to help Truth get on the streetcar.

    C. The streetcar came to an abrupt halt when Truth stepped in front of it.

    D. People watched curiously as the argument continued between the two women and the conductor.

____ **12.** When Truth says she "*ascended* the platform," she means she

    A. walked along

    B. went up

    C. went down

    D. got off

Essay

13. Based on the information in "An Account of an Experience with Discrimination," what can you infer about the two women Truth refers to in her account, Josephine S. Griffing and Laura S. Haviland? Explain your answer.

14. Truth ends the letter by commenting that "It is hard for the old slaveholding spirit to die. But die it must." What does she mean?

15. **Essential Question: What makes American literature American?** Courage is a key element in Sojourner Truth's writing. Who is a more recent writer or activist who has shown the same kind of courage in speaking up about injustices or to make people aware of other important issues? You may consider someone who fights for a global or national cause, or someone who takes up a cause in your own community. In an essay, describe the cause, and discuss the courage needed to prmote it.

"An Account of an Experience with Discrimination" by Sojourner Truth
Selection Test B

MULTIPLE CHOICE

Critical Reading *Identify the letter of the choice that best answers the question.*

_____ 1. Sojourner Truth experienced difficulty in riding streetcars because she was
   A. African American
   B. female
   C. elderly
   D. stubborn

_____ 2. What is Truth's purpose in writing this letter?
   A. to entertain
   B. to persuade
   C. to inform
   D. to explain

_____ 3. What happens during the first incident with the streetcar?
   A. The conductor treats Truth civilly because she is with a white woman.
   B. The conductor refuses to stop the streetcar.
   C. The conductor closes the door in Truth's face.
   D. The conductor overcharges Truth because she is black.

_____ 4. What happens to the conductor who was involved in the first incident that Truth describes?
   A. He is promoted.
   B. He is arrested.
   C. He is dismissed.
   D. He is assigned to a new route.

_____ 5. What does Truth's companion, Josephine Griffing, do as a result of how the conductor treated Truth during the first incident?
   A. She reports the conductor to the president of the streetcar company.
   B. She gets off herself and walks along with Truth the rest of the way.
   C. She reminds Truth that black people are often treated unfairly.
   D. She apologizes for getting on first instead of letting Truth go first.

_____ 6. What does Mrs. Haviland mean when she says Truth "does not belong to me, but she belongs to humanity"?
A. Truth was once was a slave, but she is now free.
B. Truth is a human being and should be treated like everyone else.
C. Truth is not a slave, but she is an African American woman.
D. Truth is working for the hospital and should be treated respectfully.

_____ 7. How did Truth sprain her shoulder?
A. A conductor grabbed her arm with both hands and tried to force her off the streetcar.
B. She fell as she tried to board the streetcar.
C. She grabbed the railing of the car as it sped up and was dragged along.
D. She stumbled getting off the streetcar and fell onto the platform.

_____ 8. What was the attitude of the president of the streetcar company toward the incidents that Truth reported?
A. He supported his conductors and dismissed Truth's complaints.
B. He warned her to be careful because more incidents would occur.
C. He scolded her for being so sensitive.
D. He supported her right to ride the streetcars like everyone else.

_____ 9. Why did the conductors try to prevent Truth from riding the streetcars but allowed her companions, Josephine Griffing and Laura Haviland, to ride?
A. They got on first.
B. They were white.
C. They had already purchased tickets.
D. They knew the conductors.

_____ 10. Which words best describe the tone Truth uses in "An Account of an Experience with Discrimination"?
A. self-satisfied
B. arrogant and vindictive
C. measured and calm
D. humble and embarrassed

Vocabulary

_____ 11. In which sentence is the meaning of the word *ascend* suggested?

    A. The passengers stepped up on the platform.

    B. The streetcar picked up speed.

    C. The streetcar slowly came to a stop.

    D. Truth got off the streetcar.

_____ 12. When the president advised the conductor's "arrest for *assault*," he meant the conductor should be arrested because he

    A. discriminated against Truth.

    B. attacked Truth.

    C. spoke harshly to Truth.

    D. refused to let Truth on the streetcar.

Essay

13. Based on the information in "An Account of an Experience with Discrimination," what can you infer about discrimination toward African Americans during the 1860s? Consider both good and bad attitudes. Give examples from the selection to explain your answer.

14. The conductor asks Laura Haviland, "Does she belong to you?" How does this question illustrate the meaning of Truth's final statement in the letter, "It is hard for the old slaveholding spirit to die. But die it must . . ."?

15. **Essential Question: What makes American literature American?** Courage is a key ingredient in Sojourner Truth's work. Can you think of a more recent writer and/or activist who has displayed the kind of courage needed to speak truth to power, to call attention to injustices, or to touch the conscience of a nation?

Vocabulary Warm-up Word Lists

Study these words from the selections. Then, complete the activities.

Word List A

compliance [kum PLY ans] *n.* the act of following another's commands or wishes
Asking nicely often leads to more willing <u>compliance</u> than making demands.

contribution [kahn tri BYOO shun] *n.* something that is given
The charity mailed us a letter asking for a <u>contribution</u> of twenty dollars.

deliberate [duh LIB er uht] *adj.* careful and slow
The old dog moves in a more <u>deliberate</u> way than she did as a puppy.

humbly [HUM blee] *adv.* in a meek and modest way
"Could you possibly give me your autograph?" the boy asked <u>humbly</u>.

monotonous [muh NAH tuh nus] *adj.* boring; dull; too much the same
That show is getting <u>monotonous</u>; let's change the channel.

narrative [NAR uh tiv] *n.* story
We looked at the snapshots as we listened to the <u>narrative</u> of their vacation.

sociable [SOH shuh bul] *adj.* pleasant and friendly in company
Lou is <u>sociable</u>, so she's always a hit at parties.

withstand [with STAND] *v.* successfully resist
Few people can <u>withstand</u> the aroma of freshly baked bread.

Word List B

conspicuous [kun SPIK yoo us] *adj.* easy to notice; standing out
Joe felt <u>conspicuous</u> walking down the street in a gorilla suit.

grandeur [GRAN jur] *n.* magnificence or splendor
The <u>grandeur</u> of the enormous palace took her breath away.

impressive [im PRES iv] *adj.* making a strong effect
Most tourists find the Grand Canyon a very <u>impressive</u> sight.

indifferent [in DIF er int] *adj.* having no strong feeling for or against
I love ice cream, but I feel <u>indifferent</u> about rice pudding.

loathe [LOHTH] *v.* hate intensely
Our cats <u>loathe</u> going to the veterinarian for their shots.

ruthless [ROOTH les] *adj.* having no compassion or pity
The gods of Greek mythology could be <u>ruthless</u> toward humans.

tranquil [TRAN kwil] *adj.* calm or peaceful
We enjoyed a quiet picnic on the shore of the <u>tranquil</u> lake.

transient [TRAN zee int] *adj.* not permanent
Her interest in stamps was <u>transient</u>; now she collects dolls instead.

"The Boys' Ambition" *from* **Life on the Mississippi** and **"The Notorious Jumping Frog of Calaveras County"** by Mark Twain
Vocabulary Warm-up Exercises

Exercise A *Fill in each blank in the paragraph below with the appropriate word from Word List A.*

Last night, my best friend called me and told me this [1] _____ about a school dance. "I didn't really want to go," my friend said. "You know me—I'm not that [2] _____, and I feel awkward in big groups. My sister was on the committee, though, and she asked so [3] _____ that I could not [4] _____ her. You'd think it was enough that she had won my [5] _____ about showing up, but no! She insisted that I had to dance, too. Well, I have to admit it was a little [6] _____ just standing around, so I agreed. I thought I was doing pretty well, concentrating hard on getting all the steps right, but my sister laughed at me and said it looked silly to dance in such a [7] _____ way. Can you believe that? Next time she asks me to make a [8] _____ by participating in something she plans, I am definitely saying no!"

Exercise B *Answer the following questions with complete explanations.*

1. What sort of person would most dislike being <u>conspicuous</u>?

   _____

2. If you were buying a house, would you look for comfort or <u>grandeur</u>? Why?

   _____

3. What makes a big thunderstorm <u>impressive</u>?

   _____

4. If you felt <u>indifferent</u> about sports, would you watch the whole Super Bowl?

   _____

5. Why do you think so many children <u>loathe</u> bedtime?

   _____

6. Would someone who is <u>ruthless</u> be likely to work in a soup kitchen?

   _____

7. Does carrying a cell phone make a person's life more <u>tranquil</u>?

   _____

8. Which is usually more <u>transient</u>, a regular student or an exchange student?

   _____

Name _____ Date _____

"The Boys' Ambition" *from* **Life on the Mississippi** and **"The Notorious Jumping Frog of Calaveras County"** by Mark Twain

Reading Warm-up A

Read the following passage. Pay special attention to the underlined words. Then, read it again, and complete the activities. Use a separate sheet of paper for your written answers.

"An American loves his family," the inventor Thomas Edison once wrote. "If he has any love left over for some other person, he generally selects Mark Twain."

Mark Twain—the pen name of Samuel Langhorne Clemens—was a huge celebrity during his life. People loved him not just for his many books, which were his <u>contribution</u> to American literature, but for his sense of humor. When he appeared in public, reporters crowded around, hoping Clemens would make a funny remark about current events in his famous slow, <u>deliberate</u> drawl. (About the death of one public figure, he said, "I didn't attend the funeral, but I sent a nice letter saying I approved of it.")

Outgoing, <u>sociable</u>, and not particularly modest, Clemens enjoyed his popularity. Though he sometimes found the endless round of dinners and events <u>monotonous</u>, he loved being the center of attention. Still, he poked fun at his own inability to accept fame <u>humbly</u>. Compliments, he said, "always embarrass me—I always feel that they have not said enough."

Clemens refused to take seriously anything he thought was foolish, such as the expectations of polite society. However, he adored his gentle, well-bred wife, Olivia, and tried to behave "properly" in <u>compliance</u> with her wishes. Often his efforts failed, as this <u>narrative</u> shows: One day, Clemens returned from a brief visit to their neighbor, the writer Harriet Beecher Stowe. Greeting him, his wife was horrified to see that he'd forgotten to put on a tie. Unable to <u>withstand</u> her pleading, he went straight up to his room in search of a tie. When he found one, he sent it over to Stowe's house. Attached was a note explaining that the rest of him had come to finish the visit.

1. Circle the word that tells what Twain's <u>contribution</u> to American literature was. What else could be a *contribution* to literature?

2. Circle the word that means something similar to <u>deliberate</u>. What would be the opposite of a *deliberate* way of speaking?

3. Circle the word that means almost the same as <u>sociable</u>. Do you think being *sociable* is an advantage for a celebrity?

4. Underline what Clemens found <u>monotonous</u>. What is a word that means the opposite of *monotonous*?

5. Circle the word that tells what Clemens did not accept <u>humbly</u>. Then, tell what *humbly* means.

6. Underline what Clemens tried to do in <u>compliance</u> with his wife's wishes. What other type of person might require *compliance*?

7. Circle the paragraph that includes a <u>narrative</u> about a tie. If it never really happened, would it still be a *narrative*?

8. Underline what Clemens could not <u>withstand</u>. What else might someone not be able to *withstand*?

Name _____ Date _____

"The Boys' Ambition" *from* **Life on the Mississippi** and **"The Notorious Jumping Frog of Calaveras County"** by Mark Twain

Reading Warm-up B

Read the following passage. Pay special attention to the underlined words. Then, read it again, and complete the activities. Use a separate sheet of paper for your written answers.

When young Samuel Clemens decided to become a riverboat pilot, he imagined it would be an easy occupation. He pictured himself steering the boat down the wide Mississippi River, passing the time between ports gazing out in awe, admiring the river's <u>grandeur</u>.

In fact, the job proved to be anything but easy; as Clemens soon discovered, being a riverboat pilot required an <u>impressive</u> store of knowledge. A pilot needed to recognize every landmark for twelve hundred miles, by day or by night, and these often turned out to be <u>transient</u>. For instance, a tall old tree might topple over, and then there would be no more landmark.

The river that had looked so <u>tranquil</u> when Clemens was a passenger, he found, was actually filled with hidden hazards. To an ordinary passenger, a "faint dimple" on the water's surface might be practically invisible; to a trained pilot, it was as <u>conspicuous</u> as a red flag, warning that a jagged rock or wrecked boat lay below.

Clemens quickly learned to <u>loathe</u> some of the less romantic aspects of his job, such as being awoken in the middle of the night to take over at the helm. The chief pilot, too, could be <u>ruthless</u> in his mockery of the inexperienced young man. "The idea of you being a pilot—*you*!" he once told Clemens. "Why, you don't know enough to pilot a cow down a lane." Despite these setbacks, Clemens continued to work hard at mastering his trade, and at last he was accepted as a riverboat pilot. Though he realized he had become rather <u>indifferent</u> to the scenic beauty of the Mississippi, he had gained as much as he had lost, for he had learned to read the river—"a wonderful book," he wrote, with "a new story to tell each day."

1. Circle two words that suggest that <u>grandeur</u> is something good. Then, tell what *grandeur* means.

2. Underline an example of the <u>impressive</u> knowledge needed by a pilot. What makes it so *impressive*?

3. Circle an example of a <u>transient</u> landmark. What other kind of landmark might be *transient*?

4. Underline the words that tell you that the river is not as <u>tranquil</u> as it appears. What could be *tranquil* besides a river?

5. Underline what was as <u>conspicuous</u> as a red flag to a pilot. Describe something that would be *conspicuous* in a classroom.

6. Underline what Clemens came to <u>loathe</u> about his job. Then, give a word that is the opposite of *loathe*.

7. Circle a word that tells you that <u>ruthless</u> is probably something bad. How would the chief pilot's behavior change if he were not *ruthless*?

8. Underline what Clemens was <u>indifferent</u> to. Then, tell what *indifferent* means.

Name _____   Date _____

"The Boys' Ambition" *from* Life on the Mississippi and "The Notorious Jumping Frog of Calaveras County" by Mark Twain

Mark Twain: Biography

Mark Twain is one of America's greatest writers and humorists. His fiction incorporates lasting impressions of America in the late nineteenth century and insightful looks into human nature. He combines an examination of serious subjects with powerful and sometimes outrageous humor. Twain remains as important and delightful a literary figure today as in his heyday, more than a century ago.

A. DIRECTIONS: *Imagine that Mark Twain managed to find a way to travel forward in time, and he has agreed to appear before a contemporary American audience. You have been asked to introduce Mark Twain by giving a brief overview of his life. Identify three points you'll make for each segment of your talk. Suggest a photograph to illustrate each part.*

Life on the River (The early years) Key points: _____

_____

Photograph: _____

A Traveling Man (The middle years) Key points: _____

_____

Photograph: _____

A Restless Soul (The latter years) Key points: _____

_____

Photograph: _____

B. DIRECTIONS: *Imagine that you are Mark Twain, and you are appearing as a guest on a late-night TV show. Respond to these questions.*

Host: You once said that you would have been happier if you had been able to spend your entire life as a riverboat pilot rather than as a writer. You weren't serious, were you? What did you mean by that comment?

Twain: _____

_____

Host: You use humor very effectively in your writing. Explain to me how important you think humor is in the success of your writing.

Twain: _____

_____

Host: You have created some wonderful characters that are entirely American. In your opinion, how would you define a typical American?

Twain: _____

_____

"The Boys' Ambition" *from* **Life on the Mississippi** and **"The Notorious Jumping Frog of Calaveras County"** by Mark Twain

Literary Analysis: Humor

Humor in literature is writing that is intended to evoke laughter. American humorists use a variety of techniques to make their writing amusing. Mark Twain, for example, commonly uses hyperbole and regional dialect. He calls attention to human foibles and to incongruities between a speaker's tone and the events he describes and between logic and illogic. He points out the inability of people to control their surroundings.

DIRECTIONS: *Decide whether the following passages are humorous because they contain hyperbole, regional dialect, incongruities, a sense of human foibles, or a combination of these elements. Write your answer on the lines following each passage.*

1. "He was the curiousest man about always betting on anything that turned up you ever see. . . ."

   _____

   _____

2. "If he even see a straddle bug start to go anywheres, he would bet you how long it would take him to get to . . . wherever . . . and if you took him up, he would foller that straddle bug to Mexico. . . ."

   _____

   _____

3. " . . . and *always* fetch up at the stand just about a neck ahead, as near as you could cipher it down."

   _____

   _____

4. 'He'd spring straight up and snake a fly off'n a counter there, and flop down on the floor ag'in as solid as a gob of mud."

   _____

   _____

5. He never smiled, he never frowned, he never changed his voice from the gentle-flowing key to which he tuned his initial sentence, he never betrayed the slightest suspicion of enthusiasm; but all through the interminable narrative there ran a vein of impressive earnestness and sincerity, which showed me plainly that, so far from his imagining that there was anything ridiculous or funny about his story, he regarded it as a really important matter, and admired its two heroes as men of transcendent genius in *finesse.*

   _____

   _____

Name _____ Date _____

"The Boys' Ambition" *from* **Life on the Mississippi** and **"The Notorious Jumping Frog of Calaveras County"** by Mark Twain

Reading Strategy: Understand Regional Dialect

Regional dialect is the informal language people use in everyday speech. Sometimes fiction writers use regional dialect to give readers a picture of certain characters. If you find it hard to understand this language when you're reading, try reading it aloud.

DIRECTIONS: *Read the following excerpts from "The Notorious Jumping Frog of Calaveras County." Write in your own words what you think each one means.*

1. ". . . he was the curiousest man about always betting on anything that turned up you ever see, if he could get anybody to bet on the other side; and if he couldn't he'd change sides."

   _____

   _____

   _____

2. "Thish-yer Smiley had a mare—the boys called her the fifteen-minute nag, but that was only in fun, you know, because of course she was faster than that—and he used to win money on that horse, for all she was so slow and always had the asthma, or the distemper, or the consumption, or something of that kind."

   _____

   _____

   _____

3. ". . . to look at him you'd think he warn't worth a cent but to set around and look ornery and lay for a chance to steal something. But as soon as money was up on him he was a different dog; his under-jaw'd begin to stick out like the fo'castle of a steamboat, and his teeth would uncover and shine like the furnaces."

   _____

   _____

   _____

4. ". . . all of a sudden he would grab that other dog jest by the j'int of his hind leg and freeze to it—not chaw, you understand, but only just grip and hang on till they threwed up the sponge, if it was a year."

   _____

   _____

   _____

"The Boys' Ambition" *from* **Life on the Mississippi** and **"The Notorious Jumping Frog of Calaveras County"** by Mark Twain

Vocabulary Builder

Using the Prefix *mono-*

A. DIRECTIONS: *The prefix* mono- *means "alone," "single," or "one." Use the clues given and what you know about the prefix* mono- *to figure out these word puzzles.*

1. knowing two languages = *bilingual;*

   knowing one language = _____

2. paralysis of one side of the body = *hemiplegia;*

   paralysis of a single limb = _____

3. a word with four or more syllables = *polysyllable*

   a word with one syllable = _____

4. having three of one type of chromosome = *trisomic*

   having a single chromosome = _____

Using the Word List

conjectured	eminence	garrulous	interminable
prodigious	monotonous	transient	

B. DIRECTIONS: *In the blank, write the letter of the Word List word that is closest in meaning to the numbered word.*

___ 1. guessed   A. transient
___ 2. celebrity   B. prodigious
___ 3. temporary   C. monotonous
___ 4. talkative   D. conjectured
___ 5. unvarying   E. interminable
___ 6. enormous   F. garrulous
___ 7. endless   G. eminence

"The Boys' Ambition" *from* **Life on the Mississippi** and **"The Notorious Jumping Frog of Calaveras County"** by Mark Twain

Grammar and Style: Fixing Misplaced and Dangling Modifiers

A **misplaced modifier** seems to modify the wrong word in a sentence because it is too far away from the word it really modifies. A **dangling modifier** seems to modify the wrong word—or no word at all—because the word it *should* modify isn't in the sentence. Misplaced and dangling modifiers can be single words, phrases, or clauses.

Misplaced:	*Sleepy,* the stores stood empty as the clerks nodded in their chairs.
Fixed:	The stores stood empty as the sleepy clerks nodded in their chairs.
Dangling:	*Turning upriver,* the next town was a few miles away.
Fixed:	Turning upriver, the steamboat headed toward the next town a few miles away.

A. PRACTICE: *Write a sentence using each phrase or word as a modifier. Then, circle the word or words that the phrase or clause modifies.*

1. that arrived at the landing

   _____

2. waiting his turn

   _____

3. lost in thought

   _____

4. looking carefully at his frog

   _____

5. who got the last laugh

   _____

B. Writing Application: *Decide whether the sentences below contain misplaced or dangling modifiers. If the sentence is written correctly, write "correct" on the line that follows it. If the sentence contains misplaced or dangling modifier, rewrite it correctly.*

1. Laughing heartily, the winning frog was cheered by the crowd.

   _____

2. Standing in the pilot house, he peered as far as he could see down the river.

   _____

3. Eager to see the steamboat arrive, the chores were left undone.

   _____

4. The passengers who left the steamboat wandered through the town.

   _____

5. Stories were often exaggerated while working as a reporter.

   _____

Name _____ Date _____

"The Boys' Ambition" *from* **Life on the Mississippi** and **"The Notorious Jumping Frog of Calaveras County"** by Mark Twain

Support for Writing

Think about Mark Twain's quote: "The humorous story may be spun out to great length, and may wander around as much as it pleases, and arrive nowhere in particular. . . . [It] is told gravely; the teller does his best to conceal the fact that he even dimly suspects there is anything funny about it." To gather information for your **analytical essay** about Twain's ideas of humor as they are reflected in "The Notorious Jumping Frog of Calaveras County," use the graphic organizer below.

Twain's Humor in "The Notorious Jumping Frog of Calaveras County"

Spins out at length (takes its time)	Arrives nowhere (doesn't have a point)	Is told gravely (with a serious tone)	Conceals humor (hides suggestions of humor)

On a separate page, draft your essay connecting each of Twain's points about humor with the example you have found in the story. When you revise, add examples to make your connections between Twain's comments and the story clearer.

Name _____ Date _____

"The Boys' Ambition" *from* Life on the Mississippi and "The Notorious Jumping Frog of Calaveras County" by Mark Twain
Enrichment: Jargon

When Mark Twain writes about life on the Mississippi, he often uses jargon specific to waterways and steamboats. **Jargon** is the collective name for special words and terms used by people in a certain profession.

DIRECTIONS: *Think about a job that you have done or that you are interested in doing someday. Using the following chart, fill in the title of the job and some examples of jargon that are used on the job. Use the second column of the chart to describe what each word of jargon means.*

Job Jargon

Job Title: _____

Term	What the Term Means

"The Boys' Ambition" *from* Life on the Mississippi, and
"The Notorious Jumping Frog of Calaveras County" by Mark Twain
Open-Book Test

Short Answer *Write your responses to the questions in this section on the lines provided.*

1. In the first few paragraphs of "The Boys' Ambition," Twain discusses the boys' dreams of working on a steamboat. From Twain's description of the town, what can you infer about the reason most boys wanted to work on a steamboat?

   _____

   _____

   _____

2. Twain often employs exaggeration to achieve comic effect. How does he use this technique in describing the importance of his father's job as justice of the peace?

   _____

   _____

3. What overall impression of the town of Hannibal does Twain convey in "The Boys' Ambition"? What is the town like before the steamboat has arrived, and after it has left?

   _____

   _____

   _____

4. In "The Boys' Ambition," when Twain hears that a boyhood friend of his had obtained a job as a steamboat engineer's apprentice, he is shaken. He writes:

   > This thing shook the bottom out of all my Sunday school teachings. That boy had been notoriously worldly, and I just the reverse; yet he was exalted to this eminence, and I left in obscurity and misery.

   Briefly summarize in your own words Twain's attitude toward this boy, and explain the humorous effect of his method of conveying his feelings.

   _____

   _____

   _____

   _____

5. Toward the end of "The Boys' Ambition," Twain says that he ran away from home. Why did he do this?

   _____

   _____

   _____

   _____

Name _____ Date _____

6. What evidence is there in the first few paragraphs of "The Notorious Jumping Frog of Calaveras County" that tells the reader this is going to be a humorous story? Find two details or quotations that indicate Twain's intent to amuse his readers.

_____

_____

_____

7. In "The Notorious Jumping Frog of Calaveras County," Wheeler's monologue is told largely in regional dialect. Review Wheeler's story, and pick out three examples of regional dialect, using the context of the sentences to determine the meaning of each. Record each example and your translation of it in the chart below.

Dialect Word or Phrase	Meaning of Dialect Word or Phrase

8. In "The Notorious Jumping Frog of Calaveras County," why does Smiley make a point of acting indifferent when the stranger asks him about his special frog, Dan'l Webster? What does he hope to gain from the stranger?

_____

_____

_____

9. In "The Notorious Jumping Frog of Calaveras County," Wheeler tells the story of Smiley and his frog with a fierce earnestness. What is it about Wheeler's retelling of the frog-jumping contest that makes the story so humorous?

_____

_____

_____

10. If you had conjectured the answers to most of the problems on a math test, is it likely that you had passed or failed? Why? Base your answer on the meaning of *conjectured* as it is used in "The Notorious Jumping Frog of Calaveras County."

_____

_____

_____

Essay

Write an extended response to the question of your choice or to the question or questions your teacher assigns you.

11. Much of "The Boys' Ambition" is devoted to describing the fascination that Twain and his friends had with steamboats and the lives of the people who worked on them. In an essay, explain why Twain and his friends found the idea of working on a steamboat to be so exciting. Support your answer with details from the story.

Unit 3 Resources: Division, Reconciliation, and Expansion
© Pearson Education, Inc. All rights reserved.
142

12. Twain uses exaggeration to achieve much of the humorous effect of "The Notorious Jumping Frog of Calaveras County." In an essay, explain how Twain uses exaggeration about the animals to humorous effect. Support your answer with examples from the story.

13. In "The Notorious Jumping Frog of Calaveras County," the storyteller Simon Wheeler weaves an improbable, amusing tale about an amazing jumping frog called Dan'l Webster. Which of these two—Wheeler or Dan'l Webster—do you think is the main character of the story? Support your opinion with examples from the story.

14. **Thinking About the Essential Question: How does literature shape or reflect society?** In "The Boys' Ambition" and "The Notorious Jumping Frog of Calaveras County," Mark Twain evokes characters and settings that are distinctly American. Do you think that Twain can be said to have defined America in his writing? Why or why not? Can you think of any other artist, writer, filmmaker, or musician whose view of America has been as genuine, as widely accepted and influential? Express your opinion in an essay supported by specific examples.

Oral Response

15. Go back to question 3, 4, or 9 or to the question your teacher assigns you. Take a few minutes to expand your answer and prepare an oral response. Find additional details in"The Boys' Ambition" or "The Notorious Jumping Frog of Calaveras County" that support your points. If necessary, make notes to guide your oral response.

Name _____ Date _____

"The Boys' Ambition" *from* **Life on the Mississippi and "The Notorious Jumping Frog of Calaveras County"** by Mark Twain

Selection Test A

Critical Reading *Identify the letter of the choice that best answers the question.*

____ 1. Based on "The Boys' Ambition," what did the boys feel toward people who worked on a steamboat?
  A. envy
  B. admiration
  C. happiness
  D. boredom

____ 2. What inference can you make from "The Boys' Ambition" about why being a steamboatman was such a desirable goal to Twain and his companions?
  A. The boys could leave Hannibal.
  B. Steamboatmen could get rich.
  C. The steamboat arrival was each day's high point.
  D. There were no other jobs in Hannibal at that time.

____ 3. Which statement shows Twain's humor about his father's job in "The Boys' Ambition"?
  A. He says it is a better job than steamboating.
  B. He says his father can hang anyone he wants.
  C. He says his father has a lot of power in town.
  D. He says his father has a special occupation.

____ 4. According to "The Boys' Ambition," which job on a steamboat is the best position?
  A. engineer
  B. mud clerk
  C. barkeeper
  D. pilot

____ 5. What exaggeration about Jim Smiley does the narrator of "The Notorious Jumping Frog of Calaveras County" make?
  A. Smiley has a frog that is a good jumper.
  B. Smiley will bet on anything, on any side.
  C. Smiley has a dog that wins fights.
  D. Smiley is tricked by a stranger.

_____ 6. In "The Notorious Jumping Frog of Calaveras County," what does this example of regional dialect mean?

"He roused up, and gave me good day."

A. He woke up and gave me the time.

B. He stood up and greeted me.

C. He went and made some food for us.

D. He showed me around the town.

_____ 7. Which aspect of "The Notorious Jumping Frog of Calaveras County" makes the story humorous?

A. The wild story is told in a voice that has no expression.

B. The story is so unbelievable it is not even funny.

C. The narrator believes it is a true story instead of a tall tale.

D. The narrator falls asleep as he is listening to the story.

_____ 8. How would you rephrase this sentence from "The Notorious Jumping Frog of Calaveras County"?

"And he had a little small bull-pup, that to look at him you'd think he warn't worth a cent but to set around and look ornery and lay for a chance to steal something."

A. And he had a small dog that was pretty worthless but he kept him around for protection.

B. And he had a small dog that looked like he hadn't cost a thing and had probably been stolen.

C. And he had a small dog whose job was to look fearsome and lie in wait to snatch something for nothing.

D. And he had a small dog that he kept trying to sell for more money than the creature was worth.

_____ 9. In "The Notorious Jumping Frog of Calaveras County," why does Smiley act uninterested when the stranger asks about the frog?

A. He wants to trick him into betting.

B. He doesn't want the frog to compete.

C. He has given up betting for good.

D. He is worried about the frog's health.

_____ **10.** How would you restate this sentence from "The Notorious Jumping Frog of Calaveras County"?

"If there was a horse race, you'd find him flush or you'd find him busted at the end of it."

A. At the end of a horse race, he'd either be flushed with victory or arrested.

B. At the end of a horse race, either he'd have won or he'd have lost.

C. At the end of a horse race, you couldn't find him to arrest him.

D. At the end of a horse race, he'd be embarrassed because he had lost.

Vocabulary and Grammar

_____ **11.** In which of these sentences is the meaning of the word *interminable* suggested?

A. I had a hard time believing his stories.

B. His story seemed to go on forever.

C. He was willing to bet on anything.

D. He was outsmarted by a stranger.

_____ **12.** Which of the following sentences contains a dangling modifier?

A. Smiley took the frog and gently set him on the floor.

B. Waiting for the contest to begin, the frogs were real jumpers.

C. Yelling "git," the frogs were urged by the men to jump.

D. Holding the box, he kept one eye on the frog and one on his opponent.

Essay

13. In "The Boys' Ambition," what do you think is the appeal of being a steamboatman? Using your impressions and the text of "The Boys' Ambition," write a brief essay about why Twain and his companions found the idea of being a steamboatman so exciting.

14. Exaggeration is a major element in "The Notorious Jumping Frog of Calaveras County." Write a brief essay to discuss which parts of the stories about the animals seem to be exaggerations. Include an explanation about why writers might use exaggeration.

15. **Thinking About the Essential Question: How does literature shape or reflect society?** In "The Boys' Ambition" and "The Notorious Jumping Frog of Calaveras County," the characters and settings are purely American. Do you think that Twain painted a picture of what America is really like? Why or why not? Does that picture still depict America today?

"The Boys' Ambition" *from* Life on the Mississippi and
"The Notorious Jumping Frog of Calaveras County" by Mark Twain
Selection Test B

Critical Reading *Identify the letter of the choice that best completes the statement or answers the question.*

____ 1. Which of the following best describes Jim Smiley?
    A. bored and annoyed
    B. suspicious and aggressive
    C. clever and competitive
    D. gentle and tranquil

____ 2. When the apprentice engineer is able to "cut out every boy in the village," he is able to
    A. beat any boy in the village in a fight.
    B. take a girl away from any boy in the village.
    C. ignore any boy in the village.
    D. outrun any boy in the village.

____ 3. For the author as a boy, the Mississippi River was above all
    A. a wonder of nature.
    B. a pathway to adventure.
    C. a means of escape from Hannibal.
    D. an opportunity to get rich.

____ 4. Base your answer on the following excerpt:
    "[Smiley's dog] would grab the other dog . . . and hang on till they throwed up the sponge."
    In this sentence, the words "throwed up the sponge" mean that the people watching the dog fight would
    A. admit that they had lost the bet.
    B. bet more money on Smiley's dog.
    C. grab Smiley's dog and tie it up.
    D. try to help the other dog beat Smiley's dog.

____ 5. The reader is led to believe that Andrew Jackson, the fighting dog, lost his last fight because of
    A. his own stupidity.
    B. the other dog's superior strength.
    C. a thrown sponge.
    D. a broken spirit after being tricked.

____ 6. What makes the steamboat such a source of fascination for the boys?
    A. It is a marvel of modern technology.
    B. It is accessible only to the rich and powerful.
    C. It is a connection to the world outside Hannibal.
    D. It is connected with stories of shady dealings.

____ 7. Which of the following does Mark Twain use to add humor to this story?
  A. unexpected plot shifts
  B. misunderstandings between characters
  C. colorful names for characters
  D. all of the above

____ 8. Twain uses exaggeration in "The Boys' Ambition" primarily to
  A. make the townspeople look ridiculous.
  B. emphasize the boys' feelings about steamboating.
  C. contrast Hannibal with St. Louis.
  D. make the story entertaining.

____ 9. In the sentence "By and by one of our boys went away," the expression "by and by" means
  A. after he said 'good-bye'.
  B. some time later.
  C. after purchasing his contract.
  D. mysteriously.

____ 10. Why did Smiley act indifferently when the stranger asked him about Dan'l Webster?
  A. Smiley was hoping to convince the stranger to bet on how well Dan'l could jump.
  B. Smiley was busy trying to teach Dan'l to jump, and the stranger interrupted.
  C. Dan'l looked like he had something wrong with him, and Smiley was worried.
  D. Simon Wheeler had cheated on a bet, and Smiley was angry.

____ 11. When Jim Smiley brought Dan'l Webster downtown and "lay for a bet," Twain means that Jim Smiley would
  A. talk for a while.
  B. put money on the frog.
  C. lie down and sleep.
  D. wait for someone to make a bet with him.

____ 12. Which of the following sayings best describes the author's attitude toward the boy who becomes an apprentice engineer?
  A. Everything comes to him who waits.
  B. Pride goes before a fall.
  C. Justice is blind.
  D. A rolling stone gathers no moss.

____ 13. One aspect of "The Notorious Jumping Frog of Calaveras County" that makes the story humorous is the fact that
  A. Simon Wheeler does not recognize how ridiculous his tale is.
  B. the narrator believes everything that Simon Wheeler tells him.
  C. Smiley refuses to believe that the frog-jumping contest was fair.
  D. the stranger thinks that he can actually fool Smiley.

Vocabulary and Grammar

____ 14. What is the probable result of a *"monotonous* narrative"?
   A. Listeners will be educated.
   B. Listeners will be bored.
   C. Listeners will either strongly agree or strongly disagree with the speaker.
   D. Listeners will be inspired to fight for the speaker's cause.

____ 15. Who is best described as *garrulous* in "The Notorious Jumping Frog of Calaveras County"?
   A. the narrator
   B. Simon Wheeler
   C. Jim Smiley
   D. the stranger

____ 16. Which of the following sentences contains a dangling modifier?
   A. The cabin boy ran down the gangplank, hoping to catch sight of his father.
   B. Waiting for the passengers to board, the pilot studied the river.
   C. The steamboat turned slowly in midstream and then pulled into its berth.
   D. Often swift and dangerous, the pilot kept the steamboat headed downstream.

____ 17. The drayman's "prodigious voice" in "The Boys' Ambition" makes him well suited to
   A. alert the town.
   B. drive a dray.
   C. be an apprentice engineer.
   D. pilot the river.

Essay

18. Who is the main character of "The Notorious Jumping Frog of Calaveras County"—the jumping frog Dan'l Webster or the storyteller Simon Wheeler? Write an essay stating your opinion. Support your argument with your definition of a main character and its role in a story, and describe how your choice of main character functions in Twain's tale. Use examples from the work to strengthen your essay.

19. Exaggeration, embellishment, and regional dialect are all techniques that can make a story humorous. Write a brief essay about how these techniques lend humor to one or both of these Twain selections. Support your points about the effectiveness of each humorous technique, using examples from the story or stories.

20. One central idea of "The Boys' Ambition" is that the unknown often has a much greater appeal than the familiar. Write a brief essay about the appeal of the unknown. Use examples from both "The Boys' Ambition" and your own life to support your essay.

21. **Thinking About the Essential Question: How does literature shape or reflect society?** In "The Boys' Ambition" and "The Notorious Jumping Frog of Calaveras County," Mark Twain evokes characters and settings that are distinctly American. Do you think that Twain can be said to have defined America in his writing? Why or why not? Can you think of any other artist, writer, filmmaker, or musician whose view of America has been as genuine, as widely accepted and influential? Express your opinion in an essay supported by specific examples.

from **The Life and Times of the Thunderbolt Kid** by Bill Bryson
Literary Analysis: Humor

Humor in literature is writing that is intended to make people laugh. American humorists use a variety of techniques to make their writing amusing. Bill Bryson, like Mark Twain, uses folk humor. Their techniques include use of **hyperbole, incongruity, regional** language and behavior, a focus on **human foibles,** and **comic characters.**

DIRECTIONS: *Decide whether the following passages are humorous because they contain hyperbole, incongruities, regional behavior or language, a display of human foibles, comic characters, or a combination of these elements. Write your answer on the lines following each passage.*

1. "The only downside of my mother's working was that it put a little pressure on her with regard to running the home and particularly with regard to dinner, which frankly was not her strong suit anyway."

   _____

2. "Like most people in Iowa in the 1950s, we were more cautious eaters in our house. On the rare occasions when we were presented with food with which we were not comfortable or familiar—on planes or trains or when invited to a meal cooked by someone who was not herself from Iowa—we tended to tilt it up carefully with a knife and examine it from every angle as if determining whether it might need to be defused."

   _____

3. "'It's a bit burned,' my mother would say apologetically at every meal, presenting you with a piece of meat that looked like something—a much-loved pet perhaps—salvaged from a tragic house fire."

   _____

4. "Hines's other proud boast was that he did not venture out of America until he was seventy years old, when he made a trip to Europe. He disliked much of what he found there, especially the food."

   _____

5. "All our meals consisted of leftovers. My mother had a seemingly inexhaustible supply of foods that had already been to the table, sometimes repeatedly."

   _____

from **The Life and Times of the Thunderbolt Kid** by Bill Bryson
Vocabulary Builder

Using the Word List

> dubious   embark

A. DIRECTIONS: *Circle the synonym for the underlined word in each sentence or phrase.*

1. You soon learned to stand aside about ten to six every evening, for it was then that she would fly in the back door, throw something in the oven, and disappear into some other quarter of the house to <u>embark</u> on the thousand other household tasks that greeted her each evening. (commence, evaluate)

2. In our house we didn't eat . . . anything with <u>dubious</u> regional names like "pone" or "gumbo," or foods that had at any time been an esteemed staple of slaves or peasants.

   (humorous, questionable)

B. DIRECTIONS: *For each item, choose the word pair that best expresses a relationship similar to the one expressed in the numbered pair. Circle the letter of your choice.*

1. CERTAIN : DUBIOUS ::
   A. wishful : thoughtful
   B. threatened : endangered
   C. hungry : starving
   D. tasteless : delicious

2. TASK : EMBARK ::
   A. victim : rescue
   B. diet : hunger
   C. painter : create
   D. teacher : study

from **The Life and Times of the Thunderbolt Kid** by Bill Bryson
Support for Writing

Prepare to write your **essay** comparing character types in the selection from Bryson's *The Life and Times of the Thunderbolt Kid* and Twain's "The Notorious Jumping Frog of Calaveras County." Enter details from the selections in the chart below.

	Mother in *Thunderbolt Kid*	**Jim Smiley in** **"Jumping Frog"**
What makes the character funny?		
What makes the character sympathetic?		
How does the writer use the character to critique society or humanity?		

On a separate page, write a draft of your essay. Be sure to use transitions and an effective comparison-contrast organization to make your ideas clear. When you revise, make sure you have supported your main ideas with details from the selections.

from **The Life and Times of the Thunderbolt Kid** by Bill Bryson
Selection Test

MULTIPLE CHOICE

Critical Reading *Identify the letter of the choice that best answers the question.*

____ 1. What is Bryson's main purpose in writing this passage from *The Life and Times of the Thunderbolt Kid*?
   A. to explain
   B. to persuade
   C. to describe
   D. to entertain

____ 2. Which of the following does Bryson point out as one of his mother's main foibles?
   A. collecting housekeeping magazines
   B. eating Chinese food
   C. shopping
   D. cooking

____ 3. Which quotation is an example of hyperbole?
   A. "Like most people in Iowa in the 1950s, we were more cautious eaters in our house."
   B. "The housewives in my mother's magazines were so collected, so organized, so calmly on top of things, and their food was perfect—their *lives* were perfect."
   C. "'It's a bit burned,' my mother would say apologetically at every meal, presenting you with a piece of meat that looked like something—a much-loved pet perhaps—salvaged from a tragic house fire."
   D. "I remember being surprised to learn at quite an advanced age that a shrimp cocktail was not, as I had always imagined, a predinner alcoholic drink with a shrimp in it."

____ 4. Why does Bryson say his parents' marriage was made in heaven?
   A. They both collected sugar, salt, pepper, and other food packets at restaurants.
   B. His mother always burned food and his father liked burned food.
   C. They worked the same hours and enjoyed sharing household chores.
   D. Neither of them liked foreign or unusual food.

____ 5. What was the "Burns Unit" in the Bryson household?
   A. kitchen
   B. refrigerator
   C. local emergency room
   D. Bryson's bedroom

_____ 6. What did the Bryson family do when confronted with an unfamiliar food?
   A. Refuse to eat it.
   B. Eat it very quickly.
   C. Examine it closely.
   D. Wait to see how others ate it.

_____ 7. What is the tone, or author's attitude, expressed in the passage from *The Life and Times of the Thunderbolt Kid*?
   A. humorous
   B. appreciative
   C. serious
   D. nostalgic

_____ 8. In what way does Bryson suggest that his family was much like that of other American families during the 1950s?
   A. They collected aluminum foil.
   B. They were not adventuresome eaters.
   C. They lived during the Great Depression.
   D. They enjoyed regional foods.

_____ 9. Which of the following is an accurate statement about both "The Notorious Jumping Frog of Calaveras County" and the excerpt from *The Life and Times of the Thunderbolt Kid*?
   A. Both works use language and word choice to create a comic effect.
   B. Both works use a dialect that reflects their common region of origin.
   C. Neither work uses hyperbole to create humor.
   D. Neither work was written primarily to entertain.

_____ 10. Both Twain and Bryson
   A. criticize the narrow-mindedness of people.
   B. explain why too much is expected of people.
   C. paint a good-natured picture of people.
   D. encourage people to try different things in life.

Vocabulary Warm-up Word Lists

Study these words from the selection. Then, complete the activities.

Word List A

aggressively [uh GRES iv lee] *adv.* boldly or energetically
When the magician called for a volunteer, Lucy's hand shot up <u>aggressively</u>.

circulation [ser kyoo LAY shun] *n.* the movement of blood around the body
Does aerobic exercise improve the <u>circulation</u>?

floundered [FLOWN derd] *v.* move in an awkward, stumbling way
Everyone cleared out of Big Bill's way as he <u>floundered</u> around the dance floor.

imperative [im PE ruh tiv] *adj.* urgent and necessary
It is <u>imperative</u> that you return the shirt you borrowed.

likewise [LYK wyz] *adv.* in the same way; also
Kyle is leaving at six; will you be leaving early <u>likewise</u>?

methodically [me THAH dik lee] *adv.* in an orderly, systematic way
Mandy plays chess <u>methodically</u>, while Lisa does not seem to think ahead at all.

panicky [PAN ik ee] *adj.* out of control with fear
His expression turned <u>panicky</u> as the bear lumbered toward him.

undesirable [un de ZY ruh bul] *adj.* not wanted; not pleasing
A large anthill is an <u>undesirable</u> spot for a picnic.

Word List B

agitation [a ji TAY shun] *n.* emotional disturbance or excitement
The man hopped around, wringing his hands, his <u>agitation</u> obvious.

arctic [AHRK tik] *adj.* very cold
Stepping into the air-conditioned house felt like being hit by an <u>arctic</u> blast.

asserted [uh SERT id] *v.* insisted on being recognized
If I had not <u>asserted</u> my rights, he would have kept that remote control forever.

capsizing [KAP syz ing] *v.* overturning
Returning to port prior to the storm kept the boat from <u>capsizing</u>.

entanglement [in TANG uhl muhnt] *n.* state of being tangled
The dog owners let go of their leashes to avoid <u>entanglement</u>.

immortality [im mohr TAL i tee] *n.* lasting fame
That book may be popular now, but do you think it will achieve <u>immortality</u>?

penalty [PEN ul tee] *n.* punishment or unfortunate result
The <u>penalty</u> for her lateness was that all the good seats had been taken.

yearned [YERND] *v.* longed
He <u>yearned</u> for a cold soda, but he had left his wallet at home.

"**To Build a Fire**" by Jack London
Vocabulary Warm-up Exercises

Exercise A *Fill in each blank in the paragraph below with the appropriate word from Word List A.*

I was sitting in the field, watching the cows peacefully and [1] _____ chewing the grass, when suddenly I noticed a large, angry-looking bull moving [2] _____ in my direction. I do not exaggerate when I say that the blood froze in my veins; it really felt as if my [3] _____ had actually stopped. Suddenly, it seemed [4] _____ that I be on the other side of the fence. I began to run. Then, looking over my shoulder, I saw that the bull was doing [5] _____, only faster. That was when I really started feeling [6] _____. As I [7] _____ my way clumsily over the fence, I decided that a field with a bull is an [8] _____ place to relax, unless you are a cow.

Exercise B *Decide whether each statement below is true or false. Circle T or F, and explain your answer.*

1. Getting three flat tires in one week would tend to cause a driver <u>agitation</u>.
   T / F _____

2. A smart fly tries to avoid <u>entanglement</u> in a spider's web.
   T / F _____

3. If you go to Texas in July, you will be sure to suffer <u>arctic</u> temperatures.
   T / F _____

4. Football players are especially happy when their team gets a <u>penalty</u>.
   T / F _____

5. Shakespeare achieved <u>immortality</u> through his great cooking.
   T / F _____

6. Cruise tickets might be a good gift for someone who has always <u>yearned</u> to travel.
   T / F _____

7. <u>Capsizing</u> the life boat is a good idea for shipwrecked passengers.
   T / F _____

8. When Rosa Parks refused to give up her seat on a bus, she <u>asserted</u> her rights.
   T / F _____

"To Build a Fire" by Jack London
Reading Warm-up A

Read the following passage. Pay special attention to the underlined words. Then, read it again, and complete the activities. Use a separate sheet of paper for your written answers.

Imagine being lost alone in the wilderness, hungry, cold, and unprepared—no cozy sleeping bag, no packets of belly-warming cocoa to heat over a campstove. If you should find yourself in this <u>undesirable</u> situation, would you know what to do?

According to survival experts, the first and most important thing is not to become <u>panicky</u>. Sit down, take a deep breath, and think carefully and <u>methodically</u> about your options. What equipment or supplies do you have with you? Even a plastic garbage bag can be extremely useful for keeping you warm and dry. <u>Likewise</u>, you can find natural shelter in unexpected spots—even in deep snow, for instance, there may be a dry, clear area under the lowest branches of a big evergreen tree.

To survive cold weather, it is <u>imperative</u> that you keep your body temperature up. Instead of sitting directly on the ground or in the snow, make a pile of branches or find a fallen tree. Be sure your head is covered—thanks to extra blood <u>circulation</u> around the brain, you can lose forty percent of your heat through your head. If possible, stuff your clothes with dry leaves for insulation. Then, curl yourself up into a ball to conserve your body heat.

Aside from staying alive, your main responsibility is to be found, so *stay in one place*. Searchers are more likely to discover you if you have not <u>floundered</u> around getting even more lost. Also, try to make yourself easy to see: stay out in the open, or use sticks and rocks to make a sign pointing to your shelter. Lastly, if a helicopter flies overhead, wave wildly and <u>aggressively</u> with *both* arms so they know you are in trouble and not just saying hello!

1. Underline what is <u>undesirable</u> about the situation. Then, describe another situation that would be *undesirable*.

2. Underline what to do to keep from getting <u>panicky</u>. What is the opposite of *panicky*?

3. Circle a word that means something similar to <u>methodically</u>. How could a pencil and paper help you think *methodically*?

4. What word could you substitute for *likewise* in this sentence?

5. Underline what is <u>imperative</u> for survival in cold weather. What would be *imperative* to know before riding a bicycle downhill?

6. Underline what <u>circulation</u> in the head has to do with keeping warm. What words mean the same as *circulation*?

7. Underline what could happen if you <u>floundered</u> around rather than staying put. Would you use the word *floundered* for someone who moved with grace and purpose?

8. Circle what you should do <u>aggressively</u> if you see a helicopter. What else might someone do *aggressively*?

Name _____ Date _____

"To Build a Fire" by Jack London
Reading Warm-up B

Read the following passage. Pay special attention to the underlined words. Then, read it again, and complete the activities. Use a separate sheet of paper for your written answers.

On a cold March morning in 1985, Libby Riddles waited at the starting line of the Iditarod, the "Last Great Race on Earth." Her fifteen sled dogs—Binga, Bug-man, Brownie, Stewpot, and the rest—were barking madly, and Riddles worked hard to hide her own <u>agitation</u>.

All the mushers had good reason to be nervous; after all, the race would cover more than a thousand miles of harsh, dangerous <u>arctic</u> terrain, from rugged mountain peaks to frozen rivers. For Riddles, though, the stakes were extra high. No woman had ever won the Iditarod—if she crossed the finish line first, she would win not just this year's race, but <u>immortality</u>.

Disaster struck, however, before she even got out of Anchorage, the city where the race began. Her excited dog team decided to take a "shortcut" through the woods. Ignoring her shouts, they dragged her through the brush, nearly <u>capsizing</u> the sled as Riddles struggled to keep the lines clear and avoid <u>entanglement</u>. She quickly <u>asserted</u> her authority, though, and soon she and her team were off again, this time for real.

Bitter subzero temperatures, sleepless nights, even briefly losing her dogs when they took off without her—nothing stopped Riddles, and soon she was in the lead. Then, a huge storm blew up, a raging, blinding blizzard with seventy-mile-an-hour winds. While her competitors hung back in the safety of a village, Riddles pushed on into the blizzard with her team.

It was a risky move, and she might very well have paid the ultimate <u>penalty</u> for her decision. Instead, thanks to her courage and skill—not to mention good luck—Riddles achieved the goal she <u>yearned</u> for: she became the first woman to win the "Last Great Race on Earth."

1. Underline the way the dogs showed <u>agitation</u>. How does a baby show *agitation*?

2. Circle the word that means something similar to <u>arctic</u>. Why would *arctic* terrain be dangerous?

3. Underline why winning the race would bring Riddles <u>immortality</u>. Name someone you admire who earned *immortality* through his or her achievements.

4. Underline what the dogs did that nearly resulted in <u>capsizing</u> the sled. Why would *capsizing* the sled be a bad thing for Riddles?

5. Underline what Riddles did to avoid <u>entanglement</u>. Then, describe another kind of *entanglement*.

6. How do you think Riddles <u>asserted</u> her authority over the dogs?

7. What would be the "ultimate <u>penalty</u>" that Riddles might have paid?

8. Underline what Riddles <u>yearned</u> to do, and did. Name another achievement that someone might *yearn* for.

Name _____ Date _____

"**To Build a Fire**" by Jack London
Literary Analysis: Conflict, Setting, Irony

Conflict is the struggle between two opposing forces or characters. An **internal conflict** is a struggle between conflicting thoughts and emotions within a character's mind. You face an internal conflict, for example, when you want to spend time studying for a test, yet you also want to go to a movie with your friends. An **external conflict** is a struggle between a character and an outside force, such as another character, society, nature, or fate. A pilot trying to land an airplane in strong winds is engaged in an external conflict—person against nature. In this last example, the **setting**—the place and time—serves as the source of the conflict. **Irony** is sometimes used to heighten the effect of the conflict by stressing a contradiction between what a character thinks and what the reader knows to be true.

DIRECTIONS: *Following are brief excerpts from "To Build a Fire." Identify the conflict in each as internal or external. Then identify the opposing forces and tell whether the setting is central to the conflict. Finally, identify any irony that may heighten the effect.*

1. "It was seventy-five below zero. Since the freezing point is thirty-two above zero, it meant that one hundred and seven degrees of frost obtained."

   _____

   _____

2. "He tried to keep this thought down, to forget it, to think of something else; he was aware of the panicky feeling that it caused, and he was afraid of the panic."

   _____

   _____

3. "He spoke to the dog . . . but in his voice was a strange note of fear that frightened the animal. . . . As it came within reaching distance, the man lost his control."

   _____

   _____

4. "High up in the tree one bough capsized its load of snow. . . . It grew like an avalanche, and it descended without warning upon the man and the fire, and the fire was blotted out!"

   _____

   _____

5. "He was very careful. He drove the thought of his freezing feet, and nose, and cheeks, out of his mind, devoting his whole soul to the matches."

   _____

   _____

6. ". . . it was a matter of life and death. This threw him into a panic, and he turned and ran up the creekbed along the old, dim trail."

   _____

   _____

7. "Well, he was bound to freeze anyway, and he might as well take it decently."

   _____

   _____

Name _____ Date _____

Reading Strategy: Make Predictions

Making predictions about what you are reading based on clues in the text and on your previous experience can increase your enjoyment of a literary work and help you be a more effective reader. In "To Build a Fire," many of the clues come from the setting. The main character fails to recognize these clues, but as a reader, you can look for them and make predictions.

DIRECTIONS: *As you read "To Build a Fire," watch for clues from the setting that can help you predict what will happen next. In the chart below, list the clues, your predictions based on those clues, and the actual outcomes from the text.*

CLUES FROM SETTING	PREDICTION	OUTCOME

"To Build a Fire" by Jack London
Vocabulary Builder

Using the Latin Root *-pend-*

The Latin root *-pend-* means "to hang or extend" and appears in many English words.

A. DIRECTIONS: *Read the list of prefixes and their meanings. Then read each sentence and explain how the prefix and the root -pend- influence the meaning of the underlined word.*

> *de-* = "down"
> *ap-* = "near; toward"
> *sus-* = "below; under"

1. Whether we head up to the cabin <u>depends</u> upon the weather.

   _____

2. The definition of the new terms can be found in the <u>appendix</u> at the back of the book.

   _____

3. Let's <u>suspend</u> the bird feeder from that branch.

   _____

Using the Word List

   appendage   conflagration   conjectural   peremptorily   unwonted

B. DIRECTIONS: *Each question consists of a related pair of words in CAPITAL LETTERS, followed by four lettered pairs of words. Choose the lettered pair that best expresses a relationship similar to that expressed in the numbered pair and circle the letter of your choice.*

1. CAMPFIRE : CONFLAGRATION::
   A. car : truck
   B. spark : match
   C. flurry : blizzard
   D. sun : desert

2. CONJECTURAL : CERTAIN ::
   A. guess : fact
   B. generous : charitable
   C. delicious : tasty
   D. shifting : fixed

3. COMMANDS : PEREMPTORILY::
   A. awakes : retires
   B. sings : ballads
   C. moves : forward
   D. dances : gracefully

4. UNWONTED : SURPRISING ::
   A. undesired : hating
   B. cruel : frightening
   C. sparse : meager
   D. routine : unusual

5. APPENDAGE : LEG ::
   A. lost : found
   B. tree : branch
   C. fruit : apple
   D. result : cause

Name _____ Date _____

"To Build a Fire" by Jack London

Grammar and Style: Using Introductory Phrases and Clauses

Using introductory phrases and clauses can help you vary your sentence structure and make your writing more interesting. A **phrase** is a group of words that acts as one part of speech but lacks a subject and a verb. A **clause** is a group of words that has a subject and a verb.

Subject First:	Old timers advised him not to set out.
Phrase First:	Knowing the danger of extreme cold, old timers advised him not to set out.
Subject First:	He set out despite the cold because he wanted to join his friends.
Clause First:	Because he wanted to join his friends, he set out despite the cold.

A. PRACTICE: *Use each phrase or clause to introduce a sentence.*

1. To build a fire in the snow and bitter cold

   _____

2. When he called to it

   _____

3. When he called to it

   _____

4. In the warm cabin

   _____

5. After his feet became soaked in the cold stream

   _____

B. Writing Application: *Rewrite each sentence, using a clause or phrase to begin your new sentence.*

1. The traveler relied upon his dog because he was alone in the wilderness.

   _____

2. Experienced Alaskans stayed inside on such bitter cold days.

   _____

3. He could not build a fire with his matches gone.

   _____

4. He nearly panicked when the snow put out the fire.

   _____

5. He walked quickly along the trail to keep warm.

   _____

Name _____ Date _____

"To Build a Fire" by Jack London
Support for Writing

Prepare to write your **literary analysis** of how the elements of "To Build a Fire" work together to communicate the story's message. Enter your thoughts and opinions in the chart below.

"To Build a Fire" — Analysis

Message of "To Build a Fire"	_____ _____ _____ _____ _____
Setting : Details supporting message	_____ _____ _____ _____ _____
Characters: Details supporting message	_____ _____ _____ _____ _____
Plot: Details supporting message	_____ _____ _____ _____ _____

On a separate page, write a draft of your literary analysis. State your thesis, as well as a main idea in each paragraph from your chart. When you revise, make sure you have supported your thesis, and add more details if you need to.

Name _____ Date _____

"To Build a Fire" by Jack London
Enrichment: Films About Survival

Stories of survival under challenging conditions abound in literature, in film, and on television. Although the main character in "To Build a Fire" does not survive, his behavior functions as a kind of negative guide to living through the rigors of a winter journey in the Arctic. The story probably also led you to think about the kind of characteristics that enable people to adapt to adverse conditions and, thus, to survive.

DIRECTIONS: *Consult a knowledgeable person or a guide to movies and videos to find one that deals with survival under challenging conditions. Here are a few examples:* Air Force One, Cool Hand Luke, Incredible Journey, Lord of the Flies, Return of the Jedi, *and* Swiss Family Robinson. *View one of these survival films or another of your choice. As you watch, note how the survivors adapt to conditions, and how this adaptability helps them survive. Then write a profile of a person with character traits that would prepare him or her to adapt to difficult situations. Support your points by citing evidence from the film you view and "To Build a Fire." Use the following lines to record some ideas before you write your profile.*

Movie and surviving characters: _____

_____

_____

How does each character adapt and survive? _____

_____

_____

_____

_____

_____

How do survivors differ from those who die? _____

_____

_____

_____

_____

Some character traits that allow people to adapt: _____

_____

_____

_____

_____

Name _____ Date _____

Open-Book Test

Short Answer *Write your responses to the questions in this section on the lines provided.*

1. There are several clues in the first paragraph of "To Build a Fire" that enable the reader to predict some of the problems or dangers that might arise later in the story. Name two of them.

   _____

   _____

2. In the third paragraph of the story, London gives several clues about the man's character. These clues help the reader predict how the man will fare in his encounter with the bitter cold. Use the chart below to list three of those clues. Then, in the column on the right, state what you can conclude or predict about the man's future actions from that clue.

London's Clue About the Man's Character	Conclusion About the Man's Future Actions

3. London includes an extensive description of the husky's awareness of the intense cold in "To Build a Fire." What might be his purpose in using the dog as part of his account of the weather conditions?

   _____

   _____

   _____

4. Although the man in "To Build a Fire" fails to anticipate many of the dangers he faces, he does show flashes of intelligence as his predicament deepens. What evidence does London provide of the man's intelligence in the face of his deepening conflict with nature?

   _____

   _____

   _____

5. In "To Build a Fire," the man "chuckled at his foolishness" at not having built a fire before he eats lunch. What does this laughter show about the man's judgment about the natural challenges he faces?

_____

_____

6. After the man has built a fire, London goes on to write that "For the moment the cold of space was outwitted." In what way does this sentence define the central conflict that goes on for most of the story?

_____

_____

7. Toward the end of "To Build a Fire," as the man begins to sense the gravity of his situation, he experiences conflicting emotions. How would you summarize this internal emotional conflict that the man experiences?

_____

_____

8. The relationship between the man and the dog is a major element of "To Build a Fire." Based on the way the man treats the dog, what can the reader infer about his character?

_____

_____

_____

_____

9. In "To Build a Fire," the man succumbs to the cold because he lacks certain qualities that are critical to survival in that extreme environment. Based on your reading of the story, name two qualities that the man lacks that might have saved him from freezing to death.

_____

_____

_____

_____

10. If your friend looked outside and commented on the unwonted heavy rainfall of the past several days, would that mean you were living in an area that normally gets lots of rain? Why or why not? Base your answer on the meaning of *unwonted* as it is used in "To Build a Fire."

_____

_____

_____

Essay

Write an extended response to the question of your choice or to the question or questions your teacher assigns to you.

11. The actions, reactions, and feelings of the dog play an important role in "To Build a Fire." Imagine that you are the dog in this story, and that you are able to express your thoughts. Write a short essay describing some of your feelings, hopes, and fears during the long trek through the bitter cold weather. Use details from the story to support your writing.

12. Both the man and the dog in "To Build a Fire" are nameless. Why do you think the author chose to leave them unnamed? What do nameless characters suggest to the reader? Express your opinions in an essay supported by details from the story.

13. In order to create suspense, authors often provide just enough clues to encourage readers to make predictions while creating enough uncertainty to leave the ending in doubt. In some cases, the outcome is obvious, whereas in others it remains in doubt until the very end. When you first read "To Build a Fire," were you uncertain about the outcome, or did you predict it early in the story? What clues led you to respond to the story as you did? Write an essay in which you explain why you found the story to be suspenseful or predictable. Support your response with details from the story.

14. **Thinking About the Essentail Question: What is the relationship between place and literature?** The elements—raw, untamed nature—can be seen as the antagonist in "To Build a Fire." Nature can be a setting of beauty and harmony, or it can be a deadly enemy. What do you think the relationship between humankind and nature should be? Develop your opinion in an essay supported by specific examples.

Oral Response

15. Go back to question 1, 3, or 5 or to the question your teacher assigns you. Take a few minutes to expand your answer and prepare an oral response. Find additional details in "To Build a Fire" that support your points. If necessary, make notes to guide your oral response.

"To Build a Fire" by Jack London
Selection Test A

Critical Reading *Identify the letter of the choice that best answers the question.*

____ 1. What is the external conflict in "To Build a Fire"?
A. between human and dog
B. between human and nature
C. between human and human
D. between human and God

____ 2. What information appears toward the beginning of "To Build a Fire" that helps readers predict that the man will soon be in trouble?
A. It will take him all day to reach camp.
B. The sun has not come above the horizon.
C. It is much colder than he thinks it is.
D. He has heavy whiskers on his face.

____ 3. How does the dog in "To Build a Fire" express his anxiety about the situation?
A. by running around in circles
B. by drooping his tail
C. by burrowing under the snow
D. by running back to the camp

____ 4. In "To Build a Fire," what can you predict when the man comes across a hidden spring?
A. The dog will fall into a hidden spring.
B. The man will fall into a hidden spring.
C. The man will follow the spring to camp.
D. The man will drink from the spring.

____ 5. What does London suggest when he writes, "The dog did not know anything about thermometers . . . But the brute had its instinct" in "To Build A Fire"?
A. The man is smarter than the dog.
B. The dog does not need a device to measure the cold.
C. A man's brain and a dog's brain are not the same.
D. Only man has awareness about danger.

____ 6. Which element of "To Build a Fire" best reflects the main external conflict of the story?

   A. the man's refusal to heed the advice of the old-timer

   B. the man's choice to smoke his pipe after eating his lunch

   C. the man's choice to try to reach the camp by nightfall

   D. the man's refusal to pay attention to the dog's behavior

____ 7. Which of these states a central message of "To Build a Fire"?

   A. To survive in the wilderness, pay attention to your surroundings.

   B. To survive in the Arctic, know when summer is due to arrive.

   C. To survive in extreme cold, dress in warm clothing and boots.

   D. To survive in extreme conditions, be sure to carry enough food.

____ 8. Which of these details emphasizes the central message of "To Build a Fire" most clearly?

   A. The man keeps his food from freezing by storing it near his skin.

   B. The man keeps watching to avoid falling into a hidden spring.

   C. The man runs as fast as he can to keep his body from freezing.

   D. The man builds a fire under a tree with snow-covered branches.

____ 9. Why does the man in "To Build a Fire" finally put aside his panic about freezing to death?

   A. He realizes he cannot light a fire if he is feeling panic.

   B. He wants to die with dignity if he cannot survive the cold.

   C. He does not want his panic to frighten his dog companion.

   D. He realizes he cannot run well if he is feeling panic.

____ 10. Which internal conflict does the man experience toward the end of "To Build a Fire"?

   A. hope versus acceptance

   B. summer versus winter

   C. anger versus sadness

   D. life versus death

Vocabulary and Grammar

____ 11. In which sentence is the meaning of the word *unwonted* suggested?

   A. The old-timer warned the man about the cold.

   B. The man did not realize he was feeling unusual cold.

   C. The dog understood cold and tried to warn the man.

   D. When the man froze to death, the dog went to find warmth.

____ **12.** Which of these sentences begins with an introductory clause?

    A. "He was bound for the old claim on the left fork of Henderson Creek, where the boys were already."

    B. "He would be in to camp by six o'clock: a bit after dark, it was true, but the boys would be there, a fire would be going, and a hot supper would be ready."

    C. "Since the freezing point is thirty-two above zero, it meant that one hundred and seven degrees of frost obtained."

    D. "The frozen moisture of its breathing had settled on its fur in a fine powder of frost, and especially were its jowls, muzzle, and eyelashes whitened by its crystalled breath."

Essay

13. Neither the man nor the dog in "To Build a Fire" has a name. Why do you think the author did this? What do nameless characters suggest to a reader? Write a brief essay to give your opinion about why the man and the dog have no names in this story.

14. At the beginning of "To Build a Fire," London describes the man in this way: "The trouble with him was that he was without imagination. He was quick and alert in the things of life, but . . . not in the significances." Write a brief essay to show how this description predicts what will happen to the man.

15. Essential Question: What is the relationship between place and literature?
Nature can be a setting of beauty and harmony, or it can be a deadly enemy. In "To Build a Fire," nature is the enemy. Which side of nature do you think most people see? Explain your opinion in an essay supported by specific examples.

"**To Build a Fire**" by Jack London
Selection Test B

Critical Reading *Identify the letter of the choice that best completes the statement or answers the question.*

_____ 1. In "To Build a Fire," there is an external conflict between
    A. the beauty of nature and the cruelty of nature.
    B. society and the individual.
    C. human beings and nature.
    D. instinct and civilization.

_____ 2. Which of the following character flaws brings about the man's tragic end?
    A. cowardice
    B. carelessness
    C. overconfidence
    D. greed

_____ 3. Toward the end of "To Build a Fire," the man has an internal conflict between his
    A. body and his will.
    B. short-term goals and his long-term goals.
    C. conscience and his needs.
    D. animal nature and his spiritual nature.

_____ 4. Which of the following themes is expressed by the contrasting ways in which the dog and the man cope with the cold?
    A. Animals are naturally superior to humans.
    B. Animals are unable to have or express emotions.
    C. Humans need to be as well attuned to nature as animals in order to survive in it.
    D. Humans are so closely tied to civilization that they cannot return to nature.

_____ 5. Until the story's end, the man's attitude toward the advice provided by the old-timer of Sulphur Creek was one of
    A. respect.
    B. curiosity.
    C. confusion.
    D. ridicule.

_____ 6. Which passage from the beginning of the story gives the strongest clue to the attitude that contributes to the man's death?
    A. "It was a steep bank, and he paused for breath at the top, excusing the act to himself by looking at his watch."
    B. "He was used to the lack of sun. It had been days since he had seen the sun, and he knew that a few more days must pass before that cheerful orb, due south, would just peep above the skyline and dip immediately from view."
    C. "The man flung a look back along the way he had come."
    D. "He was a newcomer in the land, a *chechaquo*, and this was his first winter."

____ 7. Which example best reflects the main external conflict of the story?
   A. the encounter between the old timer and the man
   B. the hostility between the man and the dog
   C. the opposing emotions of the man near the end of the story
   D. the conflict of the man's animal nature and his spiritual nature

____ 8. Which of the following details reflects the story's central theme most clearly?
   A. The fire was put out by an avalanche of snow from the branches that the man had inadvertently agitated.
   B. Even though it was high noon, there was no sun in the sky.
   C. At precisely the expected time, the man arrived at the forks of the creek.
   D. While attempting to build a fire, the man burned his hands.

____ 9. Which internal conflict does the man experience toward the end of the story?
   A. terror versus faith
   B. reality versus hope
   C. sorrow versus stoicism
   D. regret versus rage

____ 10. In "To Build a Fire," London's attitude toward the Alaskan wilderness can best be described as
   A. nostalgic.
   B. respectful.
   C. apprehensive.
   D. affectionate.

____ 11. Which of the following clues is most likely to lead a reader to predict that the man will make it to camp?
   A. "For the moment, the cold of space was outwitted."
   B. "He had forgotten to build a fire and thaw out."
   C. "He was pleased at the speed he had made. If he kept it up, he would certainly be with the boys by six."
   D. "Once in a while the thought reiterated itself that it was very cold and that he had never experienced such cold."

____ 12. Which of the following is the correct way to predict while reading a story?
   A. Don't try to correct your first prediction, but just read on quickly to the end of the story.
   B. Start making predictions about the end of the story about halfway through it.
   C. Check your predictions as you read, and revise them if necessary.
   D. Avoid using your own experience when making predictions about your reading.

Vocabulary and Grammar

____ 13. Choose the correct vocabulary word to complete the sentence.
   If the man had been more given to _____ thoughts from the beginning, he might have survived.
   A. unwonted
   B. peremptory
   C. conjectural
   D. none of the above

____ **14.** Which of these sentences begins with an introductory clause?
  A. "Day had broken cold and gray, exceedingly cold and gray, when the man turned aside from the main Yukon trail and climbed the high earth-bank. . . ."
  B. "He was a newcomer in the land, a *chechaquo,* and this was his first winter."
  C. "That there should be anything more to it than that was a thought that never entered his head."
  D. "He was quick and alert in things of life, but only in the things, and not in the significances."

____ **15.** Which word best suggests the way the man treats the dog in the story?
  A. unwonted
  B. conjectural
  C. peremptorily
  D. none of the above

Essay

16. The man in "To Build a Fire" has taken on a great challenge by choosing to work in a very remote and cold place. If you had to choose a great physical challenge of some type, what would you choose to do? Write an essay describing what your own challenge would be like. What do you think you might gain from such an experience? How would you use the experience of the man in the story to help you survive your challenge?

17. Sometimes an author will include a minor character who has virtues that the protagonist lacks. In Jack London's "To Build a Fire," that minor character is a dog. The dog consistently displays more innate common sense and wisdom than the man. Write an essay in which you compare and contrast the dog's and the man's attitudes toward the dangerously cold journey they are taking. Include at least three specific actions of the dog that show its instincts, under the circumstances, to be superior to the man's judgment.

18. To maintain suspense, authors may provide clues that lead readers to predict the outcome but also give readers details that make them uncertain about the outcome. In some cases, the outcome may be predictable, but how the ending works out keeps readers in suspense. When you first read "To Build a Fire," were you uncertain about the outcome, or did you know what would happen, but not how? What clues made you respond to the story the way you did? Write an essay relating your thought and prediction process as you read "To Build a Fire." Use examples from the selection where necessary.

19. Essential Question: What is the relationship between place and literature? The elements—raw, untamed nature—can be seen as the antagonist in "To Build a Fire." Nature can be a setting of beauty and harmony, or it can be a deadly enemy. What do you think the relationship between humankind and nature should be? Develop your opinion in an essay supported by specific examples.

"**Heading West**" by Miriam Davis Colt
"**I Will Fight No More Forever**" by Chief Joseph
Primary Sources: Personal History and Speech

Documents such as memoirs and speeches that describe historical events from a personal point of view may contain opinions and beliefs as well as facts. Opinions and beliefs may depend upon **assumptions** by the writer. Often these are implied.

DIRECTIONS: *Read each passage from one of the two selections. Then, analyze and describe the assumption implied by the writer or speaker.*

1. **April 24th.** A hot summer day. The men in our company are out in the city, purchasing wagons and farming implements, to take along on the steamer up to Kansas City. —"Heading West"

    _____

    _____

2. **April 28th.** The steamer struck a "snag" last night. . . .

    April 30th. Here we are, at Kansas City, all safely again on terra firma. Hasten to the hotel—find it very much crowded. Go up, up, up, and upstairs to our lodging rooms. —"Heading West"

    _____

    _____

3. **May 3rd.** Father, it seems, fell back a little and found a place to camp in a tavern (not a hotel), where he fell in with the scores of Georgians who loaded a steamer and came up the river the same time that we did. He said he had to be very shrewd indeed not to have them find out that he was a "Free States" man.—"Heading West"

    _____

    _____

4. **May 12th**. . . . Look around and see the grounds all around the camp-fire are covered with tents, in which the families are staying. Not a house is to be seen. In the large tent here is a cook stove—they have supper prepared for us. . . .—"Heading West"

    _____

    _____

5. I want to have time to look for my children and see how many I can find. Maybe I shall find them among the dead.—"I Will Fight No More Forever"

    _____

    _____

Name _____   Date _____

"Heading West" by Miriam Davis Colt
"I Will Fight No More Forever" by Chief Joseph
Vocabulary Builder

A. DIRECTIONS: *Decide whether each statement below is true or false. Circle* **T** *or* **F.** *Then use the space provided to explain each of your answers.*

1. If you had *shares* in a piece of land you might enjoy owning it.
   T / F _____

2. If a *levee* lay between your home and a large river, you might have reason to worry about flooding during times of heavy rain.
   T / F _____

3. The native people feared that the new settlers were gaining a *foothold* on the land and would grow stronger and stronger.
   T / F _____

4. The heavily forested *prairie* seemed to stretch on for many miles.
   T / F _____

5. The wagons *forded* the river at a shallow place.
   T / F _____

Using the Word List

emigrants   pervading   profusion   ravine

B. DIRECTIONS: *Rewrite each sentence below, replacing the italicized word or phrase with an appropriate word from the Word List.*

1. There were *people who moved* from many lands in the West.

   _____

2. As far as the eye could see, the prairie was covered by a *great abundance* of wild flowers.

   _____

3. The feeling *prevalent throughout* the Nez Perce camp was despair.

   _____

4. The people followed a *long, deep hollow in the ground* until they came to some water.

   _____

Name _____ Date _____

"Heading West" by Miriam Davis Colt
"I Will Fight No More Forever" by Chief Joseph
Selection Test

MULTIPLE CHOICE

Critical Reading *Identify the letter of the choice that best answers the question.*

____ 1. Where are the families going in "Heading West"?
   A. California
   B. Missouri
   C. Kansas
   D. New York

____ 2. "Heading West" includes excerpts from
   A. letters.
   B. a historical account.
   C. a journal.
   D. newspaper stories.

____ 3. What is the perspective of the narrator of "Heading West"?
   A. Native American watching settlers
   B. storekeeper in Kansas City
   C. historian telling about settlers
   D. settler heading west

____ 4. How do the settlers travel the final miles from Kansas City to their new settlement?
   A. wagon
   B. steamship
   C. train
   D. barge

____ 5. Unlike the settlers in "Heading West," the Georgians
   A. supported slavery in the western territories.
   B. opposed the use of alcohol and eating meat.
   C. opposed slavery in the territory of Kansas.
   D. were traveling west to the new territories.

___ 6. What is the mood of the settlers when they reach Octagon City?
A. elated
B. depressed
C. thoughtful
D. sorrowful

___ 7. Why were the settlers disappointed when they reached their destination?
A. No land had been set aside for them.
B. The directors had disappeared with all their savings.
C. Native Americans had retaken the land.
D. No mills or settlement had been built.

___ 8. "I Will Fight No More Forever" is a
A. speech.
B. letter.
C. newspaper report.
D. journal entry.

___ 9. What is Chief Joseph's perspective in "I Will Fight No More Forever"?
A. victorious leader of a group of Native Americans
B. Native American leader who believes his people can live with the new settlers
C. Native American leader who has seen his people defeated and scattered
D. successful leader of a large group of settlers in Kansas

___ 10. Why does Chief Joseph say he "will fight no more forever"?
A. Victory is won.
B. His people cannot win.
C. He is tired of bloodshed.
D. The people are united.

"The Story of an Hour" by Kate Chopin
Vocabulary Warm-up Word Lists

Study these words from the selection. Then, complete the activities.

Word List A

absolutely [ab suh LOOT lee] *adv.* totally; without exception
   Jody is a vegetarian, so she eats <u>absolutely</u> no meat.

countless [KOWNT les] *adj.* too many to count
   Uncle Pete has driven here <u>countless</u> times, and yet he still gets lost.

intention [in TEN shun] *n.* purpose
   My <u>intention</u> was to draw a puppy, but it came out looking like a cow.

paralyzed [PAR uh lyzd] *adj.* unable to move
   The deer stared into the headlights, as if <u>paralyzed</u> by fear.

perception [per SEP shun] *n.* awareness or understanding
   Lee's <u>perception</u> of what happened is completely different from mine.

powerful [POW er fuhl] *adj.* strong; mighty
   The weightlifter flexed his <u>powerful</u> arms.

revealed [ri VEELD] *v.* made known
   Her so-called best friend <u>revealed</u> her secret to the whole school.

significance [sig NIF i kans] *n.* meaning
   I read the motto on her T-shirt, but its <u>significance</u> was unclear to me.

Word List B

eaves [EEVZ] *n.* overhanging edge of a roof
   Have you noticed the vines growing underneath the <u>eaves</u>?

illumination [i loo mi NAY shun] *n.* enlightenment
   Reading the instructions turned my confusion to <u>illumination</u>.

imploring [im PLOR ing] *v.* begging
   "Please, I am <u>imploring</u> you," she said. "Don't wear that ugly shirt!"

inability [in uh BIL i tee] *n.* lack of ability
   Jen loves to sing but gets frustrated by her <u>inability</u> to carry a tune.

persistence [per SIS tens] *n.* stubborn refusal to give up
   She did not want to lend him the CD, but his <u>persistence</u> wore her down.

striving [STRY ving] *v.* trying very hard
   I am <u>striving</u> to be nicer to my brother, but I don't always succeed.

subtle [SUH tuhl] *adj.* not obvious
   There was a <u>subtle</u> sweetness in the air—roses, perhaps?

trivial [TRI vee uhl] *adj.* unimportant
   Charlie tends to get overexcited about <u>trivial</u> things.

"The Story of an Hour" by Kate Chopin
Vocabulary Warm-up Exercises

Exercise A *Fill in each blank in the paragraph below with the appropriate word from Word List A.*

When I went downtown, my only [1] _____ was to return a book to the library. Honestly, I had [2] _____ no plan to go in the dumpling shop. When I walked by, though, I smelled the [3] _____ aroma of fried dumplings and my stomach growled. A moment's thought [4] _____ the obvious [5] _____ of that growl: I had not had lunch. I stood there, [6] _____ by indecision. Should I save my money and go home and make a sandwich, or give in to the temptation as I had done [7] _____ times before? Of course, I gave in. All right, maybe I have no willpower, but it is not my fault— the dumplings made me do it. At least, that is my [8] _____ of what happened!

Exercise B *Decide whether each statement below is true or false. Circle T or F, and explain your answer.*

1. If you do not know the meaning of a word, a dictionary can provide <u>illumination</u>.
   T / F _____

2. Dumping an entire shakerful of salt into your food will give the dish a <u>subtle</u> flavor.
   T / F _____

3. The <u>inability</u> to tell green from red is a sign of color blindness.
   T / F _____

4. <u>Persistence</u> is advised by the saying, "If at first you don't succeed, try, try again."
   T / F _____

5. The <u>eaves</u> of a house are usually found in the basement, behind the furnace.
   T / F _____

6. If begging and pleading do not get you what you want, <u>imploring</u> might work better.
   T / F _____

7. Happy, easygoing people tend to lose their temper over <u>trivial</u> problems.
   T / F _____

8. People who read a lot of self-help books may be <u>striving</u> to improve themselves.
   T / F _____

"**The Story of an Hour**" by Kate Chopin
Reading Warm-up A

Read the following passage. Pay special attention to the underlined words. Then, read it again, and complete the activities. Use a separate sheet of paper for your written answers.

You may have heard irony mentioned <u>countless</u> times: "Isn't it ironic?" Yet, as you will discover if you ask for a definition, many people who talk about irony do not really understand the <u>significance</u> of the word.

One reason for this confusion is that *irony* can mean several different things. For instance, there is *verbal irony*, in which the speaker's <u>intention</u> is the opposite of what he or she is saying. "Can't wait to run out and buy *that*," your friend says after a commercial. Her tone of voice, however, makes it clear that she has <u>absolutely</u> no desire to do so.

Have you ever sat motionless in a movie theater, staring in <u>paralyzed</u> horror at the screen as the main character strolls into danger? "Watch out!" you want to scream. "The bad guy's right behind that door!" This is an example of *dramatic irony*, in which there is a conflict between the character's <u>perception</u> of events and that of the audience (or reader). You see things differently than the character because more has been <u>revealed</u> to you: an earlier scene showed the "bad guy" in his hiding place.

Dramatic irony often has a strong impact on our emotions, but a third type, *situational irony*, can be even more <u>powerful</u>. Situational irony occurs when something happens that contradicts our expectations.

In the classic novel *Howard's End*, a dying woman writes a note in which she leaves her home to a young friend, Margaret. Her rich widower and children burn the note and keep the house. Since nobody else knows about the note, we do not expect that the friend will ever own the house. Ironically, however, the widower later falls in love with Margaret. In the end, he marries her and gives her the house that should have been hers all along.

1. Circle a word in this paragraph that means something similar to <u>countless</u>. What is an antonym of *countless*?

2. Circle a word that, like <u>significance</u>, has to do with meaning. If you wanted to know the *significance* of a word, what would you do?

3. Underline what shows the friend's true <u>intention</u>. If your *intention* was to spend money, where would you start?

4. Underline what the friend has <u>absolutely</u> no wish to do. Would somebody who was *absolutely* full order dessert?

5. Circle the word that means almost the same as <u>paralyzed</u>. If you were *paralyzed* with laughter, would you be rolling around on the floor?

6. Underline the words that mean "You have a different <u>perception</u>." What could change your *perception* of someone?

7. Circle the word that means <u>revealed</u>. How do you feel when the ending of a movie is *revealed* before you see it?

8. Circle the word that means the same as <u>powerful</u>. What else might be described as *powerful*?

"The Story of an Hour" by Kate Chopin
Reading Warm-up B

Read the following passage. Pay special attention to the underlined words. Then, read it again, and complete the activities. Use a separate sheet of paper for your written answers.

"Kevin," my mother reminded me, "don't forget you promised to take Blue to his appointment at the vet this afternoon, okay?"

I grunted a reply and went off to search for the dog, wondering why I always got stuck with these <u>trivial</u> chores when I had so many more important things to do.

Blue lay in his usual spot by the porch, resting in the shade under the <u>eaves</u>. When he saw me, he sprang up and dashed over with his ratty old tennis ball. "Not now," I told him, but he dropped it at my feet, then pushed at me with his nose. Annoyed at his <u>persistence</u>, I snapped on his leash, kicked the ball away, and pulled him to the car.

The visit to the veterinarian went fine, as usual, and I'd forgotten all about it when the phone rang a week later. It was the vet, saying a routine blood test had turned up a problem.

"But he seems perfectly normal!" I protested.

"Early symptoms can be <u>subtle</u>," she explained. "We'll repeat the test, but if the results are consistent, Blue may be seriously ill."

I wandered outside, <u>striving</u> to grasp the meaning of this news. Blue trotted over and flopped down beside me, <u>imploring</u> me to pet him with a gaze that made me feel about two inches tall. How long had it been since I'd responded to that look by rubbing him behind the ears, instead of telling him to quit bothering me? Suddenly, it seemed obvious that tossing a ball took less energy than getting irritated over Blue's <u>inability</u> to take a hint.

The story has a happy ending—Blue wasn't sick after all. But that moment of <u>illumination</u> stayed with me, and I knew I would never take my dog for granted again.

1. Circle the word that means the opposite of <u>trivial</u>. Do you think taking a pet for a checkup is a *trivial* task?

2. Underline the words that hint at where you might find <u>eaves</u>. Then, name a kind of dwelling that does not have *eaves*.

3. Underline the words that show Blue displaying <u>persistence</u>. Describe a time when you or someone else showed *persistence*.

4. Would you describe the symptoms of a bad cold as <u>subtle</u>? Explain.

5. Underline the news that Kevin is <u>striving</u> to grasp. What would be the opposite of *striving*?

6. Circle what Blue is <u>imploring</u> Kevin to do. Then, give another word for *imploring*.

7. Earlier in the passage, how did Blue show his <u>inability</u> to take a hint? (Look for lines you already underlined, but answer in your own words.)

8. Circle the paragraph in which Kevin experiences a moment of <u>illumination</u>. If you wanted to learn how to care for a pet, where would you go for *illumination*?

Name _____ Date _____

"The Story of an Hour" by Kate Chopin
Literary Analysis: Irony

Irony is a contrast or a difference between what is stated and what is meant, or between what is expected to happen and what actually happens. **Situational irony** occurs when a result turns out differently than expected. For example, from the actions of Mrs. Mallard and her friends, readers expect that she will be overcome with grief at the news of her husband's death. Instead she exults in her freedom. **Dramatic irony** occurs when readers know something a character does not know. Readers know a few seconds before Mrs. Mallard, for example, that her husband is actually alive. Think of other stories you have read that use irony.

DIRECTIONS: *On the lines provided, identify stories you have read that use irony. Quote or summarize a passage that is an example of situational irony and one that is an example of dramatic irony. Then explain the irony in each passage.*

1. **Situational irony:**

_____

_____

_____

_____

_____

_____

_____

_____

_____

2. **Dramatic irony:**

_____

_____

_____

_____

_____

_____

_____

_____

_____

Name _____ Date _____

"The Story of an Hour" by Kate Chopin
Reading Strategy: Analyze the Philosophical Argument

In their stories, authors sometimes express philosophical arguments in which they believe. When you **analyze the philosophical argument,** you examine details about the story's plot, characterization, or other story elements that illustrate or convey the argument.

DIRECTIONS: *On the chart below, list details about the plot and characters of Kate Chopin's story and explain how they illustrate or convey her philosophy.*

Details	How It Illustrates the Author's Philosophy

"The Story of an Hour" by Kate Chopin
Vocabulary Builder

Using the Word List

elusive   forestall   repression   tumultuously

A. DIRECTIONS: *Each question consists of a related pair of words in CAPITAL LETTERS, followed by four lettered pairs of words. Choose the lettered pair that best expresses a relationship similar to that expressed in the numbered pair. Circle the letter of your choice.*

___ 1. FORESTALL : DELAY ::
    A. hurry : rush
    B. worry : disregard
    C. despair : believe
    D. deserve : forgive

___ 2. SERENELY : TUMULTUOUSLY ::
    A. precisely : accurately
    B. possibly : remotely
    C. recklessly : cautiously
    D. strictly : resentfully

___ 3. DICTATOR : REPRESSION ::
    A. dancer : music
    B. judge : justice
    C. actor : theater
    D. student : school

___ 4. ELUSIVE : VAGUE ::
    A. stout : harmless
    B. sincere : delicate
    C. resourceful : troubled
    D. scholarly : studious

B. DIRECTIONS: *Select the Word List word that relates best to each situation, and write the word on the line.*

1. Mrs. Mallard's previous actions regarding her feelings about her marriage

_____

2. the way Mrs. Mallard's imaginings about the free days ahead of her went through her mind

_____

3. Richards's attempt to keep the shock of seeing her husband alive from Mrs. Mallard

_____

4. the mysterious, unsolvable nature of love

_____

"The Story of an Hour" by Kate Chopin
Support for Writing

Prepare to write a **reflective essay** about a time in which your life changed dramatically, such as a move from one home to another. Enter your memories and reflections on the event in the graphic organizer below.

Sometimes Life Changes Quickly

Event that changed my life:

_____

_____

_____

_____

Life before event:

_____

_____

_____

_____

_____

_____

Life after event:

_____

_____

_____

_____

_____

My feelings about the change:

_____

_____

_____

_____

On a separate page, write a draft of your reflective essay. Organize your thoughts either in chronological order or in their order of importance. When you revise your essay, be sure your thoughts and feelings about the dramatic event have been made clear to the reader. Add or eliminate information to strengthen the impression you wish to make.

"The Story of an Hour" by Kate Chopin
Enrichment: Social Studies

DIRECTIONS: *Form a group with some classmates to discuss "The Story of an Hour." First, research society's attitudes toward love and marriage in the late 1800s. Then, prior to your discussion, answer the first three questions, using an extra sheet of paper if needed.*

1. In what ways, if any, is the story dated?
   _____
   _____

2. In what ways, if any, does it represent universal feelings and attitudes?
   _____
   _____

3. Imagine that the roles are reversed—the husband is told that his wife has been killed. How might he react to the message?
   _____
   _____

   Hold the discussion with your group. Start by comparing your answers to the questions above. Share your research with other group members. Try role-playing some of the ideas about the relationship that come out of the discussion. After the discussion, answer these questions:

1. What were the group's consensus answers to the first three questions?
   _____
   _____

2. How did your own answers differ from the group's answers?
   _____
   _____

3. Were there any gender differences in the responses? If so, what were they?
   _____
   _____

4. What insights did reading and discussing the story give you into the relationship of marriage and what it takes to make it succeed?
   _____
   _____

"The Story of an Hour" by Kate Chopin
Open-Book Test

Short Answer *Write your responses to the questions in this section on the lines provided.*

1. At the time "The Story of an Hour" was written—in the late nineteenth century—it was considered so shocking that several publishers rejected it. Why do you think the story seemed so shocking in its day?

   _____

   _____

   _____

   _____

2. In "The Story of an Hour," after Mrs. Mallard hears the news of her husband's death, she looks out the window and observes the scene outside. What is ironic about the kinds of sights she sees? How do they contrast with the news she received?

   _____

   _____

   _____

3. In "The Story of an Hour," after Mrs. Mallard's fit of weeping upon hearing the news of her husband's death, she retires to her room. There, she begins to experience a different kind of emotional response. What is that response? What kind of irony does it exemplify?

   _____

   _____

   _____

   _____

4. In "The Story of an Hour," as Mrs. Mallard retreats to her room, she prefers to remain alone. Why does she refuse her sister's offer to keep her company?

   _____

   _____

   _____

5. Toward the end of "The Story of an Hour," Josephine says to Louise that by staying alone in her room, "you will make yourself ill." This statement is an example of which kind of irony? Explain your answer.

   _____

   _____

   _____

6. There are several uses of irony in "The Story of an Hour." Using the chart below, list one example of verbal irony (words that suggest the opposite of their usual meaning), dramatic irony (when the reader or audience is aware of something that a character does not know), and situational irony (where the outcome is not what the reader would expect).

Verbal Irony	Dramatic Irony	Situational Irony

7. At the end of "The Story of an Hour," we read that the doctors attribute Louise's death to a heart attack caused by "the joy that kills." What can the reader conclude that the doctors assume about Louise when they pronounce her dead? What was Louise really feeling at the moment of her death?

_____

_____

_____

_____

8. Chopin chose the title of this story carefully. Does the title "The Story of an Hour" seem appropriate or inappropriate to you? Why or why not?

_____

_____

_____

_____

9. The double surprise of the ending of "The Story of an Hour"—the return of the supposedly dead husband and the sudden death of Louise—is an example of what kind of irony? Explain your answer.

_____

_____

_____

10. If someone accused you of trying to forestall the inevitable, would he be implying that you are welcoming or avoiding your fate? Why? Base your answer on the meaning of *forestall* as it is used in "The Story of an Hour."

_____

_____

_____

Essay

Write an extended response to the question of your choice or to the question or questions your teacher assigns you.

11. In "The Story of an Hour," Louise first sobs at the news of her husband's death but then later experiences a sense of relief and renewal. Do you find her reactions and emotions appropriate or inappropriate? Why? Explain your answer in an essay supported by examples from the text.

12. In "The Story of an Hour," Chopin makes this comment on Louise's sense of independence following her husband's death:

    > There would be no powerful will bending hers in that blind persistence with which men and women believe they have a right to impose a private will upon a fellow creature.

    What view of marriage is conveyed in this passage in particular and in the story in general? Develop your thoughts in an essay supported by examples from the story.

13. It seems that Josephine and Richards are very much aware of Louise's "heart trouble." Is Chopin using this description of a physical disease straightforwardly or ironically? Use details from "The Story of an Hour" to support an essay about what the use of the term "heart trouble" may imply.

14. **Thinking About the Essential Question: How does literature shape or reflect society?** In "The Story of an Hour," the narrator makes this comment about Louise's possibilities for independence after her husband's death: "There would be no powerful will bending hers in that blind persistence with which men and women believe they have a right to impose a private will upon a fellow creature." Does this sentence merely reflect a viewpoint about the possibilities for independence within marriage, or does it imply advice for people who are already married or who are considering marriage? Express your views in an essay based on clear logic and details from the story.

Oral Response

15. Go back to question 2, 3, or 8 or to the question your teacher assigns you. Take a few minutes to expand your answer and prepare an oral response. Find additional details in "The Story of an Hour" that support your points. If necessary, make notes to guide your oral response.

"The Story of an Hour" by Kate Chopin
Selection Test A

Critical Reading *Identify the letter of the choice that best answers the question.*

_____ 1. In "The Story of an Hour," why is Josephine afraid to tell Mrs. Mallard that her husband died?
A. Mrs. Mallard has a mental problem.
B. Mrs. Mallard has a heart condition.
C. Mrs. Mallard is expecting a baby.
D. Mrs. Mallard is planning to leave him.

_____ 2. In "The Story of an Hour," what is ironic about the sounds Mrs. Mallard hears after she has been told of her husband's death?
A. They are all sounds of ongoing life.
B. They are all sounds from outdoors.
C. They are all sounds from far away.
D. They are all sad and lonely sounds.

_____ 3. In "The Story of an Hour," the thing that Mrs. Mallard feels approaching her is described as "creeping" and as something that will "possess her." Why are these words ironic?
A. It is her sudden death she feels coming.
B. It is her widowhood she feels coming.
C. It is her mourning she feels coming.
D. It is her freedom she feels coming.

_____ 4. Which moment in "The Story of an Hour" is an example of situational irony?
A. when Mrs. Mallard wishes to be alone after hearing the news of her husband's death
B. when Mrs. Mallard weeps wildly after hearing the news of her husband's death
C. when Mrs. Mallard whispers, "free, free, free," after hearing of her husband's death
D. when Mrs. Mallard says, "Go away," after hearing the news of her husband's death

_____ 5. When Mrs. Mallard says "free, free, free" in "The Story of an Hour," what becomes clear?
A. Mr. Mallard has not been killed in an accident.
B. Mrs. Mallard does not have heart trouble.
C. Mrs. Mallard is happy to be free of her husband.
D. Mrs. Mallard's sister is worried about her.

_____ **6.** What is a major theme of Chopin's "The Story of an Hour"?
  A. personal freedom
  B. open marriage
  C. sad widowhood
  D. loss of love

_____ **7.** In "The Story of an Hour," whom does Mrs. Mallard believe she will live for when she thinks her husband has been killed?
  A. for his memory
  B. for her sister
  C. for Mr. Richards
  D. for herself

_____ **8.** In "The Story of an Hour," what is ironic about these words: "She breathed a quick prayer that life might be long . . . only yesterday she had thought with a shudder that life might be long"?
  A. Yesterday she thought she would die young.
  B. She gets her wish after she stops wishing for it.
  C. She has never had a prayer answered before.
  D. Her wishes changed after her husband died.

_____ **9.** What happens toward the end of "The Story of an Hour" that changes the entire story?
  A. Richards says he loves Mrs. Mallard.
  B. Mr. Mallard walks through the door.
  C. Josephine comes down the stairs.
  D. Mrs. Mallard goes downstairs.

_____ **10.** In "The Story of an Hour," what is ironic about the death of Mrs. Mallard after she sees her husband still alive?
  A. Her heart problem should have been cured by now.
  B. Her sister and Mr. Mallard are in love with each other.
  C. She had thought she had accepted the fact of his death.
  D. She had thought she had her whole life ahead of her.

_____ **11.** Why might readers interpret the title "The Story of an Hour" as an ironic title?
  A. A character gains her freedom and loses her life in a single hour.
  B. A character loses her husband in a single hour.
  C. A character learns that her heart disease is fatal in a single hour.
  D. A character dies from a severe emotional reaction in a single hour.

Vocabulary

____ 12. In which of these sentences is the meaning of the word *tumultuously* suggested?

A. Mr. Richards checked the news before he went to see Mrs. Mallard.

B. Mrs. Mallard wept wildly in her sister's arms at the bad news.

C. The sounds from outside spoke of new life to Mrs. Mallard.

D. Mr. Mallard was not killed in the accident after all.

____ 13. Which answer choice is a synonym for the underlined word? "She was young, with a fair, calm face, whose lines bespoke <u>repression</u> and even a certain strength."

A. calm

B. restraint

C. stubbornness

D. intelligence

Essay

14. The final words of "The Story of an Hour," are these: "When the doctors came they said she had died of heart disease—of joy that kills." In what way do these words suggest the opposite of what really happened? Write a brief essay to explain the irony of the story's final sentence.

15. Reread this passage from "The Story of an Hour": "There would be no powerful will bending hers in that blind persistence with which men and women believe they have a right to impose a private will upon a fellow creature." What view of marriage do you think Chopin is communicating in this story? Write a brief essay to give your response.

16. **Thinking About the Essential Question: How does literature shape or reflect society?** "The Story of an Hour" paints a pessimistic picture of marriage: Louise is privately relieved at her husband's death and stricken when he reappears. Do these plot elements just reflect one view about marriage, or do they seek to influence the reader's approach to marriage? Express your views in an essay based on clear logic and details from the story.

Name _____ Date _____

"**The Story of an Hour**" by Kate Chopin
Selection Test B

Critical Reading *Identify the letter of the choice that best completes the statement or answers the question.*

_____ 1. Readers in Kate Chopin's time must have found "The Story of an Hour" particularly shocking because of the contrast between Mrs. Mallard's response to her husband's death and
 A. the response that society would consider appropriate.
 B. the love that Mr. Mallard feels for his wife.
 C. her response to the discovery that he is actually alive.
 D. her professions of affection for her husband.

_____ 2. When Mrs. Mallard reflects that, "It was only yesterday she had thought with a shudder that life might be long," she becomes aware of the irony that she
 A. had worried about a life that she now knows will be short.
 B. has not been punished for such unacceptable thoughts.
 C. now desired something she has previously feared.
 D. had not valued her husband properly until she lost him.

_____ 3. Mrs. Mallard's reflection that she had recently wished for a short life soon has additional irony for the reader because
 A. the reader knows that she still wants her life to be short.
 B. she gets what she wanted after she stopped wanting it.
 C. the reader sees her as a less worthy person than her husband.
 D. she has too much intensity of feeling to wish for a short life.

_____ 4. Why does Mrs. Mallard refuse her sister Josephine's offer to keep her company?
 A. Mrs. Mallard does not want to upset her sister.
 B. Mrs. Mallard prefers not to display emotion to others.
 C. Mrs. Mallard needs privacy to confront her true feelings.
 D. Mrs. Mallard wants Josephine to keep Richard company.

_____ 5. How does Mrs. Mallard "hear the story" of her husband's death?
 A. with a paralyzed inability to accept its meaning
 B. with sudden, wild weeping
 C. with a shriek of joy and relief
 D. with a sigh and a dull stare in her eyes

_____ 6. What is the meaning of the following passage from the story?
 A kind intention or a cruel intention made the act seem no less a crime as she looked upon it in that brief moment of illumination.
 A. Mrs. Mallard finally realizes that her husband had been cruel to her when she thought he was being kind.
 B. She hadn't known until now whether her husband's intention had been cruel or kind.
 C. She now understands that imposing your own will on someone is a crime, no matter whether the intention is cruel or kind.
 D. She suddenly understands that her self-assertion is a crime, whether her intention was cruel or kind.

Unit 3 Resources: Division, Reconciliation, and Expansion

193

____ 7. Under which type of irony would you classify Josephine's fear that her sister will "make herself ill" by grieving alone in her room?
   A. situational
   B. dramatic
   C. verbal
   D. none of the above

____ 8. In "The Story of an Hour," Kate Chopin is primarily concerned with the
   A. sacrilege of rejoicing at someone's death.
   B. importance of confirming reports of tragic events.
   C. difficulty of distinguishing between illusion and reality.
   D. individual's right to self-expression.

____ 9. After the initial storm of tears, Mrs. Mallard's response to the news of her husband's death is motivated largely by a wave of
   A. self-assertion.
   B. anger.
   C. self-pity.
   D. vengeance.

____ 10. Which of the following excerpts from "The Story of an Hour" best illustrates the author's use of irony?
   A. "She wept at once, with sudden, wild abandonment, in her sister's arms."
   B. "She was young, with a fair, calm face, whose lines bespoke repression and even a certain strength."
   C. "And yet she had loved him—sometimes. Often she had not. What did it matter!"
   D. "'Louise, open the door! I beg; open the door—you will make yourself ill.'"

____ 11. Kate Chopin's "The Story of an Hour" is a powerful illustration of the
   A. cruel irony of fate.
   B. tragedy of thwarted love.
   C. emptiness of marriage.
   D. injustice of life.

____ 12. What is the best reason for considering the title "The Story of an Hour" ironic?
   A. The events in the story take much longer than an hour.
   B. It is really a story about people.
   C. The title is deceptively undramatic compared to the events.
   D. The words suggest the opposite of their usual meaning.

____ 13. What word best characterizes this statement about Louise's feeling for her husband?
   And yet she had loved him—sometimes.
   A. joyful
   B. sorrowful
   C. ironic
   D. insincere

Vocabulary

____ 14. What did Richards do when he learned of Brently Mallard's death in order to *forestall* some less tender friend from announcing the tragedy?
A. acted quickly
B. double-checked the facts
C. went to lunch
D. paused to think over his course of action

____ 15. Which vocabulary word best suggests Mrs. Mallard's emotional state regarding her marriage before she hears of her husband's death?
A. elusive
B. repression
C. tumultuously
D. forestall

____ 16. When Kate Chopin refers to the feeling stealing over Louise Mallard as *elusive*, she means the feeling is
A. terrifying to face.
B. painful to imagine.
C. necessary to escape.
D. difficult to grasp.

Essay

17. Do you admire Mrs. Mallard for daring to take joy in this revelation of freedom, or do you condemn her for reacting with such callousness to her husband's death? Explain your answer in an essay, and cite details from the selection to support it.

18. How might Josephine and Richards have reacted if they had learned about Mrs. Mallard's true feelings regarding her husband's death? Imagine their reactions and write an essay describing and explaining them. Cite examples from the selection to explain what you know about each character, as well as the attitudes of the period. Use these examples to support your conclusions.

19. The Victorian world in which Kate Chopin lived and wrote was one of strong social restraints. The rules and expectations of marriage, the exaltation of romantic love, and the dominance of the husband over the wife prevented many Victorian women from viewing their circumstances honestly. Do you think Mrs. Mallard is a victim of Victorian attitudes toward marriage? Why or why not? Write an essay in which you give your opinion of Mrs. Mallard and her circumstances. Support your argument with evidence from Mrs. Mallard's thoughts in the aftermath of her husband's presumed death.

20. **Thinking About the Essential Question: How does literature shape or reflect society?** "The Story of an Hour" paints a pessimistic picture of marriage: Louise is privately relieved at her husband's death and stricken when he reappears. Do these plot elements just reflect one view about marriage, or do they seek to influence the reader's approach to marriage? Express your views in an essay based on clear logic and details from the story.

Vocabulary Warm-up Word Lists

Study these words from the selections. Then, complete the activities.

Word List A

devious [DEE vee uhs] *adj.* deceptive; crooked
We mistrusted Dana, since we had heard that he had proved to be <u>devious</u> before.

grins [GRINZ] *v.* smiles widely
When Mom points the camera and says, "Say cheese," everybody <u>grins</u>.

harsh [HARSH] *adj.* severe; cruel
The winters in Canada can be <u>harsh</u>, with sub-zero temperatures and much snow.

mask [MASK] *n.* covering that conceals the face
Clowns usually wear a <u>mask</u> that covers their face.

passionate [PASH uh nuht] *adj.* full of emotion
Bill is a <u>passionate</u> follower of baseball.

swarm [SWORM] *v.* to gather or collect in large numbers; to throng
Bees have been known to <u>swarm</u> on that cherry tree in springtime.

tempest [TEM puhst] *n.* bad storm
Last year's category-4 hurricane was a <u>tempest</u> we will never forget.

tortured [TOR chuhrd] *adj.* tormented; violently injured
<u>Tortured</u> by his conscience, the traitor finally confessed to the authorities.

Word List B

bark [BARK] *n.* boat or ship
A Spanish fleet surrounded the pirate <u>bark</u> as it tried to escape.

dissension [di SEN shuhn] *n.* disagreement; conflict
There was a lot of <u>dissension</u> among the members of the political party.

ebb [EB] *n.* flow of water back toward the sea, as the tide falls
When we noticed the <u>ebb</u> of the tide, we moved closer to the water.

guile [GYL] *n.* slyness; trickery
<u>Guile</u> was not part of his nature; he was totally open and honest.

myriad [MIR ee uhd] *adj.* very numerous
When we looked through the telescope, we could see <u>myriad</u> stars.

salient [SAY lee uhnt] *adj.* prominent; very important
A <u>salient</u> part of the governor's philosophy was her belief in human rights.

subtleties [SUT uhl teez] *n.* fine distinctions; delicately skillful or clever points
It took some time for me to appreciate the <u>subtleties</u> of Professor Coburn's argument.

vile [VYL] *adj.* vicious; corrupt; hateful
Several newspapers denounced the recent kidnapping of a child as a <u>vile</u> crime.

"Douglass" and "We Wear the Mask" by Paul Laurence Dunbar
Vocabulary Warm-up Exercises

Exercise A *Fill in each blank in the paragraph below with the appropriate word from Word List A.*

Some people are hard to figure out. They are not really deceptive or
[1] _____, but they seldom let their guard down or reveal their true
opinions. My friend Ken is an example. He is always cheerful and outgoing and never
seems [2] _____ or even saddened by conflicts or disappointments.
Whatever the situation, Ken [3] _____ happily and never passes up a
chance to use his quick wit. I can't escape the feeling, though, that Ken lives behind a
happy-go-lucky [4] _____. He doesn't seem [5] _____
about anything: school, sports, or future careers. Lots of my classmates envy him for
his good looks and trouble-free attitude, and they [6] _____ to be his
friends. Maybe Ken is lucky. I wonder, though, how he might react to a storm or
[7] _____ of real trouble: a setback that would teach him that life sometimes contains [8] _____ realities.

Exercise B *Decide whether each statement below is true or false. Circle T or F, and explain your answer.*

1. The proper place to look for a <u>bark</u> is on the water.
   T / F _____

2. The opposite of "harmony" is <u>dissension</u>.
   T / F _____

3. The tide's <u>ebb</u> occurs when the water is advancing up the beach.
   T / F _____

4. People with <u>guile</u> can generally be trusted.
   T / F _____

5. The adjective <u>myriad</u> refers to a very small number.
   T / F _____

6. A <u>salient</u> argument typically receives a lot of emphasis and attention.
   T / F _____

7. The <u>subtleties</u> of a literary work are conspicuous and readily apparent.
   T / F _____

8. It makes sense to avoid associating with people who are known to be <u>vile</u>.
   T / F _____

"Douglass" and **"We Wear the Mask"** by Paul Laurence Dunbar
Reading Warm-up A

Read the following passage. Pay special attention to the underlined words. Then, read it again, and complete the activities. Use a separate sheet of paper for your written answers.

As Karen swings her leg in front of her and leans on her crutches, she nods to the other cheerleaders on their way to practice and <u>grins</u> happily as if nothing in the world was wrong. She has been going through each day wearing the <u>mask</u> of brave cheerfulness ever since the accident at the cheering competition, where she broke her leg and shattered her squad's hopes for earning the state title.

Inside her, however, rages a <u>tempest</u> of painful emotions. Though the other girls have been kind and concerned only about her recovery, she feels responsible for the loss of the championship and full of guilt. She often scolds herself in <u>harsh</u> tones when she is alone. "How could you have been so clumsy? We had practiced that throw hundreds of times! You knew it perfectly! How could you have managed to land so badly?" Time after time, the words have filled the air like a <u>swarm</u> of angry bees, and time after time she has cried with frustration.

As she sits on the sidelines of the gym, watching her friends warming up, and wishing she could join them, the coach comes over and sits next to her.

"You look <u>tortured</u>, Karen. You have to stop punishing yourself."

Karen looks away so the coach cannot see her eyes. She does not want to be <u>devious</u> and try to trick the coach, but she is afraid she is going to cry.

"I know you are <u>passionate</u> about cheerleading. It is something you truly love, and you are one of the best."

"Was, maybe," Karen whispers.

"Are," replies the coach. "Present tense. And remember, Karen, no one blames you but yourself. All the rest of us admire your courage."

Karen looks at the coach and smiles, genuinely smiles, for the first time in two weeks.

1. Underline the words that give a clue to the meaning of <u>grins</u>. What is a synonym for *grins*?

2. Circle the words that give a clue to the meaning of <u>mask</u>. Is this word used literally or figuratively here?

3. Underline the words in this sentence that hint at the meaning of <u>tempest</u>. Name a synonym for *tempest*.

4. Circle the word that gives a clue to the meaning of <u>harsh</u>. What are two synonyms for *harsh*?

5. Circle the words that offer clues to the meaning of <u>swarm</u>. Name something else that might *swarm*.

6. Underline the word that is close in meaning to <u>tortured</u>. Rewrite the sentence using a synonym for *tortured*.

7. Underline the phrase that has almost the same meaning as <u>devious</u>. Write an original sentence using the word *devious*.

8. Circle the words in this sentence that give a clue to the meaning of <u>passionate</u>. Name two antonyms for *passionate*.

"Douglass" and **"We Wear the Mask"** by Paul Laurence Dunbar
Reading Warm-up B

Read the following passage. Pay special attention to the underlined words. Then, read it again, and complete the activities. Use a separate sheet of paper for your written answers.

Masks have been used by <u>myriad</u> cultures, probably beyond counting, throughout the world. Mask makers have used an astonishing variety of materials, including wood, metal, clay, shells, paper, cloth, fiber, ivory, horn, stone, leather, and feathers. One of the most important, <u>salient</u> features of a mask, of course, is that it covers the face, hiding a person's identity. Simultaneously, however, a mask may establish another identity, suggesting both a personality and a mood.

Occasions and functions for mask wearing are as varied as the materials used. In some African cultures, the first masks are believed to have been used for disciplining children. A mother, for example, might paint a hideous, <u>vile</u> face at the bottom of her water gourd. The face would warn her child not to follow her to the well. Other masks have been used to call on the spirits of ancestors, to initiate young people, to help in hunting, or to protect or frighten troops in battle. On Roman warships, for instance, a terrifying mask was sometimes fixed to the prow of the <u>bark</u> to frighten opponents.

In other cultures, judges have worn masks to protect themselves from people seeking revenge and to reduce conflict, or <u>dissension</u>. The elaborate, complex <u>subtleties</u> of masks used to protect people from disease are striking features of Sri Lankan "devil masks." Masks used at festivals, such as Halloween and Mardi Gras, are often linked with humor, <u>guile</u> or cunning, and naughty pranks.

The <u>ebb</u> and flow of masks used in the theater are especially interesting. With origins in ancient Greek religion, masks in Western theater have been popular in a number of periods, including the Middle Ages and the Renaissance. On Java and Bali in Indonesia, masks have been used in dance dramas ever since the eighteenth century.

1. Underline the words in this sentence that give a clue to the meaning of <u>myriad</u>. Use the word *myriad* in an original sentence.

2. Circle the words in this sentence that give a clue to the meaning of <u>salient</u>. Write two words meaning the opposite of *salient*.

3. Underline the word in this sentence that hints at the meaning of <u>vile</u>. What are two antonyms for *vile*?

4. Underline the words in this sentence that give a clue to the meaning of <u>bark</u>.

5. Circle the word in this sentence that gives a clue to the meaning of <u>dissension</u>. Write two words meaning the opposite of *dissension*.

6. Underline the words in this sentence that hint at the meaning of <u>subtleties</u>. Use the word *subtleties* in an original sentence.

7. Underline the words in this sentence that give a clue to the meaning of <u>guile</u>.

8. Circle the words in this sentence that hint at the meaning of the word <u>ebb</u>. Is this word used literally or figuratively here?

Name _____   Date _____

"Douglass" and **"We Wear the Mask"** by Paul Laurence Dunbar
Literary Analysis: Formal Verse

Formal verse is poetry that follows a regular structure. Many formal poems follow a **rhyme scheme,** which is the regular pattern of rhyming words at the end of lines. One of the traditional forms of formal verse is the **sonnet,** which has fourteen lines that follow a specific rhyme scheme. Some sonnets consist of an eight-line octave followed by a six-line sestet. Some have three four-line quatrains and a final couplet.

DIRECTIONS: *Read the following lines from the poems. Identify the rhyme schemes.*

1.

Ah, Douglass, we have fall'n on evil days,

    Such days as thou, not even thou didst know,

    When thee, the eyes of that harsh long ago

Saw, salient, at the cross of devious ways,

And all the country heard thee with amaze.

    Not ended then, the passionate ebb and flow,

    The awful tide that battled to and fro;

We ride amid a tempest of dispraise.

Rhyme scheme: _____

2.

Now, when the waves of swift dissension swarm,

    And Honor, the strong pilot, lieth stark,

Oh, for thy voice high-sounding o'er the storm,

    For thy strong arm to guide the shivering bark,

The blast-defying power of thy form,

    To give us comfort through the lonely dark.

Rhyme scheme: _____

3.

We wear the mask that grins and lies,

It hides our cheeks and shades our eyes,

This debt we pay to human guile;

With torn and bleeding hearts we smile,

And mouth with myriad subtleties.

Rhyme scheme: _____

200

"Douglass" and "We Wear the Mask" by Paul Laurence Dunbar
Reading Strategy: Analyze the Effect of the Historical Period

When interpreting a poem, you sometimes need to **analyze the effects of the historical period** on the meaning of the poet's words and lines. "Read between the lines"—carefully examining the words for what they say and imply about the period.

DIRECTIONS: *Answer these interpretive questions about the historical period of Dunbar's poetry. Refer to the selection if you need to.*

1. In "Douglass," who is the "we" in the excerpt "Ah, Douglass, we have fall'n on evil days"?

_____

_____

2. In "Douglass," what is the "awful tide that battled to and fro"?

_____

_____

_____

3. In "Douglass," what does the "shivering bark" signify?

_____

_____

4. In "Douglass," what is the "lonely dark"?

_____

_____

5. Why does Dunbar address the poem "Douglass" to Frederick Douglass, an American abolitionist?

_____

_____

_____

6. What is the mask hiding in "We Wear the Mask"?

_____

_____

7. Why does Dunbar want to "hide our cheeks" and "shade our eyes" in "We Wear the Mask"?

_____

_____

_____

"Douglass" and "We Wear the Mask" by Paul Laurence Dunbar
Vocabulary Builder

Related Words: Forms of *guile*

The word *guile* means "craftiness." The word *beguile* means "to mislead by craftiness or deceit." *Guile* and *beguile* are related words.

A. DIRECTIONS: *Form other words from* guile *and* beguile *by adding the suffixes listed. Write the meaning of each word on the lines.*

1. *beguile + -ed* _____

   _____

2. *guile + -less* _____

   _____

3. *beguile + -er* _____

   _____

4. *beguile + -ing* _____

   _____

Using the Word List

   guile   myriad   salient   stark   tempest

B. DIRECTIONS: *Circle the word that best completes each sentence.*

1. The error was salient and stood _____ all the rest.
   A. out from   **B.** below   **C.** by   **D.** to the right

2. The tempest that occurred was more violent than any _____.
   A. game   **B.** criminal   **C.** color   **D.** windstorm

3. The stark trees stood out _____ against the rest of the landscape.
   A. boldly   **B.** subtly   **C.** darkly   **D.** colorfully

4. The guile shown by the con artist demonstrated her level of _____.
   A. brashness   **B.** trickiness   **C.** perkiness   **D.** voicelessness

5. The myriad colors made the room seem like a _____.
   A. paintbrush   **B.** airbrush   **C.** rainbow   **D.** gray color

Name _____ Date _____

"Douglass" and **"We Wear the Mask"** by Paul Laurence Dunbar
Support for Writing

Use library and Internet resources to find information on how critics responded to Dunbar's poetry. Record your findings on the chart below. Identify each source of your information.

Source	Details of Positive and Negative Reviews

On a separate page, write your report, summarizing your findings. Include examples, quotations, and other details to support your summary.

"Douglass" and "We Wear the Mask" by Paul Laurence Dunbar

Enrichment: Art

Dunbar's "We Wear the Mask" suggests that he and others like him wear a mask for the rest of the world to see. Masks are a common way to convey certain images or emotions—they have been used for this purpose in ancient Greek dramas and African ceremonies as well as in modern celebrations such as Mardi Gras.

DIRECTIONS: *Analyze your reaction to one of the poems. Describe an image or emotion that reflects this reaction. Think of how certain facial images can be used to portray that emotion. Use the questions below to guide your thinking. Then design a mask that portrays that image or emotion. Draw your mask in the space provided.*

The image or emotion I would like to portray with my mask is:

_____

_____

Characteristics of my mask:

_____

_____

_____

_____

_____

Drawing of my mask:

Name _____ Date _____

"Douglass" and "We Wear the Mask" by Paul Laurence Dunbar
Open-Book Test

Short Answer *Write your responses to the questions in this section on the lines provided.*

1. In "Douglass," Dunbar makes extensive use of the image of a boat in a stormy sea. What historical circumstance is Dunbar trying to evoke with this image?

   _____

   _____

   _____

2. Read the opening lines of "Douglass":

   > Ah, Douglass, we have fall'n on evil days/Such days as thou, not even thou didst know, . . .

   In your own words, provide a brief interpretation of the meaning of these lines.

   _____

   _____

   _____

3. What is the rhyme scheme of "Douglass"?

   _____

   _____

4. Why is "Douglass" a sonnet?

   _____

   _____

   _____

5. Dunbar ends the poem "Douglass" with the phrase "lonely dark." Based on what you know of the overall context of the poem, briefly explain what you think Dunbar meant by this phrase.

   _____

   _____

   _____

6. Briefly describe the mood of the last stanza of "We Wear the Mask." Which words and sounds contribute to the mood?

   _____

   _____

   _____

   _____

7. In "We Wear the Mask," the mask represents what tendency of human behavior?

_____

_____

_____

8. Read the following lines from "We Wear the Mask":

   Nay, let them only see us, while/We wear the mask.

   Explain whom the poet is referring to with the words "them" and "we," and give a brief overall interpretation of these lines.

_____

_____

_____

_____

9. Rhyme is a key feature of both "Douglass" and "We Wear the Mask." Examine the poems, and fill in the chart below with examples of end rhymes from both poems. The first set is provided as an illustration.

End Rhymes in "Douglass"	End Rhymes in "We Wear the Mask"
days, ways	lies, eyes

10. If a museum exhibit featured a myriad of painting styles, would you expect to find only a narrow range of styles represented? Why or why not? Base your answer on the meaning of *myriad* as it is used in "We Wear the Mask."

_____

_____

_____

_____

Essay

Write an extended response to the question of your choice or to the question of questions your teacher assigns you.

11. The poem "Douglass" clearly shows that Dunbar admired the life and work of the African American antislavery activist Frederick Douglass. In an essay, explain how the poem serves as a tribute to Douglass. Does Dunbar praise Douglass as a visionary, orator, inspiring political leader, or a combination of all three? Support your answer with details from the poem.

12. In "We Wear the Mask," Dunbar says that African Americans feel they have to wear masks when they deal with white people to hide their true feelings. In an essay, explain why Dunbar feels that this is the case. Support your answer with details from the poem.

13. Both "Douglass" and "We Wear the Mask" make powerful statements against the indignities and suffering caused by social and racial inequality and injustice. Which poem do you think is more effective as a cry of protest against the conditions faced by African Americans? Why? Explain your answer in an essay supported by details from the poems.

14. **Thinking About the Essential Question: How does literature shape or reflect society?** "Douglass" and "We Wear the Mask" by Paul Laurence Dunbar both express the writer's anger and indignation over injustices faced by African Americans. Do you consider these poems merely a record of social realities or a cry of protest against them? Develop your thoughts based on details from the poems.

Oral Response

15. Go back to question 1, 3, or 5 or to the question your teacher assigns you. Take a few minutes to expand your answer and prepare an oral response. Find additional details in "Douglass" and "We Wear the Mask" that support your points. If necessary, make notes to guide your oral response.

"Douglass" and **"We Wear the Mask"** by Paul Laurence Dunbar
Selection Test A

Critical Reading *Identify the letter of the choice that best answers the question.*

_____ 1. What does Dunbar mean in these opening lines of "Douglass"?

"Ah, Douglass, we have fall'n on evil days, / Such days as thou, not even thou didst know"

A. African Americans are better off now than in the days of slavery.

B. African Americans are worse off now than in the days of slavery.

C. Frederick Douglass did not understand the times in which he lived.

D. Frederick Douglass would not understand the new ways.

_____ 2. What end rhymes occur in these lines from "Douglass"?

"Such days as thou, not even thou didst know, / When thee, the eyes of that harsh long ago"/Saw, salient, at the cross of devious ways

A. *know* and *thou*

B. *thou* and *thou*

C. *eyes* and *ways*

D. *know* and *ago*

_____ 3. What kind of poem is "Douglass"?

A. sonnet

B. ode

C. informal poem

D. limerick

_____ 4. What does the line "Honor, the strong pilot, [who] lieth stark" in "Douglass" suggest about the historical period of the poem?

A. Honor died when Douglass died.

B. A pilot without honor is a liar.

C. Douglass's strength was his honor.

D. The honorable Douglass lies dead.

_____ 5. What does Dunbar suggest in "Douglass" when he refers to the great man's voice speaking over "the storm" and his "strong arm to guide the shivering bark"?

A. Douglass had a loud voice.

B. Douglass was physically strong.

C. Douglass was like the captain of a ship.

D. Douglass kept people warm.

_____ **6.** Which statement is true about "We Wear the Mask"?

    A. It uses a fixed form.

    B. It has no aesthetic qualities.

    C. It has no formal elements.

    D. It has a rhyme scheme.

_____ **7.** According to "We Wear the Mask," when is the only time that the white world is willing to see African Americans?

    A. when they are crying

    B. when they hide their feelings

    C. when they are praying

    D. when they are wounded

_____ **8.** In "We Wear the Mask," what does Dunbar say is shown on the masks worn by African Americans?

    A. anger

    B. blood

    C. happiness

    D. frustration

_____ **9.** What does Dunbar convey with the line "And mouth with myriad subtleties" from "We Wear the Mask"?

    A. a mouth that can only smile or frown

    B. a mouth that can express subtle feelings

    C. a mouth that makes speeches

    D. a mouth that is covered by a mask

_____ **10.** In "We Wear the Mask," why do the speakers wear masks?

    A. They are attending a costume party.

    B. They are going skiing.

    C. They are cold in the winter.

    D. They are hiding their feelings.

Vocabulary

_____ **11.** In which sentence is the meaning of the word *dissension* suggested?

    A. People wear masks to hide feelings.

    B. Douglass guides people through waves of disagreement and tension.

    C. The poet wants Douglass to be alive.

    D. The people sing but their hearts are sad.

____ **12.** Which word means nearly the opposite of *myriad*?
   A. absolute
   B. few
   C. countless
   D. singular

Essay

13. In "We Wear the Mask," why does Dunbar say that African Americans feel they have to wear masks when they deal with white people? Write a brief essay to give your response. Support your ideas with examples from the poem.

14. The second stanza of "Douglass" reads as follows:

> Now, when the waves of swift dissension swarm,
> And Honor, the strong pilot, lieth stark,
> Oh, for thy voice high-sounding o'er the storm,
> For thy strong arm to guide the shivering bark

What central image of Douglass and African Americans does Dunbar set up? What are the people in the poem doing? Write a brief essay to explain the images in this stanza.

15. **Thinking About the Essential Question: How does literature shape or reflect society?** "Douglass" and "We Wear the Mask" by Paul Laurence Dunbar both express the writer's anger over injustices faced by African Americans. Do you consider these poems merely a record of these problems or a cry of protest against them? Develop your thoughts based on details from the poems.

Name _____ Date _____

"Douglass" and "We Wear the Mask" by Paul Laurence Dunbar
Selection Test B

Critical Reading *Identify the letter of the choice that best completes the statement or answers the question.*

_____ 1. In "We Wear the Mask," Dunbar suggests the world sees his fellow African Americans
    A. in a harsh and honest light.
    B. only when they hide their feelings.
    C. when they are filled with "tears and sighs."
    D. as they are praying to Christ.

_____ 2. What is symbolized in these lines from "We Wear the Mask"?
    but oh the clay is vile
    Beneath our feet, and long the mile;
    A. an evil person
    B. a long, hard life
    C. a broken promise
    D. an act of revenge

_____ 3. In "Douglass," Dunbar uses the image of a boat in a stormy sea mainly to symbolize the
    A. joy and excitement of African Americans immediately after slavery was abolished.
    B. parallel between nature's power and the enduring quality of African American culture.
    C. seafaring traditions of many African cultures.
    D. turmoil and hardships African Americans still faced after emancipation.

_____ 4. The speaker in "We Wear the Mask" believes that wearing the mask is
    A. evil.
    B. foolish.
    C. impossible.
    D. essential.

_____ 5. In "We Wear the Mask," the overall emotional tone that Dunbar uses is one of
    A. aggression.
    B. defeat.
    C. hopefulness.
    D. bitterness.

_____ 6. What makes "Douglass" an example of formal verse?
    A. It treats a serious subject seriously.
    B. It follows the strict structure of a sonnet.
    C. It conveys a mood of bitter despair.
    D. It makes references to a historical figure.

_____ 7. What is the mood of "We Wear the Mask"?
    A. urgent but hopeful
    B. humorously ironic
    C. bitter and despairing
    D. playful and clever

____ 8. In "We Wear the Mask," Dunbar suggests that the mask shows
   A. anger.
   B. despair.
   C. happiness.
   D. strength.

____ 9. What is an appropriate interpretation of the following lines from "We Wear the Mask"?
   Why should the world be overwise,
   In counting all our tears and sighs?

   A. We should not think that anyone is able to guess our thoughts.
   B. Too much knowledge brings misery and hardship to the world.
   C. We must realize that we are really no wiser than anyone else.
   D. Why should we think anyone cares what we really feel?

____ 10. According to "We Wear the Mask," why do African Americans wear the mask?
   A. to pretend that they are white
   B. to convince themselves that they have made more gains than they actually have
   C. to hide their feelings about slavery and racial violence
   D. to display their material and intellectual success

____ 11. Which of the following presents the most appropriate interpretation of these lines from the first stanza of "Douglass"?
   Not ended then, the passionate ebb and flow.
   The awful tide that battled to and fro;
   We ride amid a tempest of dispraise.

   A. When slavery ended, African Americans began to quarrel among themselves as some individuals competed to gain power and influence over the rest of the African American community.
   B. The struggle for equality and against prejudice is not over; in fact, it's worse.
   C. The Civil War did not end when slavery was abolished but continued for several years afterward.
   D. The strength and character of African Americans were not destroyed by slavery but continued to grow in spite of it.

____ 12. In "Douglass," Dunbar leaves the reader feeling
   A. that no improvements will happen soon for African Americans.
   B. that Frederick Douglass was a great speaker.
   C. afraid to travel by ocean because of tempests.
   D. the world is slowly getting more racially tolerant.

____ 13. Which definition most closely distinguishes a poem's aesthetic qualities?
   A. the sense of art and beauty it conveys
   B. the emotion it conveys
   C. its fixed structure
   D. its pattern of rhyming words at the ends of lines

Vocabulary

____ **14.** In "We Wear the Mask," how does a mouth with *myriad* subtleties help pay a debt to human *guile*?

  A. By saying countless small things, we can be very crafty in how we humans portray ourselves.

  B. By smiling broadly, we can give back something to the human spirit.

  C. By seeing each mouth as a human being, we can better visualize human society.

  D. When communicating in eloquent speech, one can make almost anyone believe in anything.

____ **15.** In "Douglass," the line "And Honor, the strong pilot, lieth *stark*" implies that honor is

  A. floating all around us.

  B. angry and seething.

  C. cold, stiff, and dead.

  D. waiting for its soldiers.

____ **16.** Which example best illustrates the meaning of *myriad*?

  A. the moon when it is full

  B. the stars in the sky

  C. a dozen eggs

  D. the items on a shopping list

Essay

17. Restate in an essay Dunbar's sentiments as expressed in "We Wear the Mask" to a person unfamiliar with the poem. Use details from the poem to support your interpretation of it.

18. Paul Laurence Dunbar was the son of former slaves. His father escaped to Canada but returned to the United States to fight in the Union army. Dunbar was the first African American to make a significant attempt to earn his living as a writer. Knowing this, reread one or both of the poems and write an essay explaining how you think Dunbar looked upon the position of African Americans in post-Civil War society. Use details from one or both of the poems in your essay, as well as historical facts of the era.

19. One critic has stated that Paul Laurence Dunbar's "We Wear the Mask" is a poem "about concealed racial fire." Write an essay in which you argue either for or against that viewpoint. Is Dunbar's poem about race, or is it more universal? Support your opinion with evidence from one or both of the poems, as well as facts from Dunbar's life and work.

20. Thinking About the Essential Question: How does literature shape or reflect society? "Douglass" and "We Wear the Mask" by Paul Laurence Dunbar both express the writer's anger over injustices faced by African Americans. Do you consider these poems merely a record of these problems or a cry of protest against them? Develop your thoughts based on details from the poems.

Study these words from the selections. Then, complete the activities.

Word List A

chiseled [CHIZ uhld] *v.* cut or shaped with a chisel (sharp hand tool)
The decoy carver quickly chiseled the wood into the shape of a duck.

discontent [dis kun TENT] *n.* dissatisfaction or displeasure
Seeing my brother's look of discontent, I offered to swap my prize for his.

medicinal [muh DIS in uhl] *adj.* having the properties of medicine
Many medicinal herbs can easily be grown in pots indoors.

memorable [MEM er uh buhl] *adj.* worth remembering
What really made that party memorable was the great band that played.

rambled [RAM buhld] *v.* wandered aimlessly
We rambled over the fields and hills, following wherever our feet took us.

repose [ri POHZ] *n.* state of being at rest
He tiptoed through the house, not wanting to disturb his father's repose.

schooled [SKOOLD] *v.* taught or trained
She has been schooled in shiatsu as well as Swedish massage.

weariness [WEER ee nes] *n.* fatigue
My weariness overcame me, and I drifted off to sleep.

Word List B

admirably [AD mer uh blee] *adv.* in a way that deserves admiration
Considering what he has been through, I think he has behaved admirably.

arrayed [uh RAYD] *v.* dressed up; decked out
Arrayed in his rented tuxedo, Sam joined his prom date in the limousine.

consistent [kuhn SIS tent] *adj.* staying the same; steadfast
Mrs. Edwards may be strict, but at least she is consistent in her rules.

crimson [KRIM sun] *adj.* deep red
"That crimson dress makes you look like a movie star," he said.

imperially [im PEER ee uhl ee] *adv.* majestically
The beauty queen sat on the float, waving imperially at the crowd.

influenced [IN floo ensd] *v.* moved or affected
His mother's being a lawyer influenced his own choice of career.

pessimistic [pes i MIS tik] *adj.* gloomy; expecting the worst
Macie is sure it will rain on our picnic, but I am feeling less pessimistic.

quench [KWENCH] *v.* put out (as a fire)
Nothing can quench my burning desire to run away with the circus.

Poetry of Edwin Arlington Robinson and Edgar Lee Masters
Vocabulary Warm-up Exercises

Exercise A *Fill in each blank in the paragraph below with the appropriate word from Word List A. Use each word only once.*

Some vacations are easily forgotten, but my summer in the country was truly
[1] _____. Every day, with nothing in particular to do, I
[2] _____ over the hills, breathing in air that was so fresh and healthy it
seemed to have a [3] _____ effect. If I ever felt sadness or
[4] _____, all I had to do was walk until the mood passed. When I was
overcome by [5] _____, I found a place to rest. One day, I stopped at an
old cemetery, where I read the words [6] _____ on the overgrown tombstones. One said, "She was [7] _____ in the ways of these hills, and now
she finds [8] _____ here."

Exercise B *Answer the questions with complete explanations.*

1. Would you expect someone who walked <u>imperially</u> to be shy and modest?
   _____

2. If someone said, "Hand me the <u>crimson</u> tie," would you give him the red one or the
   blue one?
   _____

3. Which would <u>quench</u> a fire better, gasoline or water?
   _____

4. In a movie, who behaves more <u>admirably</u>, the hero or the villain?
   _____

5. Would a report card filled with *D*s and *F*s be <u>consistent</u> with plans to go to college?
   _____

6. Do you think someone who is very <u>pessimistic</u> is a lot of fun to be around?
   _____

7. If you saw a girl <u>arrayed</u> in her best clothes, would you think she was going to a
   party or getting ready to take out the garbage?
   _____

8. Do you think a shopper with only a dollar is likely to be <u>influenced</u> by price?
   _____

Name _____ Date _____

Read the following passage. Pay special attention to the underlined words. Then, read it again, and complete the activities. Use a separate sheet of paper for your written answers.

When I picture Grandpa Lou, I see his hands—strong, brown, weather-beaten hands. This <u>memorable</u> image in my mind is not a photo, but a video clip, because the hands were always in motion: hammering a board in place on the henhouse, hauling buckets of scraps to the pigs, slapping the rump of a stray cow that had <u>rambled</u> away from the herd.

Grandpa Lou believed in hard work, for himself and for everyone else, especially his grandchildren. Long ago, he had been <u>schooled</u> in the idea that a boy with a few minutes of free time was a boy looking for trouble. "Idle hands find mischief," he would say, and find me yet another chore to do. By dinnertime, I was ready to drop with <u>weariness</u>, but Grandpa Lou, who had been working alongside me all day, showed no sign of exhaustion himself.

He was eighty-five when he had the operation on his heart. It was strange to see him in the hospital room, with its white walls and faint <u>medicinal</u> smell. He rested on his back, eyes closed, his hands folded across his chest in <u>repose</u>. Grandpa Lou was not doing as well as they had hoped, one of my aunts told me in a whisper. "He never complains," she said, "but we know he's unhappy."

Looking at the still hands, I thought I knew the reason for his <u>discontent</u>. "Grandpa," I said, "look what I brought you." He turned his head slowly and opened his eyes without much interest, expecting, I was certain, more chocolates or another flower arrangement. When he saw the small woodcarving set, however, his expression changed.

I still have the wooden cow he <u>chiseled</u> for me during his hospital stay; when I look at it, what I see is Grandpa Lou's hands.

1. Underline the <u>memorable</u> image the writer has of Grandpa Lou. Then, describe a *memorable* feature of someone you have met.

2. Circle what you would call a cow that <u>rambled</u> away from the herd. Then, suggest another word that you could substitute for *rambled* in this sentence.

3. Underline what Grandpa Lou was <u>schooled</u> in. What else might someone be *schooled* in?

4. Circle the word that means the same as <u>weariness</u>. What is a good cure for *weariness*?

5. Underline what had a <u>medicinal</u> smell. Name an item that is *medicinal*.

6. Underline what aspect of Grandpa Lou suggests <u>repose</u>. Is *repose* something Grandpa Lou seems to enjoy?

7. Circle the word that means something similar to <u>discontent</u>. How do you know if someone is feeling a sense of *discontent*?

8. Underline what Grandpa Lou <u>chiseled</u> with his new carving set. What word could you use here instead of *chiseled*?

Poetry of Edwin Arlington Robinson and Edgar Lee Masters
Reading Warm-up B

Read the following passage. Pay special attention to the underlined words. Then, read it again, and complete the activities. Use a separate sheet of paper for your written answers.

As I accept this Academy Award, I would like to thank everyone who contributed to the film and to my career; but, also, I would like to take a moment to express my tremendous gratitude to the person who first <u>influenced</u> me as an actress: my high school drama teacher, Ms. Veronica Graham.

I remember the day I walked into Ms. Graham's class to find her <u>arrayed</u> in a toga for our first reading of *Julius Caesar*. I was a skinny girl who went to any length to avoid showing my legs, so you can imagine my horror when Ms. Graham told us we all had to wear togas, too. As I stood there, blushing <u>crimson</u> with embarrassment, my deepest wish was that I had chosen wood shop or home economics for my elective. Then, Ms. Graham strode <u>imperially</u> out onstage, and my everyday world disappeared; in the way she walked, the way she spoke, she had actually transformed herself into Julius Caesar. At that moment, I knew that I had to be an actress.

Ms. Graham taught as <u>admirably</u> as she acted, and with apologies to my director, I have to say that I learned everything I know about acting from her. The most important thing she taught me, however, was not to give up. Over the years, the memory of Ms. Graham has been a <u>consistent</u> source of support and encouragement for me. Whenever I felt most <u>pessimistic</u> about my chances in Hollywood, I would think of her favorite saying: "Never let anything <u>quench</u> your fire, and you'll never find your-self out in the cold." So, thank you for everything, Ms. Graham, and I accept this Oscar in your honor.

1. Who might have <u>influenced</u> the speaker, besides her drama teacher? What is a synonym for *influenced*?

2. Circle what Ms. Graham was <u>arrayed</u> in. Then, tell what *arrayed* means.

3. What else might be *crimson* besides a blush?

4. Circle what Ms. Graham did <u>imperially</u>. Who else might behave *imperially*?

5. Circle two things Ms. Graham did <u>admirably</u>. What else might someone do *admirably*?

6. Underline what was a <u>consistent</u> source of support to the speaker. Then, tell what *consistent* means.

7. Why might the speaker have felt <u>pessimistic</u> about her chances as an actress?

8. If you wanted to do the opposite of <u>quench</u> a fire, what would you do?

"Luke Havergal" and "Richard Cory" by Edwin Arlington Robinson
"Lucinda Matlock" and "Richard Bone" by Edgar Lee Masters
Literary Analysis: Speaker

Often, the **speaker** of a poem is the poet, but when the speaker is a fictional character, as in the poems by Edwin Arlington Robinson and Edgar Lee Masters, the poem may not only communicate a message, but also reveal the attitude of the speaker and possibly the development of his or her character. For example, in "Richard Cory," the speaker looks with envy and admiration on Cory for his wealth and breeding. This provides insight into the character speaking the poem—that he or she is not of the same economic or social class.

DIRECTIONS: *In some poems, the speaker's identity is obvious, but in other poems, such as "Luke Havergal," the speaker's identity and purpose are more mysterious. Read "Luke Havergal" again, and then answer the questions below. Cite examples from the poem to support your answers.*

1. What details from "Luke Havergal" provide clues to the speaker's identity?

   _____

   _____

2. Do you think the woman whom the speaker mentions is alive or dead? Why or why not?

   _____

   _____

   _____

3. Is the speaker of this poem providing advice about a physical journey or a supernatural one? How can you tell?

   _____

   _____

4. Does the speaker of this poem expect Luke Havergal to find happiness? How can you tell?

   _____

   _____

5. What do you think happened to Luke Havergal before the speaker began speaking?

   _____

   _____

Name _____ Date _____

"**Luke Havergal**" and "**Richard Cory**" by Edwin Arlington Robinson
"**Lucinda Matlock**" and "**Richard Bone**" by Edgar Lee Masters
Reading Strategy: Comparing and Contrasting

When you read poems by a single writer, on a similar theme, or dating from the same or even a different time period, it often helps you understand each poem if you apply the skill of **comparing and contrasting.** By comparing the poems' **formal elements, point of view,** and **theme,** you can gain insight into each poem as well as into the characteristics of the group.

DIRECTIONS: *Use this chart to help you compare and contrast the poems by Edwin Arlington Robinson and Edgar Lee Masters. For each poem, describe the characteristics at the top of each column. Use your finished chart to consider how they are alike and different.*

	Formal Elements	**Point of View**	**Theme**
"Luke Havergal"			
"Richard Cory"			
"Lucinda Matlock"			
"Richard Bone"			

"Luke Havergal" and **"Richard Cory"** by Edwin Arlington Robinson
"Lucinda Matlock" and **"Richard Bone"** by Edgar Lee Masters

Vocabulary Builder

Using the Latin Root -*genus*-

A. DIRECTIONS: *The Latin root* -genus- *means "birth, race, species, or kind." Define each underlined word below based on its use in the sentence and what you know about the word root* -genus-.

1. The physician explained that the disease was <u>congenital</u> and even the healthiest lifestyle would not have prevented its onslaught.

   _____

   _____

2. Poetry is one of the most intense, compact of all literary <u>genres.</u>

   _____

   _____

3. The beautiful stitching and vivid colors convinced her that the quilt was <u>genuine.</u>

   _____

   _____

4. Each <u>generation</u> of Americans has its own priorities and interests.

   _____

   _____

Using the Word List

    chronicles   degenerate   epitaph   repose

B. DIRECTIONS: *Above each underlined word in the following paragraph, write a synonym from the Word List.*

During her life, Arliss's accusers claimed she was a <u>corrupt</u> person, but when she died, the

community maintained a respectful silence as she was lowered into her final <u>rest</u>. The

headstone above her grave bore the <u>legend</u> "A loyal sister, a wise leader, loved by all." Still, the

<u>stories</u> of her many deceits and exploits persisted.

Name _____ Date _____

"Luke Havergal" and **"Richard Cory"** by Edwin Arlington Robinson
"Lucinda Matlock" and **"Richard Bone"** by Edgar Lee Masters
Support for Writing

Use the outline to organize ideas for your fictional narrative based on one of the poems in this grouping.

Poem: _____

I. Beginning: _____

   A. _____

      1. _____

      2. _____

   B. _____

      1. _____

      2. _____

I. Middle: _____

   A. _____

      1. _____

      2. _____

   B. _____

      1. _____

      2. _____

I. End: _____

   A. _____

      1. _____

      2. _____

   B. _____

      1. _____

      2. _____

Name _____ Date _____

"Luke Havergal" and "Richard Cory" by Edwin Arlington Robinson
"Lucinda Matlock" and "Richard Bone" by Edgar Lee Masters
Enrichment: Dance

Each of the poems in this selection reveals some aspects of the character's personality and values, while other parts remain a mystery. The reader of a poem must often imagine what a character in the poem is like, judging from clues in the poem. For example, Edgar Lee Masters tells us that part of Richard Bone's job is to chisel epitaphs on headstones, but he does not tell us what Richard Bone looks like. However, the reader can surmise that Richard Bone can both lift a heavy headstone and chisel fine details. So, we can guess that he is probably able-bodied and dexterous. From this image we can picture how Richard Bone might move.

DIRECTIONS: *Try to picture each character in each of the poems. (Remember that the speaker is not always the main character of the poem.) Look for the clues in each poem that reveal its main character's personality. What does each character look like while moving? Now think about what each character would look like when dancing. What would he or she dance to—music, sounds of nature, or maybe silence? Weave body movements and sounds together to create a dance that the character might do. Use the space below to plan your dance.*

Poem/Character	Body Movements	Sounds
Luke Havergal		
Richard Cory		
Lucinda Matlock		
Richard Bone		

"Luke Havergal" and **"Richard Cory"** by Edwin Arlington Robinson
"Lucinda Matlock" and **"Richard Bone"** by Edgar Lee Masters
Open-Book Test

Short Answer *Write your responses to the questions in this section on the lines provided.*

1. In the first line of "Luke Havergal," the speaker says, "Go to the western gate, Luke Havergal, . . ." Who is the speaker who issues this command? Where does the speaker come from?

   _____

   _____

   _____

2. In the first stanza of the poem, the speaker tells Luke Havergal, "But go, and if you listen she will call." Who is "she," and what is the nature of her relationship with Luke Havergal?

   _____

   _____

3. Each stanza of "Luke Havergal" begins and ends with the same line. Why does Robinson use this device? What message or theme does it emphasize in this poem?

   _____

   _____

   _____

4. Who is the speaker in "Richard Cory"? Whose views does the speaker represent?

   _____

   _____

   _____

5. Why is the ending of "Richard Cory" so surprising? What theme or philosophy of life is underscored by this ending?

   _____

   _____

   _____

   _____

6. "Richard Cory" cites the many advantages that Cory had in life: wealth, good looks, nice manners, and so on. Based on the poem's ending, what do you think Cory lacked, despite all his advantages, that made him so unhappy?

   _____

   _____

   _____

7. Richard Bone says of his work chiseling epitaphs onto tombstones, "And made myself party to the false chronicles/Of the stones." What does this line say about his attitude toward his work?

_____

_____

_____

8. Richard Bone compares himself to a historian in these lines:

> Even as the historian does who writes/Without knowing the truth/Or because he is influenced to hide it.

What is Richard Bone implying about the accuracy of the historian's record of the past?

_____

_____

_____

_____

9. Compare and contrast the outlook on life expressed in "Lucinda Matlock" and "Richard Bone." Cite details from the poems to support your answer.

_____

_____

_____

_____

10. If someone told you she was longing for repose, how would she likely respond to a proposal to go out for a three-mile run? Explain your answer, basing it on the definition of *repose* as it is used in "Lucinda Matlock."

_____

_____

_____

_____

Essay

Write an extended response to the question of your choice or to the question or questions your teacher assigns you.

11. The speaker and townspeople of "Richard Cory" have a picture of Richard Cory that turns out to be very different from the reality of his life. In an essay, explain why the townspeople might have had such a mistaken perception of Cory's life. Support your answer with examples from the poem.

12. Choose the character or speaker from these four poems—"Luke Havergal," "Richard Cory," "Lucinda Matlock," or "Richard Bone"—that you find to be most interesting. In an essay, write a brief biographical sketch of the character, drawing on details from the poem and your imagination. Explain why you find the character so interesting.

13. The speaker of "Luke Havergal" keeps urging Luke Havergal to "go to the western gate." The poem begins with this command and ends with it. What do you think the speaker is urging Luke Havergal to do? Explain your answer in an essay supported by details from the poem.

14. **Thinking About the Essential Question: What is the relationship between place and literature?** All of the poems in this grouping—"Luke Havergal," "Richard Cory," "Lucinda Matlock," or "Richard Bone"—evoke a strong sense of place or setting. Choose one of the poems and, in an essay, explain how a sense of place enhances the overall mood and/or message of the poem. Support your answer with details from the poem.

Oral Response

15. Go back to question 1, 3, or 6 or to the question your teacher assigns you. Take a few minutes to expand your answer and prepare an oral response. Find additional details in "Luke Havergal," "Richard Cory," "Lucinda Matlock," or "Richard Bone," or in a combination of the poems, that support your points. If necessary, make notes to guide your oral response.

Name _____ Date _____

"Luke Havergal" and **"Richard Cory"** by Edwin Arlington Robinson
"Lucinda Matlock" and **"Richard Bone"** by Edgar Lee Masters
Selection Test A

Critical Reading *Identify the letter of the choice that best answers the question.*

_____ 1. In "Luke Havergal," what does the speaker want Luke to do?
   A. to visit her grave
   B. to join her in death
   C. to climb the western gate
   D. to meet her at twilight

_____ 2. In "Luke Havergal," what relationship has existed between Luke and the speaker?
   A. They were sweethearts.
   B. They were mother and son.
   C. They were sister and brother.
   D. They were father and daughter.

_____ 3. In "Luke Havergal," how does the speaker show Luke the importance of what she wishes him to do?
   A. by describing the eastern dawn
   B. by comparing hell and paradise
   C. by repeating "Out of a grave I come,"
   D. by reminding him of her kiss

_____ 4. In "Richard Cory," whose ideas does the speaker reflect?
   A. his own
   B. Richard Cory's
   C. the townspeople's
   D. the Cory family's

_____ 5. In "Richard Cory," what is the general feeling Richard Cory inspires in the townspeople up until the last lines?
   A. confusion
   B. envy
   C. approval
   D. pity

_____ 6. In "Richard Cory," what attitude would you expect the speaker to have as he writes the final lines of the poem?
  A. satisfaction
  B. shock
  C. acceptance
  D. admiration

_____ 7. In "Lucinda Matlock," what is the title character's attitude toward life?
  A. She thinks life is hard.
  B. She thinks life ends too soon.
  C. She thinks life is worthwhile.
  D. She thinks life is boring.

_____ 8. Which of these might the title character say to young people at the end of "Lucinda Matlock"?
  A. Life will get better as you get older.
  B. All life has some sorrow.
  C. You can sleep after you die.
  D. It takes strength to engage in life.

_____ 9. What attitude can you assume Lucinda Matlock would have toward Richard Cory's final actions?
  A. sympathy
  B. disgust
  C. relief
  D. agreement

_____ 10. What job does the title character have in "Richard Bone"?
  A. He is an undertaker.
  B. He is an epitaph carver.
  C. He is a stonecutter.
  D. He is a historian.

_____ 11. Why does the speaker in "Richard Bone" carve lies about the dead?
  A. He does not know they are lies.
  B. He does not care about truth or lies.
  C. He is paid to carve what he is told.
  D. He wants to make survivors feel better.

Vocabulary

____ **12.** In which sentence is the meaning of the word *repose* suggested?

    A. A ghost called from the grave to Luke Havergal.

    B. Everyone thought Richard Cory lived a charmed life.

    C. Lucinda Matlock rested only when she died.

    D. Richard Bone questioned the value of his life's work.

____ **13.** What is the meaning of the word *chronicles* when Richard Bone says I "made myself party to the false *chronicles* / Of the stones"?

    A. habits

    B. actions

    C. stories

    D. feelings

Essay

14. Why do you think the speaker and the townspeople in "Richard Cory" had a picture of Richard Cory that was different from the real person? Write a brief essay to suggest reasons why the townspeople might have been so wrong about someone they saw every day.

15. Richard Bone in the poem of the same name compares himself to a historian. How could a person who carves epitaphs be like a person who writes history? Write a brief essay using your own ideas and the material from the poem to give your opinion on Richard Bone's belief.

16. Thinking About the Essential Question: What is the relationship between place and literature? All of the poems in this grouping—"Luke Havergal," "Richard Cory," "Lucinda Matlock," and "Richard Bone"—convey a strong sense of place or setting. Choose one of the poems and, in an essay, explain how a sense of place helps the poet communicate his message. Support your answer with details from the poem of your choice.

Name _____ Date _____

"**Luke Havergal**" and "**Richard Cory**" by Edwin Arlington Robinson
"**Lucinda Matlock**" and "**Richard Bone**" by Edgar Lee Masters
Selection Test B

Critical Reading *Identify the letter of the choice that best completes the statement or answers the question.*

____ 1. What is the speaker's main motive for talking to Luke Havergal in this poem?
A. to comfort Luke
B. to convince Luke to act on his feelings
C. to chastise Luke for being overly emotional
D. to provide Luke with hope for a brighter future

____ 2. Which of the following best describes the tone of "Luke Havergal"?
A. angry
B. hopeful
C. indifferent
D. brooding

____ 3. Which of the following most likely explains the relationship between Luke Havergal and the woman mentioned in the poem?
A. The woman was Luke's lover, but she died.
B. The woman was Luke's enemy, and she destroyed his life.
C. The woman was a homeless vagrant whom Luke saw and pitied.
D. The woman was a murderer who killed Luke's family.

____ 4. Who is the speaker of "Luke Havergal"?
A. Luke Havergal
B. a living woman
C. a ghost
D. Edwin Arlington Robinson

____ 5. Who is the speaker of "Richard Cory"?
A. Richard Cory
B. a person in the town
C. a member of Richard Cory's family
D. Edwin Arlington Robinson

____ 6. Why did the speaker of "Richard Cory" envy Richard Cory?
A. because he was wealthy and admirable
B. because he had a large family
C. because he led a happy life
D. because he was a community leader

____ 7. Which of the following passages from "Richard Cory" shows that the speaker admired Richard Cory's character and manners?
A. "He was a gentleman from sole to crown,"
B. "But still he fluttered pulses when he said, / 'Good-morning'"
C. ". . . and he glittered when he walked."
D. "And he was rich—yes, richer than a king—"

_____ 8. Which sentence best describes Lucinda Matlock's view of life?
    A. The parties and explorations of youth are the best part of life; old age is full of pain, suffering, and loneliness.
    B. You need anger to get you through the hardships of life; the angrier you are, the more likely you are to survive to an old age.
    C. You must work hard and you may encounter sorrow, but life is basically fulfilling and rewarding.
    D. People's lives are determined by fate, and no one really cares about what you think or how you feel.

_____ 9. How would you Contrast Lucinda Matlock's view of life with that of Richard Cory?
    A. She thinks life is hard but worthwhile; he gives up on life.
    B. She thinks joy is for everyone; he thinks it is only for the rich.
    C. She focuses on everyday concerns; he is more philosophical.
    D. She takes people at face value; he is more cynical.

_____ 10. Which of the following excerpts gives the best insight into the personality of Lucinda Matlock?
    A. "One time we changed partners,"
    B. "Enjoying, working, raising the twelve children,"
    C. "And by Spoon River gathering many a shell,"
    D. "Anger, discontent, and drooping hopes?"

_____ 11. Which of the following passages from "Richard Bone" shows that the speaker feels uncomfortable about chiseling deceptive epitaphs?
    A. "I did not know whether what they told me/Was true or false."
    B. "And I chiseled them whatever they wished,/All in ignorance of its truth."
    C. "I knew how near to the life/Were the epitaphs that were ordered . . . "
    D. "And made myself party to the false chronicles/Of the stones,"

_____ 12. What does this passage from "Richard Bone" suggest about the speaker's attitude?
    But still I chiseled whatever they paid me to chisel
    And made myself party to the false chronicles

    A. He is indifferent to the truth.
    B. He has been influenced to hide the truth.
    C. He prefers not to know the truth.
    D. He will chisel only true epitaphs.

Vocabulary

_____ 13. What does the narrator in "Lucinda Matlock" mean by the word *degenerate* in these lines?
    Degenerate sons and daughters,
    Life is too strong for you—
    It takes life to love Life.

    A. innocent
    B. morally corrupt
    C. passionate
    D. self-deceived

____ 14. Which of the following statements most accurately paraphrases the following excerpt from "Lucinda Matlock"?

> At ninety-six I had lived enough, that is all
> And passed to a sweet *repose*.

   A. At age ninety-six, I moved into a nursing home.
   B. At age ninety-six, I stopped working and started having fun.
   C. At age ninety-six, I decided to stop working and retire.
   D. At age ninety-six, I died and got a long overdue rest.

____ 15. In the following passage from "Richard Bone," what does the word *epitaph* mean?

> They would bring me the *epitaph*
> And stand around the shop while I worked

   A. inscription
   B. headstone
   C. grave marker
   D. dead body

Essay

16. Choose one of the poems in this selection and write a short biographical essay on the title character. Draw conclusions about the life the character led or is leading, and support those conclusions with details from the poem. Consider the tone of the poem you choose, and use that as a clue to the kind of life the person led.

17. How would you describe Lucinda Matlock's attitude toward younger people? Write an essay describing how she comes to give the advice she does in the poem. Do you think she despises people who are younger than she, or is she motivated by a desire to ensure that they do not miss out on life? Support your conclusions with details from the poem.

18. What do you think the speaker of "Luke Havergal" wants Luke Havergal to do? Write an essay, using evidence from the poem to answer the question and support your answer.

19. **Thinking About the Essential Question: What is the relationship between place and literature?** All of the poems in this grouping—"Luke Havergal," "Richard Cory," "Lucinda Matlock," and "Richard Bone"—convey a strong sense of place or setting. Choose one of the poems and, in an essay, explain how a sense of place helps the poet communicate his message. Support your answer with details from the poem of your choice.

Vocabulary Warm-up Word Lists

Study these words from the selection. Then, complete the activities that follow.

Word List A

alight [uh LYT] *v.* to get down or set foot on a platform or sidewalk
As the train slowed to a stop, I prepared to <u>alight</u> on the platform.

comprehend [kahm pree HEND] *v.* to understand
That theory is so complex that it is difficult to <u>comprehend</u>.

conjuror [KAHN juh ruhr] *n.* magician
The entertainer was a famous <u>conjuror</u> who performed magic tricks.

eluding [i LOOD ing] *v.* evading; escaping
<u>Eluding</u> the police, the cat burglar slipped away in the night.

haggard [HAG uhrd] *adj.* drawn; pale
Sam looked <u>haggard</u>, as if he hadn't slept for days.

legacy [LEG uh see] *n.* inheritance; anything handed down from the past
Grandmother's stories about her own youth are a precious family <u>legacy</u>.

pitiless [PIT ee les] *adj.* without pity or compassion
The weather has been <u>pitiless</u>, with extremely cold winters and very hot summers.

vainly [VAYN lee] *adv.* to no effect; emptily
Mark tried <u>vainly</u> to persuade Mom, but she would not accept his arguments.

Word List B

absurdities [ab SERD uh teez] *n.* irrational or illogical things or situations
Among other <u>absurdities</u>, the comedian introduced a hilarious talking parrot.

characteristically [kar ik tuh RIS tik lee] *adv.* typically; in a predictable fashion
Cyrus was <u>characteristically</u> melancholy, seldom cracking a smile.

frenzy [FREN zee] *n.* state of great excitement or madness
The cornered cat shrieked in a <u>frenzy</u> of fear.

harmonious [har MOH nee uhs] *adj.* in tune or harmony with
Sue's neighbors are a <u>harmonious</u> group of people.

immobility [i moh BIL i tee] *n.* motionless state
Do not be fooled by the possum's <u>immobility</u>; it is still very much alive!

pathetic [puh THET ik] *adj.* pitiful; worthy of compassion
The condition of the refugees was <u>pathetic</u>; many of them even lacked shoes.

pedestal [PED uhs tuhl] *n.* base for a statue or sculpture
The statue stood on a magnificent <u>pedestal</u> of polished granite.

wholly [HOHL ee] *adv.* entirely
Trent's story was <u>wholly</u> unbelievable, and we dismissed it out of hand.

Name _____ Date _____

"A Wagner Matinée" by Willa Cather
Vocabulary Warm-up Exercises

Exercise A *Fill in each blank in the paragraph below with the appropriate word from Word List A.*

After his parents took him to see a magic show, Lenny decided he wanted to become a magician, or [1] _____. He imagined himself preparing his performances and getting ready to [2] _____ on stage in front of the audience. They would try desperately but [3] _____ to [4] _____ the secrets of his tricks, and Lenny, [5] _____ all their efforts, would remain mysterious as ever. He would work hard to keep up with new trends in the magic business. Putting up with a harsh and [6] _____ schedule on tour might make him so tired that he would look weary, or even [7] _____. However, he would have the greatest magic show in the country, and a lasting reputation for unbelievable tricks would be his [8] _____ to future generations.

Exercise B *Decide whether each statement below is true or false. Circle T or F, and explain your answer.*

1. <u>Absurdities</u> are worth taking seriously.
   T / F _____

2. If someone is <u>characteristically</u> optimistic, he or she generally looks on the bright side.
   T / F _____

3. A person in a <u>frenzy</u> might act wildly and unpredictably.
   T / F _____

4. Nations that sign a peace treaty expect that their relations will not be <u>harmonious</u>.
   T / F _____

5. Paralysis causes a state of <u>immobility</u>.
   T / F _____

6. A <u>pathetic</u> state of affairs often inspires pity.
   T / F _____

7. A <u>pedestal</u> often supports a statue or sculpture.
   T / F _____

8. If a house has been <u>wholly</u> renovated, parts of it remain to be refurbished.
   T / F _____

"A Wagner Matinée" by Willa Cather
Reading Warm-up A

Read the following passage. Pay special attention to the underlined words. Then, read it again, and complete the activities. Use a separate sheet of paper for your written answers.

In the late nineteenth and early twentieth centuries, millions of immigrants streamed off ships from Europe to alight on American soil for the first time. The majority of these newcomers settled in eastern cities, such as New York, Philadelphia, Boston, and Baltimore. Many of them joined relatives who were already here. These family members could help the new arrivals comprehend the challenges of building a new life. They could assist with learning an unfamiliar language, finding a place to live, and securing a job.

A number of immigrants, however, traveled westward to the Great Plains. In return for cheap land, these settlers were prepared to endure a pitiless climate of scorching summers and freezing winters. Many of these Midwestern farmers were from Scandinavia and central Europe.

In many of her novels, Willa Cather celebrated the Czech and Slovak farmers of Nebraska. She thought of them as unsung heroes. Their legacy of courage and endurance, passed down to their descendants, deserved commemoration, Cather believed. In his book *Giants in the Earth,* published in 1927, the novelist Ole Edvart Rölvaag wrote about the Norwegian homesteaders of the Dakota Territory.

Both Cather and Rölvaag were realistic in their portrayals of the immigrants' farm life. The farmers' existence was so harsh that many homesteaders became haggard—worn out with fatigue. Some of the characters struggle vainly against misfortune and are crushed by the obstacles they encounter. Other characters are luckier, eluding disaster and disappointment. In the end, for both authors, a person winning out in this challenging environment is almost like a conjuror, whose magical abilities suffice to build a new life full of hope and promise.

1. Underline the words in this sentence that give a clue to the meaning of alight. Use the word *alight* in an original sentence.

2. Circle the words in this and the next sentence that give a clue to the meaning of the word comprehend. What is a synonym for *comprehend*?

3. Underline the words that give a clue to the meaning of pitiless. What is an antonym for *pitiless*?

4. Circle the words that offer a clue to the meaning of legacy here. What is a synonym for the word *legacy*?

5. Circle the words in this sentence that offer clues to the meaning of haggard. Write two words meaning the opposite of *haggard*.

6. Underline the words in this sentence that give a clue to the meaning of vainly. What are two antonyms for *vainly*?

7. Circle the words in this sentence that give a clue to the meaning of eluding. Use the word *eluding* in an original sentence.

8. Underline the words in this sentence hinting at the meaning of conjuror. Use the word *conjuror* in an original sentence.

Name _____   Date _____

"**A Wagner Matinée**" by Willa Cather
Reading Warm-up B

Read the following passage. Pay special attention to the underlined words. Then, read it again, and complete the activities. Use a separate sheet of paper for your written answers.

As an art form, opera is over 400 years old. Developed in Italy in the early 1600s, operas are unique fusions of song, orchestral accompaniment, and stage effects. These effects include costumes, scenery, and lighting. In an ideal performance, all these elements exist in a <u>harmonious</u>, balanced combination.

Many people find opera difficult to understand, however. Some critics mock operatic works as <u>absurdities</u> that no reasonable person can take seriously. Critics claim that operas <u>characteristically</u> possess unrealistic plots, which depend on coincidence so much that they are <u>wholly</u> unbelievable. According to these skeptics, operatic characters exemplify ridiculous extremes. At some points, they exhibit a <u>frenzy</u> of wild emotions, and at others they lapse into static <u>immobility</u>.

Opera's fans, on the other hand, claim that no other art form contains such rich possibilities of expression. Without unduly glorifying opera, or putting it on a <u>pedestal</u>, it must be acknowledged that the form afforded great composers like Richard Wagner and Giuseppe Verdi wonderful artistic opportunities. For example, two or more characters singing together could express varying or conflicting emotions at the same time. Orchestral themes could function like flashbacks or foreshadowing in literature, signaling a memory of the past or a hint about the future. Profound emotions could be illustrated on stage, ranging from the triumphant to the <u>pathetic</u>.

In the end, opera has not turned out to be everybody's cup of tea. People like Aunt Georgiana in Willa Cather's story, "A Wagner Matinée," are still in the minority, and opera has never been hugely popular, at least in America. Let there be no doubt, however, that opera's fans are passionate, if they are anything!

1. Underline the words in this sentence that give a clue to the meaning of <u>harmonious</u>. Write two words meaning the opposite of *harmonious*.

2. Circle the words in this sentence that give a clue to the meaning of <u>absurdities</u>. Are *absurdities* logical or illogical?

3. What is a synonym for <u>characteristically</u>? What is an antonym for *characteristically*?

4. Underline the words in this sentence that give a clue to the meaning of <u>wholly</u>. What is a synonym for *wholly*?

5. Circle the words in this sentence that give a clue to the meaning of <u>frenzy</u>. Write two words meaning the opposite of *frenzy*.

6. Underline the word in this sentence that hints at the meaning of <u>immobility</u>. What is a synonym for *immobility*?

7. Underline the words in this sentence that give a clue to the meaning of <u>pedestal</u>. Is this word used literally or figuratively here?

8. Circle the words in this sentence that hint at the meaning of the word <u>pathetic</u>.

Name _____   Date _____

"A Wagner Matinée" by Willa Cather
Literary Analysis: Characterization

Most readers enjoy a story more when they feel as if they know the characters as people. **Characterization** is the way in which a writer reveals a character's personality. A writer can make direct statements about a character, give a physical description, describe the character's actions, and/or tell the character's thoughts and comments.

DIRECTIONS: *Read each excerpt from the selection, and write down what each tells you about the character of Aunt Georgiana.*

1. "Whatever shock Mrs. Springer experienced at my aunt's appearance she considerately concealed."
   _____
   _____

2. ". . . a plain, angular, spectacled woman of thirty."
   _____
   _____
   _____

3. ". . . she eloped with him, eluding the reproaches of her family and the criticism of her friends by going with him to the Nebraska frontier."
   _____
   _____
   _____

4. ". . . in those days I owed to this woman most of the good that ever came my way, . . ."
   _____
   _____
   _____

5. "Don't love it so well, Clark, or it may be taken from you."
   _____
   _____

6. "When the violins drew out the first strain of the Pilgrims' chorus, my Aunt Georgiana clutched my coat sleeve."
   _____
   _____
   _____

7. "Poor old hands! They were stretched and pulled and twisted into mere tentacles to hold, and lift, and knead with; . . ."
   _____
   _____
   _____

8. "She burst into tears and sobbed pleadingly, 'I don't want to go, Clark, I don't want to go!'"
   _____
   _____

Name _____ Date _____

"A Wagner Matinée" by Willa Cather
Reading Strategy: Clarify

As you read, it is important to **clarify,** or check your understanding of, the details in what you read. You can clarify the details by reading a footnote, looking up a word in the dictionary, rereading a passage to refresh your memory, or reading ahead to find additional details.

DIRECTIONS: *Read each phrase from the selection. Answer the question using one clarifying strategy.*

1. ". . . the gangling farmer boy my aunt had known, scourged with chilblains . . ."
   What is a chilblain?

   _____

   _____

2. "[Aunt Georgiana] had come all the way in a day coach. . . ."
   What was the origin of Aunt Georgiana's trip, and what was her destination?

   _____

   _____

3. "One summer, which she had spent in the little village in the Green Mountains where her ancestors had dwelt for generations, . . ."
   Where are the Green Mountains?

   _____

   _____

4. "I suggested our visiting the Conservatory and the Common before lunch, . . ."
   Why would Aunt Georgiana be interested in the Conservatory?

   _____

   _____

5. ". . . with the bitter frenzy of the Venusberg theme and its ripping of strings, . . ."
   What is the significance of the term *Venusberg*?

   _____

   _____

6. "Soon after the tenor began the 'Prize Song,' I heard a quick-drawn breath, and turned to my aunt. Her eyes were closed, but the tears were glistening on her cheeks, . . ."
   Why did the "Prize Song" make Aunt Georgiana cry?

   _____

   _____

Unit 3 Resources: Division, Reconciliation, and Expansion
© Pearson Education, Inc. All rights reserved.
237

Name _____ Date _____

"A Wagner Matinée" by Willa Cather
Vocabulary Builder

Using Words From Music

Words from music can often have two meanings—one specific musical meaning and one for use in a nonmusical context.

A. DIRECTIONS: *Each sentence below contains a word from music. On the line below the sentence, write either* musical *or* nonmusical *to show how the word is used in the sentence.*

1. The team practiced as a <u>prelude</u> to the big game.
   _____

2. His <u>key</u> didn't fit in the new lock.
   _____

3. When we heard the <u>prelude</u>, we knew the performance had just started.
   _____

4. They played the song in a <u>minor</u> key.
   _____

Using the Word List

    inert   jocularity   prelude   reverential   tremulously

B. DIRECTIONS: *Each sentence includes a word or phrase that means about the same as one of the words in the Word List. Underline that word or phrase and write the Word List word in the blank.*

1. The orchestra began with the overture to the opera. _____
2. Aunt Georgiana was emotional and spoke with a quivering voice. _____
3. In the concert hall, she seemed somewhat less unable to move. _____
4. Clark's attempts at light-hearted joking seemed lost on Aunt Georgiana.
   _____

5. Clark had very respectful feelings for his aunt. _____

Name _____ Date _____

Support for Writing

As you prepare to write an **editorial** on Willa Cather's portrayal of Nebraska, enter your arguments in the chart below. Keep in mind that you will be writing as though you are the editor of a Nebraska newspaper.

Why Willa Cather's "A Wagner Matinée" Is Fair/Not Fair to Nebraskans

Example from story: Why it supports my opinion

_____
_____
_____
_____
_____
_____

Example from story: Why it supports my opinion

_____
_____
_____
_____
_____
_____

Example from story: Why it supports my opinion

_____
_____
_____
_____
_____
_____

On a separate page, put your examples in order of importance and write a draft of your editorial. When you revise your work, make sure you have used persuasive language to make your point of view clear and powerful.

"A Wagner Matinée" by Willa Cather
Enrichment: Music

Identity in Song

DIRECTIONS: *Among some African tribes, a baby's mother develops a song for the child. The mother teaches the song to the rest of the village, and the music becomes the child's song. The village sings the song at important times throughout the child's life—celebrations of achievement, recovery from wounds or illness, and other ceremonies.*

Find or write a song that represents you as a person—your song. Write the name of your song and describe it. Tell why you identify with the song.

My Song: _____

This is my song because:

_____
_____
_____
_____
_____
_____
_____
_____

Some lines from the song that best describe me are:

_____
_____
_____
_____
_____
_____
_____
_____
_____
_____
_____

Name _____ Date _____

"**A Wagner Matinée**" by Willa Cather
Open-Book Test

Short Answer *Write your responses to the questions in this section on the lines provided.*

1. In "A Wagner Matinée," Paul is struck very forcefully by the condition of his Aunt Georgiana when he first sees her. What initial impression does she make on her nephew?

_____

_____

2. If you wanted to clarify why Clark went to live with his aunt as a boy, what would you find out about this from "A Wagner Matinée"?

_____

_____

3. The narrator of "A Wagner Matinée" provides richly detailed descriptions of the life his aunt has lived on the farm in Nebraska. Based on these descriptions, what can the reader infer about Aunt Georgiana's feelings about the life she left in Boston? Use a detail or two from the story to support your answer.

_____

_____

_____

4. A hundred years ago train travel posed hardships that are not familiar to present-day train riders. Cite two details from "A Wagner Matinée" and its accompanying footnotes that would help a reader clarify what difficulties a long-distance train rider might have suffered.

_____

_____

_____

5. What can the reader infer about Aunt Georgiana's character from the following passage from "A Wagner Matinée"?

> She questioned me absently about various changes in the city, but she was chiefly concerned that she had forgotten to leave instructions about feeding half-skimmed milk to a certain weakling calf

_____

_____

_____

_____

6. The narrator of "A Wagner Matinée" gives an extensive description of the orchestra's appearance. What does his attention to detail tell you about the narrator's character? What does it tell you about how Aunt Georgiana may have contributed to his development?

_____

_____

_____

7. In "A Wagner Matinée," Clark takes great pains to mention the ways in which his aunt sustained him during his years on the Nebraska farm. Use the chart below to list examples of both painful and pleasant memories he has of those days.

Painful Memories	Pleasant Memories

8. In "A Wagner Matinée," during the second half of the concert, Clark experiences a sense of confusion, wondering how his aunt is responding to the music she has just heard. What is the source of his confusion? Why is he uncertain if she enjoyed the music?

_____

_____

_____

9. If your teacher tended to speak in a tone of jocularity, would she be likely to have a good sense of humor? Base your answer on the meaning of *jocularity* as it is used in "A Wagner Matinée."

_____

_____

_____

10. In "A Wagner Matinée," Cather's portrait of Aunt Georgiana yields several important main ideas or themes. Summarize one of these key ideas from the story.

_____

_____

_____

Essay

Write an extended response to the question of your choice or to the question or questions your teacher assigns you.

11. In "A Wagner Matinée," Cather makes it clear that Aunt Georgiana never lost her love of music despite her long years of isolation on the farm in Nebraska. In an essay, discuss the details that show that music remained important to Aunt Georgiana for years after she left the conservatory in Boston.

Unit 3 Resources: Division, Reconciliation, and Expansion

12. In "A Wagner Matinée," Clark is trying to repay his Aunt Georgiana for her many years of kindness to him. He believes he is giving her a meaningful gift by taking her to a concert. In a few paragraphs, discuss whether his gift is appropriate. In your essay, consider Aunt Georgiana's state of mind at the beginning and end of the story.

13. In "A Wagner Matinée," during their years together on the farm, when young Clark shows a passion for music, Aunt Georgiana tells him, "Don't love it so well Clark, or it may be taken from you." What do you think she means by this? And how does this remark underscore a key idea of the story? Develop your ideas in an essay supported by details from the story.

14. **Thinking About the Essential Question: What is the relationship between place and literature?** "A Wagner Matinee" is a tale of two places: the desolate Nebraska farm where Aunt Georgiana spent most of her adulthood, and the thriving culture of Boston, where she spent her youth and to which she returns for a visit many years later. How does each setting influence her character? Develop your thoughts in an essay based on details from the story.

Oral Response

15. Go back to question 1, 2, or 3 or to the question your teacher assigns you. Take a few minutes to expand your answer and prepare an oral response. Find additional details in "A Wagner Matinée" that support your points. If necessary, make notes to guide your oral response.

Name _____ Date _____

"**A Wagner Matinée**" by Willa Cather
Selection Test A

Critical Reading *Identify the letter of the choice that best answers the question.*

____ 1. In "A Wagner Matinee," which method of characterization does the author use here to describe Aunt Georgiana?

". . . her linen duster had become black with soot."?

A. a character's thoughts and words

B. a physical description of the character

C. comments made by other characters

D. the character's statements

____ 2. In "A Wagner Matinee," how would a reader clarify the meaning of this passage?

"He requested me to meet her at the station, and render her whatever services might prove necessary."

A. use a map to find the station

B. find out what city the station is in

C. look up the meaning of the word *prove*

D. look up the meaning of the word *render*

____ 3. In "A Wagner Matinee," what can the reader infer about Aunt Georgiana from reading that she "would often stand until midnight at her ironing board . . . gently shaking me when my drowsy head sank down over a page of irregular verbs"?

A. She preferred ironing to learning.

B. She started her working-day late.

C. She disliked the study of Latin verbs.

D. She cared about her nephew's schooling.

____ 4. In "A Wagner Matinee," how does the narrator feel about how his aunt once cared for him?

A. unhappy

B. bored

C. grateful

D. angry

____ 5. Which word or phrase describes Aunt Georgiana's adult life on the farm in "A Wagner Matinee"?

A. full of life

B. quiet and lonely

C. comfortable

D. city-like

_____ 6. In "A Wagner Matinee," which life event causes the most pain?

    A. the realization of one's loss

    B. the failure of prairie farming

    C. the insensitivity of youth

    D. the absence of dreams

_____ 7. In "A Wagner Matinee," what do readers learn by reading that Aunt Georgiana was worried because she had not told her daughter to cook the mackerel in the cellar so it wouldn't spoil?

    A. She often neglects her daughter.

    B. She takes her responsibilities seriously.

    C. She hates to use any food that isn't fresh.

    D. She has trouble enjoying her travels.

_____ 8. In "A Wagner Matinee," how can a reader clarify this passage?

    "When the musicians came out . . . she . . . looked with quickening interest down over the rail . . . perhaps the first wholly familiar thing that had greeted her eye since she had left old Maggie and her weakling calf."

    A. do research on musicians

    B. look up the word *familiar*

    C. reread to identify who Maggie is

    D. find information on calves

_____ 9. In "A Wagner Matinee," how would a reader clarify the information in this passage?

    "Shortly afterward he had gone to town on the Fourth of July, lost his money at a faro[14] table, ridden a saddled Texas steer . . . and disappeared with a fractured collarbone."

    A. read the information in footnote 14

    B. do research on Texas gambling

    C. look up the meaning of *steer*

    D. do research on the Fourth of July

_____ 10. In "A Wagner Matinee," which of these is used to express Aunt Georgiana's emotional state?

    A. her hair

    B. her hands

    C. her love of music

    D. her love for her nephew

Vocabulary

____ 11. In which sentence is the meaning of the word *inert* suggested?
   A. Aunt Georgiana arrived flustered on the morning train.
   B. I remembered her constant work at the farm in Nebraska.
   C. She sat motionless as we listened to the Wagner music.
   D. She cried when she had to leave and return to Nebraska.

____ 12. What does *prelude* mean in this line from the story?
   "I watched her closely through the prelude to *Tristan and Isolde,* trying vainly to conjecture what that warfare of motifs, that seething turmoil of strings and winds, might mean to her."
   A. loud section
   B. closing section
   C. most dramatic section
   D. introductory section

Essay

13. In "A Wagner Matinee," Aunt Georgiana says to Clark, "Don't love it so well Clark, or it may be taken from you." What do you think she means by this? Write a brief essay to discuss this quote. Use what you have learned about Aunt Georgiana in the story in your discussion.

14. At the end of "A Wagner Matinee," the author writes, "For her, just outside the door of the concert hall, lay the black pond with the cattle-tracked bluffs, the tall, unpainted house, naked as a tower. . . ." Does the author mean that Aunt Georgiana's home is located outside the concert hall? Write a brief essay to explain why you think the author ends the story this way.

15. **Thinking About the Essential Question: What is the relationship between place and literature?** "A Wagner Matinee" tells about two places: the lonely Nebraska farm where Aunt Georgiana spent most of her adulthood, and Boston, where she spent her youth and to which she returns for a visit many years later. How does each setting influence her character? Develop your thoughts in an essay based on details from the story.

Name _____ Date _____

"A Wagner Matinée" by Willa Cather
Selection Test B

Critical Reading *Identify the letter of the choice that best completes the statement or answers the question.*

____ 1. The description of Aunt Georgiana as having "an incessant twitching of the mouth and eyebrows . . . resulting from isolation and monotony, and from frequent physical suffering" reveals her character through
   A. a dialogue with another character.
   B. the narrator's observations of her physical appearance.
   C. her own thoughts and comments.
   D. Mrs. Springer's reactions.

____ 2. The selection says that Aunt Georgiana and her husband "took a homestead in Red Willow County."[6] The "6" tells us we can find out more about Red Willow County
   A. in footnote number six.
   B. in the sixth definition under *County* in a dictionary.
   C. in the sixth map at the end of the book.
   D. by reading six paragraphs ahead.

____ 3. As a young boy, Clark appears to have been
   A. oblivious and lazy.
   B. tough and quick-witted.
   C. studious and dull.
   D. diligent and sensitive.

____ 4. We learn in the first paragraph that the letter announcing Aunt Georgiana's arrival comes from Nebraska. Therefore, we assume she lives in Nebraska. We can find out Aunt Georgiana lives on a small homestead in Red Willow County by
   A. using an atlas.
   B. reading a footnote.
   C. reviewing past sentences.
   D. reading ahead.

____ 5. Which of the following aspects of Aunt Georgiana's life does the author appear to value most highly?
   A. piety
   B. poverty
   C. modesty
   D. devotion

____ 6. The description of the Nebraska farm creates an atmosphere of
   A. adventure and tension.
   B. desolation and hardship.
   C. boredom and apathy.
   D. productivity and vitality.

Name _____ Date _____

_____ 7. Which of the following factors probably contributed most to Aunt Georgiana's general bewilderment during her visit?
A. the long and difficult journey to Boston
B. her age, which had brought about a certain forgetfulness
C. the contrast in settings between Boston and the Nebraska farm
D. the suddenness of her departure from Nebraska

_____ 8. What is the central idea of "A Wagner Matinée"?
A. the oppression of women by men
B. the high price of foolish young love
C. the pain of realizing what you have lost
D. the hardships of frontier

_____ 9. What can the reader infer about Aunt Georgiana's character from the following passage?
> She questioned me absently about various changes in the city, but she was chiefly concerned that she had forgotten to leave instructions about feeding half-skimmed milk to a certain weakling calf.

A. She tended to be absent-minded in her daily chores.
B. She found it difficult to rely on others.
C. She focused more on her responsibilities than on what gives her pleasure.
D. She disliked the city and longed to be back on the farm.

_____ 10. Why does Clark come to live with Aunt Georgiana as a boy?
A. He was orphaned when he was a young boy.
B. His parents sent him there while they traveled in Europe.
C. He was an apprentice farmer for his Uncle Howard.
D. The selection does not explain.

_____ 11. Which is a reading strategy for clarifying?
A. knowing how other characters feel about the main character
B. knowing what tense the sentence is written in
C. memorizing sections of texts
D. rereading a previous passage to refresh your memory

_____ 12. The tone of "A Wagner Matinée" can best be described as
A. sympathetic.
B. distant.
C. accusatory.
D. apologetic.

_____ 13. Which of the following passages is an example of characterization?
A. "There they measured off their eighty acres by driving across the prairie in a wagon. . . . "
B. "When the musicians came out and took their places, she gave a little stir of anticipation. . . . "
C. "The world there is the flat world of the ancients. . . . "
D. ". . . the people filed out of the hall chattering and laughing, glad to relax and find the living level again. . . . "

Unit 3 Resources: Division, Reconciliation, and Expansion

Vocabulary

____ 14. Which word is closest in meaning to the underlined word in the following excerpt?

"Well, we have come to better things than the old *Trovatore* at any rate, Aunt Georgie?" I queried, with well-meant <u>jocularity.</u>

A. love
B. shyness
C. caution
D. humor

____ 15. Clark uses the word *reverential* to describe his feelings for his aunt, meaning he
A. fears her.
B. respects her.
C. ignores her.
D. dislikes her.

____ 16. Which word means most nearly the opposite of *inert*?
A. moving
B. motionless
C. vivid
D. basic

Essay

17. There are several indications that Aunt Georgiana retained her love of music throughout her time in Nebraska. In an essay, describe which details in the selection indicate that music remained alive in Aunt Georgiana's heart, even years after she left the conservatory.

18. At the end of the story, Aunt Georgiana pleads with Clark that she does not want to leave the concert. Write an essay in which you interpret the deeper meaning of her response to the end of the concert. What does leaving the concert hall symbolize for Aunt Georgiana? Support your explanation with details from the story.

19. In first-person narration, the reader learns only as much about the narrator as the narrator chooses to reveal. A person reading "A Wagner Matinée" learns a great deal more about Aunt Georgiana than about her nephew Clark. Write a descriptive essay about Clark, the narrator, based on information in the story. Although nothing is said about Clark's appearance, you can infer his personality from his thoughts, statements, and actions. Be as specific as possible, and support your observations with examples from the text.

20. **Thinking About the Essential Question: What is the relationship between place and literature?** "A Wagner Matinee" tells about two places: the lonely Nebraska farm where Aunt Georgiana spent most of her adulthood, and Boston, where she spent her youth and to which she returns for a visit many years later. How does each setting influence her character? Develop your thoughts in an essay based on details from the story.

Name _____ Date _____

Writing Workshop—Unit 3
Research: Historical Investigation Report

Prewriting: Choosing Your Topic

Answer the questions in the chart below to choose a topic of interest for your research.

What broad subjects like the environment, politics, sports, technology, or literature interest you?	
What specific categories of that subject do you find appealing?	
What people in history or current events would you like to understand better?	

Drafting: Using a Formal Outline

Complete the outline below to organize your ideas and supporting information before writing.

    I. Introduction
       A. Interesting Opening
       B. Thesis Statement
   II. Body Paragraph 1
       A. Topic Sentence
       B. Supporting Evidence
       C. Supporting Evidence
  III. Body Paragraph 2
       A. Topic Sentence
       B. Supporting Evidence
       C. Supporting Evidence
  IV. Body Paragraph 3
       A. Topic Sentence
       B. Supporting Evidence
       C. Supporting Evidence
   V. Body Paragraph 4
       A. Topic Sentence
       B. Supporting Evidence
       C. Supporting Evidence
  VI. Conclusion
       A. Restatement of Thesis
       B. Memorable Closing

Name _____ Date _____

Historical Investigation Report: Revising Your Paragraphs

As you introduce blocks of information in your report, help the reader follow your train of thought from one paragraph to another. When you revise, **add transitions to improve the flow of ideas.** Transitional words and phrases show the relationships between ideas and clarify the connections you want readers to make. The following chart shows common transitions used to show different kinds of relationships:

chronological order	first, next, recently, later, finally
comparison-and-contrast	both, like, unlike, however, on the other hand
cause-and-effect	as a result, therefore, because
details that support a main idea	in addition, furthermore, for instance, for example

DIRECTIONS: *Copy the following paragraphs from a research report. Then revise the paragraphs by adding transitions where they are needed to show the relationships between ideas.*

Two early American writers who promoted a spirit of individualism were Ralph Waldo Emerson and Henry David Thoreau, who were neighbors in Concord, Massachusetts. Fourteen years older than Thoreau, Emerson was a major influence on his younger friend. Emerson's essay, called "Self-Reliance," inspired Thoreau to trust his own instincts about right and wrong.

Thoreau believed in self-reliance. He put his ideas to the test in more extreme ways. He lived by himself in a cabin at Walden Pond for two years, where he observed nature and wrote his best-known work, *Walden*. He once spent a night in jail rather than pay a tax that might help support a war he did not believe in. This experience led to his famous essay "Civil Disobedience," which has inspired generations of social activists, including Martin Luther King, Jr.

Name _____ Date _____

Oral Interpretation of a Literary Work

Choose a literary work for an oral interpretation. Use the form to help you analyze the work, plan your interpretation, and evaluate your work.

ORAL INTERPRETATION PLANNER

Title and Author of Literary Work: _____

Analysis of Work

—*Form:* _____

—*Tone(s):* _____

—*Style:* _____

—*Imagery:* _____

_____

—*Rhythm, meter, "melody" of language:* _____

_____

—*Author's intention:* _____

Oral Interpretation Techniques

—*Gestures and movements:* _____

_____

—*Vocalization*

Tone(s) of voice: _____

Words to emphasize: _____

Dialect/other special vocalization: _____

—*Media elements:*

Music/sound effects? _____

Visuals? _____

EVALUATION OF ORAL INTERPRETATION

Interpreter: _____ **Title of Work:** _____

1. What impression of the work did the interpreter create? _____

_____

2. What gestures and movements were more effective? Less effective?

_____

_____

3. What vocal techniques were more effective? Less effective?

_____

_____

4. If the interpreter used media elements, which ones were especially effective? Which were not?

_____

5. Was the oral interpretation effective? Why or why not? _____

_____

Unit 3 Vocabulary Workshop
Words from Mythology and Religious Traditions

Words derived from mythology and the Bible are often easy to remember if you know the characters and stories behind them. For example, to the ancient Greeks, a huge Titan named Chronos represented time. In English, a *chronology* is a timeline, a *chronicle* records events during a time period, and a *chronometer* is a clock.

A. DIRECTIONS: *For each item below, read the origin of the word and answer the question.*

1. **atlas** In Greek mythology, Atlas was a Titan who supported the heavens on his shoulders. What would you find in an *atlas*—a history, mathematical formulas, or a group of maps?

_____

2. **cereal** In Roman mythology, Ceres was the goddess of agriculture. Explain why you think *cereal* is named after this goddess.

_____

3. **gorgon** In Greek mythology, Gorgons were sisters so horrible that anyone who looked at them turned to stone. If a woman is described as a *gorgon*, is she gentle or terrifying?

_____

4. **edenic** In the Bible, Eden was the garden home of Adam and Eve. Why did many people imagine America as *edenic*?

_____

B. DIRECTIONS: *Use a dictionary to identify the mythological or biblical origins of the following words. Then use each word in a sentence that illustrates its meaning.*

1. **oracular** Origin: _____

   Sentence: _____

2. **volcano** Origin: _____

   Sentence: _____

3. **chimera** Origin: _____

   Sentence: _____

Essential Questions Workshop—Unit 3

In their stories, poems, and nonfiction, the writers in Unit Three express ideas that relate to the three Essential Questions framing this book. Review the literature in the unit. Then, for each Essential Question, choose an author and at least one passage from his or her writing that expresses a related idea. Use this chart to complete your work.

Essential Question	Author/Selection	Literary Passage
How does literature shape or reflect society?		
What is the relationship between place and literature?		
What makes American literature American?		

Unit 3: Division, Reconciliation, and Expansion
Benchmark Test 5

MULTIPLE CHOICE

Literary Analysis and Reading Skills

Answer the following questions.

1. Which is the best definition of diction?
   A. the dictionary definitions of the words an author uses
   B. a writer's choice of sentence structure and length
   C. saying words aloud to another person who writes them down
   D. a writer's choice and arrangement of words

2. Which of the following could serve as an opposing force in a survival story?
   A. plot
   B. internal conflict
   C. irony
   D. setting

3. Which of the following is *not* a feature of a periodical abstract?
   A. a list of the article's key points
   B. photos or other elements from the original article
   C. direct quotations from the article
   D. the article's title, author's name, and publication information

Read the passage. Then, answer the questions that follow.

Thish-yer Smily had a mare—the boys called her the fifteen-minute nag, but that was only in fun, you know, because, of course, she was faster than that—and he use to win money on that horse, for all she was so slow and always had the asthma, or the distemper, or the consumption, or something of that kind. They use to give her two or three hundred yards' start, and then pass her under way; but always at the fag-end of the race she'd get excited and desperate-like, and come cavorting and spraddling up, and scattering her legs around limber, sometimes in the air, and sometimes out to one side amongst the fences, and kicking up m-o-r-e dust, and raising m-o-r-e racket with her coughing and sneezing and blowing her nose—and always fetch up at the stand just about a neck ahead, as near as you could cipher it down.

–from "Jim Smily and His Jumping Frog" by Mark Twain

4. Which phrase from the passage does *not* use regional dialect?
   A. of course, she was faster than that
   B. he use to win money on that horse, for all she was so slow
   C. as near as you could cipher it down
   D. Thish-yer Smily had a mare

5. What is the author's purpose in using regional dialect in the passage?
   A. to show that the narrator is uneducated
   B. to mimic the speech used in the region where the story takes place
   C. to teach the reader how to speak in this dialect
   D. to make the reader research the origin of unknown expressions

6. What is the tone of passage?
   A. pessimistic
   B. confused
   C. humorous
   D. matter-of-fact

7. What is the main technique that author Mark Twain uses to create humor in the passage?
   A. ridicule
   B. exaggeration
   C. joke telling
   D. puns and word play

8. Which word from the passage best characterizes the horse?
   A. insensitive
   B. determined
   C. clever
   D. lucky

9. Which detail is relevant when explaining why the mare wins races?
   A. The boys call her the fifteen-minute nag.
   B. She raises a racket with her coughing and sneezing and blowing her nose.
   C. She always has asthma, distemper, consumption, or something of that kind.
   D. Always toward the end of the race, she would get excited and desperate.

10. Which value is part of the cultural context of the passage by Mark Twain?
    A. fierce family loyalty
    B. an appreciation of horse racing
    C. a love of all sports
    D. a fear of diseases

Answer the following questions.

11. Which is an example of internal conflict?
    A. A character struggles with the guilt he feels about a crime he committed as a child.
    B. A character struggles to distinguish herself from her many siblings.
    C. A character struggles against the restrictions of traditional gender roles.
    D. A character struggles to survive after being lost in blizzard.

12. What literary technique do writers use to make a forceful contrast between expectations and results?
    A. hyperbole
    B. irony
    C. analogy
    D. oxymoron

13. Which of the following is an example of narrative poetry?
    A. a sonnet
    B. an ode
    C. an epic
    D. a haiku

Read the passage. Then, answer the questions that follow.

It was a soft, reposeful summer landscape, as lovely as a dream, and as lonesome as Sunday. The air was full of the smell of flowers, and the buzzing of insects, and the twittering of birds, and there were no people, no wagons, there was no stir of life, nothing going on. The road was mainly a winding path with hoof-prints in it, and now and then a faint trace of wheels on either side in the grass—wheels that apparently had a tire as broad as one's hand.

–from *A Connecticut Yankee in King Arthur's Court* by Mark Twain

14. What inference can you make when the author writes that the road was mainly a path with hoof-prints in it?
    A. The narrator is retelling a dream.
    B. The road is also used by animals such as horses, cows, or sheep.
    C. The road leads to a farm.
    D. The narrator does not know where he or she is.

Read the introduction and the passage. Then, answer the questions that follow.

In this excerpt from "Old Ironsides," the poet protests the destruction of a historic battleship. The poem helped save the ship, which is now a national memorial.

Her decks, once red with heroes' blood,
Where knelt the vanquished foe,
When winds were hurrying o'er the flood,
And waves were white below,
No more shall feel the victor's tread,   5
Or know the conquered knee—
The harpies of the shore shall pluck
The eagle of the sea!
Oh, better that her shattered hulk
Should sink beneath the wave;   10
Her thunders shook the mighty deep,
And there should be her grave;
Nail to the mast her holy flag,
Set every threadbare sail,
And give her to the god of storms,   15
The lightning and the gale!

—from "Old Ironsides" by Oliver Wendell Holmes

15. Who is the speaker in the poem?
    A. the ship
    B. a sailor
    C. the god of storms
    D. the poet

16. This passage from "Old Ironsides" is an example of which of the following?
    A. blank verse
    B. free verse
    C. heavy verse
    D. formal verse

17. Which of these true historical details would be the least helpful in your understanding of this poem?
    A. In 1830, the Secretary of the Navy recommended that the ship be disposed of.
    B. The ship has a length of 204 feet.
    C. "Old Ironsides" defeated a British frigate in the War of 1812.
    D. "Old Ironsides" is the nickname of the battle frigate *USS Constitution*.

18. Which of the following questions would *least* help to clarify meaning in your reading of "Old Ironsides"?
    A. Why were the decks "once red with heroes' blood"?
    B. Who is the "god of the storms"?
    C. Who are the "harpies of the shore"?
    D. Why is the ship now a national memorial?

Read the following passage. Then, reread the passage on the previous page. Use both passages to answer the questions below.

> I know why the caged bird sings, ah me,
> When his wing is bruised and his bosom sore,—
> When he beats his bars and he would be free;
> It is not a carol of joy or glee,
> But a prayer that he sends from his heart's deep core,
> But a plea, that upward to Heaven he flings—
> I know why the caged bird sings!
> —from "Sympathy" by Paul Laurence Dunbar

19. How are the themes of the two poems similar?
    A. Both cope with the issues of destruction and honorable death.
    B. Both support the necessity of a dramatic struggle.
    C. Both deal with the fight for individual freedom.
    D. Both argue for patience and faith.

20. Which of the following accurately compares the underlying structure of the two poems?
    A. The focus of the first poem is directed downward, toward the sea. The second poem looks upward, to Heaven.
    B. The first poem considers the eventual silencing of the ship, while a relentless voice penetrates the second poem.
    C. Both poems utilize end rhyme and meter which add momentum to the speaker's emotional language.
    D. All of the above.

21. Which best characterizes the speakers of the two poems?
    A. adamant
    B. haughty
    C. disappointed
    D. violent

Answer the following questions.

22. What background knowledge would best help you to understand the following sentences?

> The Northern soldiers ached for home. They were restless and angry. Was this Union really worth it?

A. the type of family members they had left behind
B. the reason the soldiers were in a war
C. each soldier's rank
D. the geography of the region

23. What is the tone of the sentences above?
A. impassioned
B. bitter
C. reflective
D. pompous

Vocabulary

24. Based on your understanding of the prefix *mono-*, choose the distinguishing characteristic of a monoplane.
A. two propellers
B. no wheels
C. no engine
D. one pair of wings

25. What is the meaning of the root shared by the words *pendulum* and *pendant*?
A. to happen
B. to look
C. to hang
D. to write

26. What is the definition of *orchestrated* in the following sentence?

> The library's directors <u>orchestrated</u> the move to the new facility.

A. convened a committee
B. arranged music
C. voted in opposition to
D. organized and directed

Grammar

27. Which of the following sentences contains a dangling modifier?
A. Walking in the park, I saw a rabbit under a bush.
B. Together, we worked to get the project finished in time.
C. Listening closely, distant thunder could be detected.
D. Standing on the beach, the children saw a school of dolphins.

28. Which sentence contains an introductory clause?
   A. If you see smoke, you know there is fire.
   B. Yes, she is going to the party.
   C. Given a choice, I would rather eat dinner early.
   D. In the corner of the room, you will find the missing shoe.

ESSAY

29. Write a field report. To prepare, take notes as you observe an event directly. Be as detailed and accurate as possible. Then write up your notes. Present you observations in a logical, well-organized manner and leave out your opinions.

30. Suppose you are writing an editorial for your school newspaper on one of the pressures that young people face. These pressures might come from family, school, peers, or culture. In your editorial, state your point of view clearly at the beginning. Then, support your viewpoint with examples. You might refer to personal experiences that have helped to shape your views. Be sure to use language and ideas that will convince your readers that your point of view is valid.

31. Select two movies, television programs, or books that share a similar subject. In an essay, compare and contrast the two movies, programs, or books by discussing the similarities and differences in content, viewpoint, and presentation.

Diagnostic Tests and Vocabulary in Context
Use and Interpretation

The Diagnostic Tests and Vocabulary in Context were developed to assist teachers in making the most appropriate assignment of *Prentice Hall Literature* program selections to students. The purpose of these assessments is to indicate the degree of difficulty that students are likely to have in reading/comprehending the selections presented in the *following* unit of instruction. Tests are provided at six separate times in each grade level—a *Diagnostic Test* (to be used prior to beginning the year's instruction) and a *Vocabulary in Context,* the final segment of the Benchmark Test appearing at the end of each of the first five units of instruction. Note that the tests are intended for use not as summative assessments for the prior unit, but as guidance for assigning literature selections in the upcoming unit of instruction.

The structure of all Diagnostic Tests and Vocabulary in Context in this series is the same. All test items are four-option, multiple-choice items. The format is established to assess a student's ability to construct sufficient meaning from the context sentence to choose the only provided word that fits both the semantics (meaning) and syntax (structure) of the context sentence. All words in the context sentences are chosen to be "below-level" words that students reading at this grade level should know. All answer choices fit *either* the meaning or structure of the context sentence, but only the correct choice fits *both* semantics and syntax. All answer choices—both correct answers and incorrect options—are key words chosen from specifically taught words that will occur in the subsequent unit of program instruction. This careful restriction of the assessed words permits a sound diagnosis of students' current reading achievement and prediction of the most appropriate level of readings to assign in the upcoming unit of instruction.

The assessment of vocabulary in context skill has consistently been shown in reading research studies to correlate very highly with "reading comprehension." This is not surprising as the format essentially assesses comprehension, albeit in sentence-length "chunks." Decades of research demonstrate that vocabulary assessment provides a strong, reliable prediction of comprehension achievement— the purpose of these tests. Further, because this format demands very little testing time, these diagnoses can be made efficiently, permitting teachers to move forward with critical instructional tasks rather than devoting excessive time to assessment.

It is important to stress that while the Diagnostic and Vocabulary in Context were carefully developed and will yield sound assignment decisions, they were designed to *reinforce*, not supplant, teacher judgment as to the most appropriate instructional placement for individual students. Teacher judgment should always prevail in making placement—or indeed other important instructional—decisions concerning students.

Diagnostic Tests and Vocabulary in Context Branching Suggestions

These tests are designed to provide maximum flexibility for teachers. Your *Unit Resources* books contain the 40-question **Diagnostic Test** and 20-question **Vocabulary in Context** tests. At *PHLitOnline,* you can access the Diagnostic Test and complete 40-question Vocabulary in Context tests. Procedures for administering the tests are described below. Choose the procedure based on the time you wish to devote to the activity and your comfort with the assignment decisions relative to the individual students. Remember that your judgment of a student's reading level should always take precedence over the results of a single written test.

Feel free to use different procedures at different times of the year. For example, for early units, you may wish to be more confident in the assignments you make—thus, using the "two-stage" process below. Later, you may choose the quicker diagnosis, confirming the results with your observations of the students' performance built up throughout the year.

The **Diagnostic Test** is composed of a single 40-item assessment. Based on the results of this assessment, make the following assignment of students to the reading selections in Unit 1:

Diagnostic Test Score	Selection to Use
If the student's score is 0–25	more accessible
If the student's score is 26–40	more challenging

Outlined below are the three basic options for administering **Vocabulary in Context** and basing selection assignments on the results of these assessments.

1. For a one-stage, quicker diagnosis using the *20-item* test in the *Unit Resources:*

Vocabulary in Context Test Score	Selection to Use
If the student's score is 0–13	more accessible
If the student's score is 14–20	more challenging

2. If you wish to confirm your assignment decisions with a *two-stage* diagnosis:

Stage 1: Administer the 20-item test in the *Unit Resources*	
Vocabulary in Context Test Score	Selection to Use
If the student's score is 0–9	more accessible
If the student's score is 10–15	(Go to Stage 2.)
If the student's score is 16–20	more challenging

Stage 2: Administer items 21–40 from *PHLitOnline*	
Vocabulary in Context Test Score	Selection to Use
If the student's score is 0–12	more accessible
If the student's score is 13–20	more challenging

3. If you base your assignment decisions on the full 40-item **Vocabulary in Context** from *PHLitOnline:*

Vocabulary in Context Test Score	Selection to Use
If the student's score is 0–25	more accessible
If the student's score is 26–40	more challenging

Unit 3 Resources: Division, Reconciliation, and Expansion

Grade 11—Benchmark Test 4

Skill Objective	Test Items	Item Number	Reading Kit
Literary Analysis			
Rhyme	1, 3		pp. 224, 225
Paradox	4		pp. 166, 167
Epic Poetry (American)	6, 7		pp. 90, 91
Refrain	8		pp. 210, 211
Biblical Allusion	9		pp. 44, 45
Allegory	10		pp. 4, 5
Free Verse	5		pp. 120, 121
Point of View	11, 12		pp. 186, 187
Stream of Consciousness	13, 14		pp. 248, 249
Autobiography	15		pp. 38, 39
Author's Purpose	2, 17		pp. 40, 41
Spirituals (Biblical Allusion)	18		pp. 44, 45
Reading Skill			
Rereading	19		pp. 2, 3
Adjust Reading Rate	21		pp. 2, 3
Evaluate Text Element	22		pp. 106, 107
Connecting to Historical Context	20		pp. 64, 65
Analyze Patterns of Organization	23		pp. 12, 13
Evaluate Cultural and Ethical Influences of a Historical Period	16		pp. 100, 101
Listening	24		pp. 146, 147
Vocabulary			
Latin Roots: -greg-, -bene-, -fin-	25, 26, 27		pp. 302, 303
Latin Root: -dict-	28, 29		pp. 298, 299
Multiple-Meaning Words	30, 31		pp. 328, 329
Grammar			
All grammar for Unit 3 is treated in BMT 5	n/a		n/a
Writing			
Multimedia Presentation	32		pp. 444, 445
Reflective Essay	33		pp. 442, 443
Critical Essay	34		pp. 432, 433

Grade 11—Benchmark Test 5

Skill Objective	Test Items	Item Number	Reading Kit
Literary Analysis			
Style, Diction	1, 3		pp. 42, 43
Setting	2		pp. 232, 233
Tone/Purpose	6, 23		pp. 262, 263
Humor	7		pp. 124, 125
Characterization	8		pp. 52, 53
Conflict	11		pp. 62, 63
Irony	12		pp. 144, 145
Narrative Poetry	13		pp. 160, 161
Speaker	15		pp. 240, 241
Formal Elements	16		pp. 118, 119
Drawing Inferences and Making Predictions	14		pp. 84, 85
Reading Skill			
Clarifying Meaning, Including Regional Dialect	4, 5		pp. 56, 57
Relevant Details	9		pp. 218, 219
Connecting to Historical Period	10, 17		pp. 64, 65
Ask Questions to Clarify Meaning	18		pp. 36, 37
Compare and Contrast Poetic Elements	19, 20, 21		pp. 60, 61
Use Background Knowledge	22		pp. 264, 265
Vocabulary			
Greek prefix: *mono-*	24		pp. 270, 271
Latin roots: *-pend-, -genus-*	25		pp. 310, 311
Words from Music	26		pp. 336, 337
Grammar			
Misplaced and dangling modifiers	27		pp. 372, 373
Introductory phrases and clauses	28		pp. 370, 371
Writing			
Historical Investigation Report	29		pp. 446, 447
Editorial	30		n/a
Compare and Contrast Essay	31		pp. 424, 425

ANSWERS

Unit 3 Introduction

Names and Terms to Know, p.2

Sample Answers

A. 1. The Confederate attack on Fort Sumter marked the start of the Civil War.

2. The Homestead Act of 1862 offered 160 western acres to anyone who would work the land.

3. During the Gilded Age of the 1880s and 1890s, cities grew, lit by electric lights, and the economy expanded.

4. The fictional character Horatio Alger went from rags to riches by working hard.

5. The muckrackers were writers who exposed corruption and incompetence in business and industry.

6. Local color was a type of writing that focussed on unique features of local, usually rural areas.

B. 1. Lasting four years and resulting in high casualties, the war disillusioned both North and South. The North grew more pragmatic and materialistic; the South was physically devastated, its economy in shambles.

2. It gave Americans both brighter and dirtier streets. It made work easier, but the resulting industrial growth accelerated pollution, exploited immigrant and child labor, and led to urban blight.

3. The Homestead Act and the growth of railroads encouraged Americans to settle the West. As settlements expaded, Native Americans were driven from their lands to "reservations." As more and more farms and towns arose, the frontier disappeared.

Essential Question: How does literature shape or reflect society? p. 3

Sample Answers

A. 1. a. They were hymns sung by slaves that used work rhythms and Bible imagery and communicated the woe of slavery and hope for freedom and happiness in heaven.

b. Frederick Douglass's autobiography, Mary Chestnut's journal

c. corruption and incompetence in business and industry.

2. a. They tell of the rise to wealth, through "luck and pluck," of hard-working, poor characters like Horatio Alger.

b. the unpredictability of life

c. Zane Grey and L. Frank Baum

3. a. it disillusioned Americans and made them less optimistic.

b. recognizable details of everyday life as lived by ordinary people, shown in an honest, factual way

c. Edward Arlington Robinson and Edgar Lee Masters

d. describing the powerlessness of individuals in the face of an indifferent universe

B. 1. They lamented slavery.

2. They saw it as a setting of romantic, escapist adventure.

3. It would portray simple, less educated members of society.

Essential Question: What is the relationship between place and literature? p. 4

Sample Answers

A. 1. a. believe that what was bigger and stronger was better

b. urban problems, such as the daily struggles, emotions, and values of people crowded into cities

2. a. It was devastated, with homes and plantations destroyed and the economy, which had depended on slavery, in ruins.

b. rural life

3. a. the unique details of life in particular American settings, usually rural areas or small towns

b. Mark Twain, Kate Chopin, Sarah Ome Jewett

c. Henry James, Edith Wharton, William Dean Howells

B. 1. stories and sketches set mostly in California

2. Eastern high society and its repressive customs

3. Hamlin Garland and Willa Cather

Essential Question: What makes American literature American? p. 5

Sample Answers

A. 1. a. uniquely American settings such as a Civil War battlefield, a California mining camp, a Mississippi riverboat

b. common speech and dialect

c. exposing human weaknesses

2. a. tried to describe the world in objective terms

b. local settings in realistic detail

c. Darwin, Marx, and Zola

d. heredity, environment, and social conditions

3. a. hard-edged pragmatism

b. war tarnished by hames, fear, and guilt

c. a man crushed by nature or society

d. ordinary, everyday characters

e. fascination with science and a belief in progress

B. 1. Naturalists like Jack London and Frank Norris

2. the Civil War

3. the mines of California and the Yukon wilderness

Following-Through Activities, p. 6

A. Students should complete the chart with concepts appropriate to the period and groups associated with these concepts.

B. Students should complete the chart with answers that will help them to research a form of spoken literature.

"An Occurrence at Owl Creek Bridge"
by Ambrose Bierce
Vocabulary Warm-up Exercises, p. 8

A.
1. assented
2. rustic
3. audibly
4. intervals
5. keen
6. assassin
7. convulsively
8. matchless

B. **Sample Answers**
1. T; The *congestion* of heavy traffic on the highway might delay travelers.
2. F; *Etiquette* stresses politeness and good manners.
3. T; *Ineffable* means "difficult or impossible to express."
4. F; A *luminous* theory would, by definition, shed light on a problem.
5. T; A *perilous* mission might be expected to hold dangers.
6. T; Since a *sentinel* functions as a guard or watchperson, it would not be suitable for him or her to fall asleep.
7. F; *Summarily* connotes rapid action.
8. F; *Velocity* refers to speed, not weight.

Reading Warm-up A, p. 9

Sample Answers
1. ruthless as the attitude; *killer, murderer*
2. (sometimes even loudly); *silently, inaudibly*
3. (strongly); *sharp*
4. then gasp spasmodically for breath; *in a twitching manner*
5. vigorously disagree; True cynics would never agree with that idea.
6. (each day at dawn and midday)
7. (overcomes all others); *incomparable, peerless, unequaled, unsurpassed*
8. "simple . . . even when they did not live in the country"

Reading Warm-up B, p. 10

Sample Answers
1. must be greeted politely according to a formal code; *Etiquette* requires you to use certain forms of address when you attend a meeting with the head of state.
2. (was leisurely indulging in a favorite pastime); *promptly*
3. to destroy the Owl Creek bridge; *safe, secure*
4. slows down . . . his fast-paced plot; *swiftness, speed*
5. (vivid . . . he sheds light on Farquhar's inner state of consciousness); The opposite of *luminous* is *obscure* or *shadowy.*

6. the overcrowding . . . of thoughts in Farquhar's mind give way to a single goal; *crowdedness*
7. (standing watchfully); All night long, a *sentinel* patrolled the perimeter of the armed camp, keeping watch.
8. he cannot translate his emotions into words; *able to be expressed*

Literary Analysis: Point of View, p. 11

Sample Answers
1. How unbelievable! Here I am not far from home, standing on a bridge, about to die. The river is swift, sparkling, just twenty feet down there. My hands hurt. They tied them too tightly with that rough cord. And the rope . . . the rope around my neck is prickly. Soon it will tighten and tighten. What will it be like? How quickly will death come?
2. As the man fell through the bridge, the watching soldiers swayed back slightly, as if they had all inhaled simultaneously and might hold their breath until he died. He did not die immediately; as he dangled in the air he seemed to come to life, if only for a short time.

Reading Strategy: Identify Chronological Order, p. 12

Sample Answers
1. The "preternatural" sensory experience suggests the heightened sensations some people believe occur just before death.
2. The whirling Farquhar does here might suggest the turning of a body at the end of a rope.
3. The scene is not natural. The large road seems untraveled, and there is no sign of life anywhere.

Vocabulary Builder, p. 13

A. Sample Answers
1. to say words that mean the opposite
2. a thing connected with words
3. to give expression to what will happen before it happens
4. the words pronouncing the truth about what happened

B.
1. summarily
2. dictum
3. ineffable
4. etiquette
5. deference
6. apprised

Enrichment: The Legal System, p. 15

Students will choose different aspects to cover in a defense trial. Sample answers:
1. Peyton Farquhar performed an act in defense of his "country." (Use to minimize sentencing.)
2. Peyton Farquhar performed an act to provide for the safety of his wife and children. (Use to invite empathy from judge and jury.)

3. Peyton Farquhar did not perform an act that would hurt or kill someone; the act involved property damage only. (Use to minimize the seriousness of the crime.)

4. Peyton Farquhar knowingly committed an illegal act with full knowledge of the punishment. (Acknowledge, but use defenses 1–3 in response.)

5. Peyton Farquhar had probably committed such acts before, although no solid evidence is provided. (Object to this statement as unproven.)

6. Peyton Farquhar acted in a time of war. (Use to justify Farquhar's actions or request reduced sentencing.)

7. Peyton Farquhar was somewhat "tricked" into this act by a Federal scout. (Use to suggest Farquhar's inherent innocence.)

8. The punishment seems too severe for the crime. (Use to minimize sentencing.)

Open-Book Test, p. 16

Short Answer

1. Given the fact that a man is about to hanged and is looking death directly in the face, the reader might expect a more charged and emotional tone.
   Difficulty: *Challenging* **Objective:** *Interpretation*

2. Bierce is making the point that war and the death that comes in its wake can sweep up ordinary, even kindly civilians as well as dedicated professional soldiers. In effect, no one is safe from the brutality of war.
   Difficulty: *Challenging* **Objective:** *Interpretation*

3. The three sections are: (1) the preparations for the hanging; (2) a background explanation of how Farquhar came to be involved in the attempted sabotage of the bridge; (3) Farquhar's fantasy of escape and the actual moment of his death by hanging.
   Difficulty: *Easy* **Objective:** *Reading*

4. In this passage the story's point of view shifts from third-person objective point of view to third-person limited point of view.
   Difficulty: *Average* **Objective:** *Literary Analysis*

5. Students might note that Section II flashes backward, to an explanation of how Farquhar became involved in trying to sabotage the bridge. Section III shifts to the present, to Farquhar's fantasy of escape and his real-world death. The effect of these shifts is to make the story more dramatic and dreamlike, in contrast to the opening section, with its objective account of the orderly preparations for the hanging.
   Difficulty: *Average* **Objective:** *Reading*

6. The horseman is a Federal scout. He goads Farquhar into trying to burn down the bridge. Although Farquhar takes the bait, he might not have thought to do it on his own, without the prodding of the scout.
   Difficulty: *Average* **Objective:** *Interpretation*

7. Trees taking the form of giant garden plants is a fantastic image, like something out of a dream.
   Difficulty: *Average* **Objective:** *Literary Analysis*

8. the expression "all is fair in love and war"
   Difficulty: *Easy* **Objective:** *Vocabulary*

9. objective third-person and limited third-person
   Difficulty: *Easy* **Objective:** *Literary Analysis*

10. The sequence is as follows; 1. Farquhar has a conversation with a Federal scout; 2. Farquhar is strung up in preparation for his hanging; 3. Farquhar sees his wife wating for him at home; 4. Farquhar dies.
    Difficulty: *Average* **Objective:** *Reading Strategy*

Essay

11. Students will probably feel that Bierce does not agree with the statement. His view of war is so grim—given the way in which circumstances overtake a decent bystander like Farquhar—that he would most likely take the view that all the things people do in war are neither fair nor justified.
    Difficulty: *Easy* **Objective:** *Essay*

12. Most students will probably view the outlook of the story as pessimistic and dark. Readers are led to believe that Farquhar will escape the noose and be reunited with his wife. In fact, all of this "action" occurs only in Farquhar's imagination as he is dying. Moreover, Farquhar's guilt is viewed as a matter of trickery and entrapment by the Federal scout, so his execution seems all the more unjust.
    Difficulty: *Average* **Objective:** *Essay*

13. Some students might prefer a straight sequence of events and a single, objective point of view because they would be able to follow the story more easily. Others might prefer to keep the story as it is written, noting that the shifts in point of view and in time sequence lend the story a variety and sense of depth and mystery that would otherwise be lacking.
    Difficulty: *Challenging* **Objective:** *Essay*

14. Students might suggest that a sense of place is not so much a matter of physical setting as of the psychological and cultural attitudes of the inhabitants. Therefore, a place that was once peaceful and idyllic—such as the rural farming environs of this story—can, in wartime, easily turn into a nest of suspicions, betrayal, and death. This is the case in "An Occurrence at Owl Creek Bridge," in which an ordinary citizen farmer loses his life because of an unexpected entrapment in the intrigues of war in a place that was once the scene of peaceful, neighborly farming.
    Difficulty: *Average* **Objective:** *Essay*

Oral Response

15. Oral responses should be clear, well organized, and well supported by appropriate examples from the selections.
    Difficulty: *Average* **Objective:** *Oral Interpretation*

Selection Test A, p. 19

Critical Reading

1. **ANS:** B   **DIF:** Easy   **OBJ:** Comprehension

2. ANS: C	DIF: Easy	OBJ: Comprehension
3. ANS: D	DIF: Easy	OBJ: Interpretation
4. ANS: C	DIF: Easy	OBJ: Comprehension
5. ANS: D	DIF: Easy	OBJ: Literary Analysis
6. ANS: B	DIF: Easy	OBJ: Interpretation
7. ANS: C	DIF: Easy	OBJ: Interpretation
8. ANS: B	DIF: Easy	OBJ: Literary Analysis
9. ANS: D	DIF: Easy	OBJ: Reading Strategy
10. ANS: B	DIF: Easy	OBJ: Reading Strategy

Vocabulary

11. ANS: B	DIF: Easy	OBJ: Vocabulary
12. ANS: C	DIF: Easy	OBJ: Vocabulary

Essay

13. Students' essays should reflect that the setup of the story is pessimistic. Readers are led to believe that Farquhar will escape the noose and be reunited with his wife. In fact, all of this "action" occurs only in Farquhar's imagination as he is dying.

   Difficulty: *Easy*

   Objective: *Essay*

14. Students' essays should reflect that the story shows war as a hopeless experience: War breaks up families; it leads men to betray one another; it leads to the deaths of many soldiers and others; it causes much grief and suffering.

   Difficulty: *Easy*

   Objective: *Essay*

15. Students should recognize that the stark contrast between the ordinarily calm and peaceful farming community and the violent, unpredictable place in wartime is a fascinating situation to explore. A writer would want to emphasize those differences and invite readers to wonder at how quickly the peaceful setting as in "An Occurrence at Owl Creek Bridge" can transform into something deadly.

   Difficulty: *Easy*

   Objective: *Interpretation*

Selection Test B, p. 22

Critical Reading

1. ANS: A	DIF: Average	OBJ: Literary Analysis
2. ANS: A	DIF: Average	OBJ: Comprehension
3. ANS: C	DIF: Challenging	OBJ: Reading Strategy
4. ANS: B	DIF: Challenging	OBJ: Interpretation
5. ANS: C	DIF: Easy	OBJ: Interpretation
6. ANS: B	DIF: Average	OBJ: Literary Analysis
7. ANS: D	DIF: Easy	OBJ: Reading Strategy
8. ANS: D	DIF: Average	OBJ: Comprehension
9. ANS: B	DIF: Average	OBJ: Reading Strategy
10. ANS: B	DIF: Challenging	OBJ: Literary Analysis

11. ANS: A	DIF: Average	OBJ: Interpretation
12. ANS: C	DIF: Average	OBJ: Literary Analysis

Vocabulary

13. ANS: D	DIF: Challenging	OBJ: Vocabulary
14. ANS: B	DIF: Easy	OBJ: Vocabulary
15. ANS: C	DIF: Average	OBJ: Vocabulary
16. ANS: B	DIF: Average	OBJ: Vocabulary

Essay

17. Students will probably feel that Bierce does *not* agree. His view of war is so grim that he clearly feels all things people do in war are neither fair nor justified.

   Difficulty: *Easy*

   Objective: *Essay*

18. Students should realize that the meeting is critical to the story: the Union army would not have captured Farquhar had he not been entrapped by the Federal scout. Students can infer from its core of deception that the rest of the story contains a key deception: Farquhar thinks that he has escaped and returned home when he has actually been hanged.

   Difficulty: *Average*

   Objective: *Essay*

19. Some students may prefer a true sequence of events and an objective point of view, perhaps because continuity could help the reader follow the story better and make it more straightforward. Other students may prefer to keep the story as written, perhaps because the changing point of view and sequence of events help make the story interesting.

   Difficulty: *Challenging*

   Objective: *Essay*

20. Students might suggest that a sense of place is not so much a matter of physical setting as of the psychological and cultural attitudes of the inhabitants. Therefore, a place that was once peaceful and idyllic—such as the rural farming environs of this story—can, in wartime, easily turn into a nest of suspicions, betrayal, and death. This is the case in "An Occurrence at Owl Creek Bridge," in which an ordinary citizen farmer loses his life because of an unexpected entrapment in the intrigues of war in a place that was once the scene of peaceful, neighborly farming.

   Difficulty: *Average*

   Objective: *Interpretation*

Primary Sources: War Correspondence, p. 25

Sample Answers

1. Were these people truly enjoying the prospect of a war?

2. Chesnut says that for once in her life she listened. How good an observer can she be?

3. Why does Goss begin his journal in such a cheerful manner?

4. What is Goss preparing to do? Go to war? Go courting?

5. Why did Goss think it would be okay to speak to the drill sergeant like this?

6. What lesson has Goss learned from these experiences?

7. Why were the soldiers ordered to attack under these circumstances?

8. Will the men succeed against such overwhelming odds?

Vocabulary Builder, p. 26

1. The *recruits* did not know how to march.

2. The enemy *intercepted* a letter that was being sent to headquarters.

3. The officers failed to make a decision, so they *adjourned* the meeting.

4. The soldiers stayed in *entrenchments* in order to avoid being shot.

5. The *brigade* prepared for battle.

6. The general was *obstinate* and wouldn't give up the fight.

7. A *spectator* stood on the distant hill.

8. Citizens held a *convention* to talk about ways they could help the wounded.

9. The battle showed a marked *fluctuation* throughout the day.

10. The commander told the officers to plan an *offensive*.

Selection Test, p. 27

Critical Reading

1. ANS: B	DIF: Easy	OBJ: Literary Analysis
2. ANS: A	DIF: Average	OBJ: Comprehension
3. ANS: B	DIF: Challenging	OBJ: Interpretation
4. ANS: C	DIF: Easy	OBJ: Reading Strategy
5. ANS: C	DIF: Average	OBJ: Interpretation
6. ANS: D	DIF: Average	OBJ: Interpretation
7. ANS: A	DIF: Average	OBJ: Literary Analysis
8. ANS: A	DIF: Easy	OBJ: Comprehension
9. ANS: D	DIF: Average	OBJ: Comprehension
10. ANS: C	DIF: Easy	OBJ: Interpretation

"An Episode of War" by Stephen Crane

Vocabulary Warm-up Exercises, p. 30

A. 1. comrades
2. bugler
3. reverberated
4. sympathetically
5. stragglers
6. spectators
7. infantry
8. lieutenant

B. Sample Answers
1. On the beach, we saw an aggregation of hundreds of seagulls.

2. Ollie appropriated Mike's bicycle, and Mike couldn't ride it for the rest of the day.

3. We were very surprised at the astoundingly large number of concertgoers.

4. Berating me soundly, Dad also grounded me for my bad report card.

5. The game was a catastrophe for our football team, which lost by a score of 35-0.

6. That school was very well endowed, with exceptionally fine facilities for athletics.

7. The time passed so slowly that the play seemed interminable.

8. The art exhibit was singular, resembling no other show that had been held before.

Reading Warm-up A, p. 31

Sample Answers

1. haunting melody, played by; The army bugler wore a splendid full-dress uniform.

2. (or another officer in charge of a regiment); The *lieutenant* was respected by those both within and outside of the military.

3. (soldiers on foot); on land

4. late, still wandering around; at the end

5. (in caring remembrance); sympathy, sympathize, sympathetic

6. in attendance; *audience*

7. those from their group; After the championship win, Tom celebrated with his comrades on the lacrosse team.

8. (these same notes); the ringing of a bell, thunder, a siren

Reading Warm-up B, p. 32

Sample Answers

1. high school students and local music fans; *group*

2. (had no money for equipment); Paul appropriated Ira's soccer ball because he needed it for the game.

3. shouting criticisms; The opposite of *berating* is *praising* or *complimenting*.

4. (disastrously); A hurricane can cause considerable damage to homes and businesses.

5. (surprisingly); *predictably*

6. (a powerful voice that provided warmth and clarity); Preston was endowed with speed and agility, so he was a nimble player on the soccer field.

7. No one had ever heard anything like his songs; *remarkable, unique*

8. applause; Math class sometimes seems *interminable*.

Literary Analysis: Realism and Naturalism, p. 33

Sample Answers

1. Naturalism: The event of being shot is a force beyond the lieutenant's control.

2. Naturalism: This passage emphasizes the lieutenant's and the women's reactions to an event outside their

control; Realism: The reaction reflects realistic responses to the lieutenant's injury.

Reading Strategy: Recognize Historical Details, p. 34

1. **War tactics:** Most battles were hand-to-hand combat, making injury likely.
2. **Medicine:** Medicine was less advanced, and wartime hospitals were short on staff and supplies, increasing the chances that an injury would become life threatening. The lieutenant's injury turns into an amputation, whether necessary or not.
3. **Communication:** Letters to families took a long time, particularly during wartime. When the lieutenant returns home, his family does not know about his amputation.
4. **Transportation:** Soldiers moved by horse or by foot. Injured men could not be rushed to an emergency room. The lieutenant has to bring himself to the field hospital, which probably made his condition worse.

Vocabulary Builder, p. 35

A. 1. gregarious; 2. egregious; 3. congregation; 4. aggregation
B. 1. A; 2. C; 3. B; 4. D
C. 1. A; 2. C; 3. B

Enrichment: Photograph, p. 37

Sample Answers

1. An interminable crowd of bandaged men were coming and going. Great numbers sat under the trees nursing heads or arms or legs.
2. He wore the look of one who knows he is the victim of terrible disease and understands his helplessness.
3. The lieutenant had been very meek, but now his face flushed, and he looked into the doctor's eyes. "I guess I won't have it amputated," he said.
4. The soldiers look resigned to their fates, an expression that might reflect dignity or simply despair.

Open-Book Test, p. 38

Short Answer

1. The first two paragraphs of "An Episode of War" portray the lieutenant absorbed in the very ordinary task of dividing coffee into squares on a rubber blanket so that he can distribute equal amounts to each squad. The task is described as a routine, everyday detail of a military camp and so establishes a naturalistic feel to the story.
   Difficulty: *Average* **Objective:** *Literary Analysis*
2. The lieutenant's wound is portrayed as an extraordinary event. This emphasizes the ordinary everydayness of the circumstances in which it occurs.
   Difficulty: *Challenging* **Objective:** *Literary Analysis*

3. The most obvious clue is the fact that the lieutenant has a sword. Swords have not been used in battle for more than a hundred years.
   Difficulty: *Easy* **Objective:** *Reading Strategy*
4. Crane prefers to let the impact of events build to an awareness of how much the injury has stunned and shocked the lieutenant rather than stating it directly. Developing this point through the events and details of the story creates a stronger impact on the reader.
   Difficulty: *Challenging* **Objective:** *Interpretation*
5. The lieutenant's distance and detachment emphasize naturalism's focus on how the course of people's lives is determined by forces outside their control.
   Difficulty: *Average* **Objective:** *Literary Analysis*
6. Sample answers: Detail 1: The lieutenant's wound; it shows how major events in a person's life can literally and suddenly come out of nowhere.
   Detail 2: An officer on the roadside scolds him for having his wound dressed incorrectly, and he proceeds to re-dress it; the officer probably dresses the wound incorrectly and may contribute to the lieutenant's loss of his arm.
   Detail 3: The field hospital is chaotic and understaffed; the hurried and impersonal atmosphere of the field hospital contributes to the drastic solution of amputating the lieutenant's wounded arm.
   The lieutenant is not in control of his own fate because external circumstances—a stray bullet, a chance encounter with an officer, an overcrowded hospital—not his own will or intention, lead to his losing his arm.
   Difficulty: *Average* **Objective:** *Literary Analysis*
7. Crane's description of the chaos and commotion of the field hospital suggests that the lieutenant will likely receive inadequate and/or incompetent treatment of his wound there.
   Difficulty: *Easy* **Objective:** *Interpretation*
8. Sample answer: Crane thought that describing the procedure would be unnecessarily gruesome and would therefore detract from his focus on the soldier's thoughts, feelings, and reactions to his situation.
   Difficulty: *Average* **Objective:** *Interpretation*
9. The primary mode of transportation is horseback, and this tells the reader that the story took place in the nineteenth century, before the invention of the automobile.
   Difficulty: *Easy* **Objective:** *Reading Strategy*
10. The comment would be unfavorable, because *disdainfully* means "in a manner that shows scorn or contempt."
    Difficulty: *Average* **Objective:** *Vocabulary*

Essay

11. Comments: "Why, man, that's no way to do. You want to fix that thing"; "Well, let's have a look at it"; "What mutton-head tied it up that way?"; "Come along. Don't be a baby." Students might note that the meaning of these comments is to make the lieutenant feel that he

does not know how to handle himself correctly, "that he did not know how to be correctly wounded." He feels scorned by the doctor and generally at the mercy of people who are indifferent to his feelings and concerns.

Difficulty: *Easy*   **Objective:** *Essay*

12. Sample answers: the officer handing out coffee to his men implies that he understands the importance of giving them support in battle; the silent reaction of the men to his wound implies a company that is unified in its respect for the lieutenant; the men "crowded forward sympathetically," so they clearly have some feeling for their leader; they view him as someone both brave and perhaps doomed.

Difficulty: *Average*   **Objective:** *Essay*

13. "An Episode of War" can be read as Crane's condemnation of the brutality and destructiveness of war. When the lieutenant suffers the wound that leads to the loss of his arm, he is not even engaged in combat—he is just distributing coffee to his soldiers. The care he receives at the field hospital shows that, in the confusion and rush of combat, the soldiers' best interests do not come first—the doctors simply do the fastest and simplest thing, which in this case is to amputate the soldier's arm. All of this seems to happen to the soldier out of nowhere, for no good reason, thus underscoring the horror and inhumanity of warfare.

Difficulty: *Challenging*   **Objective:** *Essay*

14. Students might argue that it is the job of the fiction writer to explore original or hidden truths of life that might go beyond the average person's understanding or worldview. For example, many citizens might support the idea of war until they get a first-hand glimpse of just how brutal it can be. In this sense, Crane and writers like him perform a public service in putting readers in touch with truths that they might otherwise never encounter or think about.

Difficulty: *Average*   **Objective:** *Essay*

Oral Response

15. Oral responses should be clear, well organized, and well supported by appropriate examples from the selection.

Difficulty: *Average*   **Objective:** *Oral Interpretation*

Selection Test A, p. 41

Critical Reading

1. ANS: D	DIF: Easy	OBJ: Reading Strategy
2. ANS: B	DIF: Easy	OBJ: Interpretation
3. ANS: D	DIF: Easy	OBJ: Reading Strategy
4. ANS: B	DIF: Easy	OBJ: Literary Analysis
5. ANS: B	DIF: Easy	OBJ: Reading Strategy
6. ANS: B	DIF: Easy	OBJ: Literary Analysis
7. ANS: A	DIF: Easy	OBJ: Interpretation
8. ANS: C	DIF: Easy	OBJ: Comprehension
9. ANS: C	DIF: Easy	OBJ: Comprehension
10. ANS: C	DIF: Easy	OBJ: Comprehension

Vocabulary

11. ANS: B	DIF: Easy	OBJ: Vocabulary
12. ANS: A	DIF: Easy	OBJ: Vocabulary

Essay

13. Students' essays should reflect that the characters are involved in a war that they did not plan and probably did not want to fight. The main character has even less control over his fate because he is not engaged in battle when he is wounded by a stray bullet. Finally, he has no control over what happens to his arm as the result of his wound.

Difficulty: *Easy*

Objective: *Essay*

14. Some students might say that it is the job of the fiction writer to help readers see life as it is, not colored over and unrealistic. In this sense, Crane and writers like him help readers come to terms with a reality they might otherwise ignore, either by wish or ignorance. Other students might say that a writer's job is to entertain and give us relief from a world that is already too brutal and severe. In this case, Crane's story is a fictionalized look at a reality that is all too close for some people already.

Difficulty: *Easy*

Objective: *Interpretation*

Selection Test B, p. 44

Critical Reading

1. ANS: B	DIF: Average	OBJ: Comprehension
2. ANS: B	DIF: Challenging	OBJ: Literary Analysis
3. ANS: D	DIF: Challenging	OBJ: Interpretation
4. ANS: D	DIF: Easy	OBJ: Interpretation
5. ANS: B	DIF: Average	OBJ: Interpretation
6. ANS: B	DIF: Average	OBJ: Reading Strategy
7. ANS: B	DIF: Challenging	OBJ: Literary Analysis
8. ANS: C	DIF: Easy	OBJ: Reading Strategy
9. ANS: D	DIF: Average	OBJ: Literary Analysis
10. ANS: A	DIF: Challenging	OBJ: Literary Analysis
11. ANS: D	DIF: Challenging	OBJ: Interpretation
12. ANS: B	DIF: Average	OBJ: Reading Strategy

Vocabulary and Grammar

13. ANS: A	DIF: Average	OBJ: Vocabulary
14. ANS: A	DIF: Easy	OBJ: Vocabulary
15. ANS: D	DIF: Average	OBJ: Vocabulary
16. ANS: B	DIF: Average	OBJ: Vocabulary

Essay

17. Students may note that the lieutenant's injury at the story's beginning makes him a sympathetic character. Accept any essay that contains a well-reasoned argument in support of the writer's opinion.

Difficulty: *Easy*

Objective: *Essay*

18. Students should define Realism as a literary movement whose advocates sought to depict real life as faithfully and accurately as possible by focusing on ordinary people faced with the harsh realities of everyday life. They may point out how the lieutenant was wounded while occupied with mundane duties and trace his journey through the harsh realities of the battle zone. They should also mention how Crane's use of vivid and historically accurate details heightens the story's realism.

Difficulty: *Challenging*

Objective: *Essay*

19. Students might argue that it is the job of the fiction writer to explore original or hidden truths of life that might go beyond the average person's understanding or worldview. For example, many citizens might support the idea of war until they get a first-hand glimpse of just how brutal it can be. In this sense, Crane and writers like him perform a public service in putting readers in touch with truths that they might otherwise never encounter or think about.

Difficulty: *Average*

Objective: *Interpretation*

from **My Bondage** and **My Freedom**
by Frederick Douglass

Vocabulary Warm-up Exercises, p. 48

A. 1. consternation
   2. incompatible
   3. congenial
   4. domestic
   5. apt
   6. variable
   7. overthrow
   8. victorious

B. Sample Answers
   1. The T-shirt label <u>chafed</u> the back of my neck and made my skin feel uncomfortable.
   2. <u>Consenting</u> to our proposal, Rose gave us permission to begin the plan's first phase.
   3. Ken was so <u>destitute</u> that he had to make do with a very small house and no automobile.
   4. When she heard that comment, Yolanda expressed her <u>mirth</u> with a smile and a chuckle.

Reading Warm-up A, p. 49

Sample Answers

1. <u>tried to hide the comic book . . . as if she might be angry</u>; To my *consternation*, the boss called me in for a thorough review of my job performance.
2. (the family meals, the after-dinner TV sessions)
3. <u>trying to make friends</u>; The opposite of *congenial* is *aloof* or *unfriendly*.

4. <u>Nate was surely old enough to know how to read . . . the fact that he couldn't seemed . . . with the intelligence she could see in his eyes</u>; *compatible, reconcilable*
5. (sometimes he understood, sometimes he didn't); *changeable, fluctuating*
6. <u>eventually grasping everything she explained to him</u>; The opposite of *apt* is *inept* or *incapable*.
7. (a gang of villains . . . the government and rule the country); *subvert, overturn*
8. <u>conquered</u>; *conquering, triumphant*

Reading Warm-up B, p. 50

Sample Answers

1. <u>many people supported . . . there was some . . . to the idea, however</u>; *resistance*
2. (against the preconceived notions); *wore away, rubbed against*
3. <u>amusement</u>; The comedian's hysterical jokes were greeted with *mirth* in the audience.
4. <u>passed two acts . . . to the enlistment of African Americans</u>; *disagreeing*
5. (was cautiously delayed); Dad urged me to drive with *prudence* during the heavy storm.
6. (runaways from the moral . . . of slavery); *evil, corruption*
7. <u>far from being . . . of courage and skill</u>; The opposite of *destitute* is *rich*.
8. <u>. . . the attention of all Americans with their heroic deeds</u>; *fastened*

Literary Analysis: Autobiography and Tone, p. 51

Sample Answers

1. The effects are strength and self-knowledge. Writing this as an autobiography makes the writer seem more real and the passage more convincing. The tone is one of insistent reasonableness and honesty that invites readers to believe his story.
2. In this passage, the perceptions and effects are pain and despair. Describing images such as a "dragon ready to pounce" from a first-hand viewpoint draws the reader into Douglass's horror at being enslaved. The tone is one of careful analysis and controlled resentment that reinforces the experience he is relating by making it sound authentic.
3. The effects of this passage are anger and sorrow. By using the first person, Douglass demonstrates anger, rather than merely reporting it. The tone is one of controlled anger, reinforcing feelings natural to his experience.

Reading Strategy: Establish a Purpose, p. 52

Sample Answers

Character: Mrs. Auld's eventual brutal opposition to Douglass's efforts to learn to read

Ethical influence: She became educated in the cultural ethics of slavery that convinced her that educating slaves was bad and dangerous and responded in the manner of people of the time.

Characters: small boys with whom Douglass talked about slavery and who sympathized with him

Ethical influence: The boys naturally thought of him as a person; they were not yet governed by the slave mentality that possessed many Southern adults of the period.

Incident: Douglass's reluctance to identify the boys who helped him learn to read because they might be embarrassed

Ethical influence: During those times, helping a slave learn to read was both illegal and unethical. It might also suggest a weakness of character or intelligence, so these helpers might be embarrassed.

Vocabulary Builder, p. 53

A. 1. beneficiary; 2. benign; 3. beneficent; 4. beneficial
B. 1. C; 2. F; 3. D; 4. A; 5. B; 6. E

Enrichment: Career as a Teacher, p. 55

Sample Answers

1. **Passage:** In teaching me the alphabet . . . my mistress had given me the "inch," and now, no ordinary precaution could prevent me from taking the "ell." **Lesson:** By learning the fundamentals, interested students will be motivated to learn more.

2. **Passage:** I used to carry . . . a copy of Webster's spelling book in my pocket; and, when sent on errands, or when play time was allowed me, I would step . . . aside, and take a lesson in spelling. I usually paid my tuition fee . . . with bread. . . . **Lesson:** As a child, Douglass learned to spell by paying boys to teach him on his free time. This anecdote could be used as inspiration for those who don't completely understand the value of reading.

3. **Passage:** When I was about thirteen years old, and had succeeded in learning to read, every increase of knowledge, especially respecting the free states, added something to the almost intolerable burden of the thought—"I am a slave for life." **Lesson:** For Douglass, reading freed his mind and made him knowledgeable about his condition of slavery. This story could be used to encourage others to learn to read.

Open-Book Test, p. 56

Short Answer

1. Students can point to the first sentence: "I lived in the family of Master Hugh . . ." as indicating both an autobiography and the story of someone who was enslaved to a master. They might cite examples from the rest of the paragraph that pertain to Douglass's childhood in the household, and his determination to learn to read despite the opposition of the master and, eventually, the mistress: "my history here," "my mistress," "shutting me up in mental darkness," "slaveholder's prerogative."

Difficulty: *Average* **Objective:** *Literary Analysis*

2. From this remark the reader can infer that Douglass believes that slavery runs against the natural human inclinations of both the slaveholder and the enslaved person—that slavery is, therefore, a completely unnatural institution.

Difficulty: *Average* **Objective:** *Interpretation*

3. Students might argue that this statement is an accurate self-assessment because, although he was the "property" of the Aulds growing up, he understood that he had a natural right to freedom and so was, as a human being, potentially more than just a slave.

Difficulty: *Challenging* **Objective:** *Literary Analysis*

4. A person who wanted to read the selection to find out more about the Aulds would probably be interested in learning more about the attitudes and practices of slaveholders before the Civil War.

Difficulty: *Easy* **Objective:** *Reading*

5. Students might conclude that even naturally goodhearted people could end up acting cruelly toward other human beings because of the dictates and pressures of the institution of slavery.

Difficulty: *Challenging* **Objective:** *Reading*

6. Most students will note that it was Mr. Auld who pressured Mrs. Auld to change her attitude because he believed that it was dangerous to teach slaves to read. Mrs. Auld allowed her loyalty to her husband to overrule her natural inclination toward kindness.

Difficulty: *Challenging* **Objective:** *Interpretation*

7. This section of Douglass's autobiography shows that young white children tended to be less corrupted by racist attitudes than adults were.

Difficulty: *Average* **Objective:** *Literary Analysis*

8. Mr. Auld probably believed that if you taught a slave to read, he or she would be more likely to develop the ability to think critically and independently and to question the justice and fairness of one human being owning and completely controlling another.

Difficulty: *Challenging* **Objective:** *Interpretation*

9. If the king was benevolent toward his subjects, he would be more likely to treat them kindly, because *benevolent* means "disposed toward doing good."

Difficulty: *Average* **Objective:** *Vocabulary*

10. Sample answers (early behavior): She had begun to teach him; she was kind and tenderhearted; she had humanity in her heart; she had simplicity of mind; she first treated him as a human being; she felt him to be more than chattel. (later behavior): She "set her face as a flint" against Douglass's learning to read; she lost all of her Christian qualities; she would rush at him to snatch reading matter from him; she would suspect him of reading, if he was even momentarily separated from the family; she was offended by his downcast look.

Difficulty: *Easy* **Objective:** *Interpretation*

Essay

11. Students might note that it was Douglass's determination to read that helped inspire his desire to

improve his lot in life and to become a free human being. They might also note that the ideas he encountered in the Columbian Orator further inspired him in his quest for freedom. These examples show that education for all—especially those with the fewest opportunities—can inspire a quest for a better, freer life and is thus an invaluable tool for all people, no matter what their background.

Difficulty: *Easy* **Objective:** *Essay*

12. Students will probably argue in favor of Douglass's viewpoint, because he persuasively supports this idea with incidents and examples throughout the selection. Students might mention the example of the young white boys who, not yet trained as slaveholders, are naturally sympathetic to Douglass's desire to learn to read and be free.

Difficulty: *Average* **Objective:** *Essay*

13. Some students might support this statement, noting that Mrs. Auld could not incorporate her husband's attitude without undergoing a complete transformation from benevolence to domineering harshness. Others might argue that her conscience could not have been that strong to begin with to collapse so readily before the dictates of her husband.

Difficulty: *Challenging* **Objective:** *Essay*

14. Students might suggest that all of these elements play a crucial role in writing that inspires social change. First, it must be skillful and eloquent—as Douglass's writing is—to command the attention of the reader. Likewise, it must convey a dedicated personality and a passion for justice—as Douglass's writing does—to have credibility. Finally, it must have the ring of truth—especially insofar as it gives people a glimpse of realities or circumstances with which they were previously unfamiliar. In Douglass's case, these circumstances include: the psychology of slaveholders and the way in which they try to limit their slaves' mental development, the openness of children and young people to feelings of equality that tend to fade in adulthood, and the ability of oppressed people to rise above their circumstances if given sufficient opportunities.

Difficulty: *Average* **Objective:** *Essay*

Oral Response

15. Oral responses should be clear, well organized, and well supported by appropriate examples from the selections.

Difficulty: *Average* **Objective:** *Oral Interpretation*

Selection Test A, p. 59

Critical Reading

1. ANS: B	DIF: Easy	OBJ: Comprehension
2. ANS: C	DIF: Easy	OBJ: Comprehension
3. ANS: C	DIF: Easy	OBJ: Literary Analysis
4. ANS: B	DIF: Easy	OBJ: Literary Analysis
5. ANS: C	DIF: Easy	OBJ: Reading Strategy
6. ANS: B	DIF: Easy	OBJ: Literary Analysis
7. ANS: B	DIF: Easy	OBJ: Interpretation

8. ANS: C	DIF: Easy	OBJ: Reading Strategy
9. ANS: C	DIF: Easy	OBJ: Interpretation
10. ANS: D	DIF: Easy	OBJ: Interpretation

Vocabulary

11. ANS: C	DIF: Easy	OBJ: Vocabulary
12. ANS: C	DIF: Easy	OBJ: Vocabulary

Essay

13. Students may say that they would have been less patient than Douglass in waiting for opportunities they knew they deserved. They may also say that they would have been able to wait, knowing that better times were ahead.

Difficulty: *Easy*

Objective: *Essay*

14. Students should mention that without education, people are limited in their activities and their ability to think about a variety of subjects. In Douglass's case, the book he bought led him to think about freedom and how he wanted to live his life.

Difficulty: *Easy*

Objective: *Essay*

15. Students might suggest that writers can have a great impact on how society responds to these causes. Writers can challenge people to think about these issues and show them new sides to issues that they perhaps never considered before. Good writers can also inspire people to take action rather than just wait for others to do something.

Difficulty: *Easy*

Objective: *Interpretation*

Selection Test B, p. 62

Critical Reading

1. ANS: D	DIF: Average	OBJ: Interpretation
2. ANS: D	DIF: Average	OBJ: Comprehension
3. ANS: A	DIF: Challenging	OBJ: Interpretation
4. ANS: D	DIF: Average	OBJ: Comprehension
5. ANS: B	DIF: Challenging	OBJ: Literary Analysis
6. ANS: D	DIF: Challenging	OBJ: Reading Strategy
7. ANS: C	DIF: Challenging	OBJ: Interpretation
8. ANS: A	DIF: Average	OBJ: Interpretation
9. ANS: C	DIF: Average	OBJ: Reading Strategy
10. ANS: B	DIF: Average	OBJ: Literary Analysis
11. ANS: D	DIF: Average	OBJ: Literary Analysis
12. ANS: C	DIF: Easy	OBJ: Reading Strategy

Vocabulary

13. ANS: B	DIF: Easy	OBJ: Vocabulary
14. ANS: A	DIF: Average	OBJ: Vocabulary
15. ANS: D	DIF: Easy	OBJ: Vocabulary
16. ANS: B	DIF: Easy	OBJ: Vocabulary

Unit 3 Resources: Division, Reconciliation, and Expansion

Essay

17. Students should provide details that show that Mrs. Auld was a benevolent and congenial woman at the outset who, after having been persuaded not to teach Frederick to read or write, became angry and harsh in her behavior toward him whenever she suspected him of attempting to read. One example of her changed behavior is the incident of her rushing at him with fury to snatch away a book or newspaper.

    Difficulty: *Easy*

    Objective: *Essay*

18. Students will probably argue in favor of this statement, since this is the position Douglass persuasively supports with incidents and examples throughout his account. Students may support their position with the example of the young white boys who, not yet trained as slaveholders, are naturally sympathetic to Douglass. Accept any answer that is well supported with examples from the text:

    Difficulty: *Average*

    Objective: *Essay*

19. Some students will support this statement, noting that Mrs. Auld could not incorporate her husband's attitude without undergoing a complete transformation from benevolent to harsh, angry, and domineering. Others may explain her behavior as a twisted sort of benevolence, arguing that Mrs. Auld hoped to spare young Frederick the recognition of his horrid situation that learning might bring.

    Difficulty: *Challenging*

    Objective: *Essay*

20. Students might suggest that all of these elements play a crucial role in writing that inspires social change. First, it must be skillful and eloquent—as Douglass's writing is—to command the attention of the reader. Likewise, it must convey a dedicated personality and a passion for justice—as Douglass's writing does—to have credibility. Finally, it must have the ring of truth—especially insofar as it gives people a glimpse of realities or circumstances with which they were previously unfamiliar. In Douglass's case, these circumstances include: the psychology of slaveholders and the way in which they try to limit their slaves' mental development, the openness of children and young people to feelings of equality that tend to fade in adulthood, and the ability of oppressed people to rise above their circumstances if given sufficient opportunities.

    Difficulty: *Average*

    Objective: *Interpretation*

"Swing Low, Sweet Chariot" and "Go Down, Moses" Spirituals

Vocabulary Warm-up Exercises, p. 66

A. 1. spiritual
   2. band

3. fugitives
4. captivity
5. legal
6. banned
7. rebellions
8. deprived

B. Sample Answers

1. F; Activists are often involved in issues and causes.
2. T; A chariot was typically owned by upper-class people in ancient times.
3. F; *Enacted* means "put into effect."
4. T; *Eventually* means "after a certain length of time."
5. T; A network is a group that is linked or associated.
6. F; *Oppressed* means "harshly put down," so oppressed people probably would feel unhappy.
7. F; A pharaoh was the Egyptian king in ancient times.
8. F; *Smite* means "to strike forcefully."

Reading Warm-up A, p. 67

Sample Answers

1. (song); "Swing Low, Sweet Chariot" is a famous spiritual that probably dates from the 1800s.
2. taken away; It would die.
3. hostages without freedom; *freedom*
4. (against the system); *revolts*
5. (forbidden); The opposite of *banned* is *permitted*.
6. lawful; *unlawful, illegal*
7. (group); Out in the desert, a band of robbers attacked the caravan of travelers.
8. running from the law; Several prisoners escaped, but the police succeeded in recapturing the fugitives.

Reading Warm-up B, p. 68

Sample Answers

1. ordering; The legislature recently enacted a law that raises the driving age in our state to twenty-one.
2. (in the ruler's house); in ancient Egypt
3. privileged to ride; a fancy car
4. after some time; The opposite of *eventually* is *immediately*.
5. (shocked and saddened); The opposite of *oppressed* is *liberated*.
6. groups . . . like-minded; Aaron called on a network of friends to help publicize the event.
7. intent on the cause; recycling, hybrid cars
8. (hitting hard); In karate class, I had to smite the wood block twice to break it in half.

Literary Analysis: Refrain, Allusion, and Allegory p. 69

Sample Answers

1. "Swing low, sweet chariot,/Coming for to carry me home" or "Coming for to carry me home"

2. The allegory in "Go Down, Moses" refers, on the literal level, to Moses freeing the Israelites who were held in bondage in Egypt. On a symbolic level, it refers to slaves in the South—the Israelites symbolizing the slaves and Egypt symbolizing the South.

3. The allusion to Jordan refers to the River Jordan in the Near East that is mentioned in the Bible. Crossing the Jordan represents crossing into freedom in the spiritual.

4. Their repetition increases the intensity and the urgency of the spiritual's message.

5. The refrains in both spirituals refer to the desire for freedom. In "Swing Low, Sweet Chariot," the refrains refer to a release—that of death and going to Heaven. In "Go Down, Moses," the refrains are couched as a demand for freedom during life. The refrains in "Go Down, Moses" are much more militant than those of "Swing Low, Sweet Chariot."

Reading Strategy: Listen, p. 70

Sample Answers

"Swing Low, Sweet Chariot"

Cell 1. In second verse *see* and *me* rhyme

Cell 2. "Swing low, sweet chariot" and "Coming for to carry me home"

Cell 3. yearning or longing

Cell 4. Encourages patience and faith in eventual freedom from hardship

"Go Down, Moses"

Cell 1. "Pharaoh" and "go"; "land" and "stand"; "said" and "dead"

Cell 2. "Go down, Moses," "Way down in Egypt land," "Tell old Pharaoh," "To let my people go"

Cell 3. persistence and determination

Cell 4. Eventually the powerless will triumph over the powerful.

Vocabulary Builder, p. 71

A. 1. suppress
   2. express
   3. pressurize
   4. press
   5. impression
   6. depression

B. 1. B; 2. A

C. 1. E; 2. C

Enrichment: Social Studies, p. 73

1. A pharaoh is a king and has a great amount of power over his subjects.

2. the owner of the plantation

---

3. They were kept down and oppressed.

4. They, too, were oppressed.

5. He told the pharaoh to let his people go.

6. The spiritual also demands freedom. The demand is directed toward the owners of the slaves.

Open-Book Test, p. 74

Short Answer

1. The surface meaning is the soul's hope of going "home" to heaven or God in the afterlife. The hidden meaning is a call for liberation from slavery—going "home" to freedom and escaping from a life of bondage and oppression.
   Difficulty: *Average*   **Objective:** *Literary Analysis*

2. The angels could be coming from heaven to carry a person's soul to an afterlife of harmony and peace after earthly life is over. On a deeper level, the angels might represent antislavery activists who have come to help free the slaves from their bondage.
   Difficulty: *Challenging*   **Objective:** *Interpretation*

3. Sample answers: ancestral home in Africa; home in heaven, far from the travails of this world; home of freedom in the North; or home in general as a sanctuary from the trials of life.
   Difficulty: *Average*   **Objective:** *Interpretation*

4. The refrain establishes the rhythm, mood, and theme of the song.
   Difficulty: *Easy*   **Objective:** *Literary Analysis*

5. The main mood and feelings suggested by the rhythm and repetition of key phrases are longing, patience, and hope.
   Difficulty: *Average*   **Objective:** *Reading Strategy*

6. Moses was an especially meaningful figure because he led his people from slavery to freedom.
   Difficulty: *Easy*   **Objective:** *Literary Analysis*

7. Students might suggest that the creators of this spiritual may have wanted to repeat this line to convey the slaves' longing for freedom. They were probably addressing the slaveowners, and they may have hoped that the slaves' repeated cry for freedom in this song would move the slaveowners to free their people.
   Difficulty: *Average*   **Objective:** *Reading*

8. The repetition of the phrase "way down in Egypt land" implies a strong connection to biblical history. This could affect the listener by making them aware of the parallel between Egypt and the South as lands of slavery.
   Difficulty: *Challenging*   **Objective:** *Reading*

9. The line is "Oppressed so hard they could not stand."
   Difficulty: *Easy*   **Objective:** *Interpretation*

10. The people would be protesting, because *oppressed* means "kept down by cruel or unjust powers."
    Difficulty: *Average*   **Objective:** *Vocabulary*

Essay

11. Sample answers: "Swing Low, Sweet Chariot": Sweet chariot; coming for to carry me home; swing low; coming; home; carry. "Go Down, Moses": Go down, Moses; Let my people go; Egypt land; Way down; Tell old Pharaoh. The phrases in both songs express a longing for a better life. Both songs use the phrases for their surface meanings as well as for their deeper meanings about freedom from slavery.

    Difficulty: *Easy*   **Objective:** *Essay*

12. Sample answers: "Swing Low": the angels, home (heaven), Jordan. Students may choose "Swing Low" as more effective, because it promises the beauty of heavenly release.

    "Go Down, Moses": Moses, Israel, Egypt, the smiting of the first-born. Students might also mention that the speaker is addressing God or some agent of God in each song. Students might choose "Go Down, Moses" as more effective because it uses biblical references more directly as a plea for freedom.

    Difficulty: *Average*   **Objective:** *Essay*

13. Students' essays might explain any of the following words or phrases: *chariot*—travel or route on the Underground Railroad; *home*—a state without slavery; *Jordan*—the Ohio River or a border between slave and free territories; *band of angels*—"conductors" on the Underground Railroad; *get there*—reach freedom; *tell my friends*—tell those who have already escaped.

    Difficulty: *Challenging*   **Objective:** *Essay*

14. Students might note that the idea of a promised land is especially evident in "Swing Low, Sweet Chariot," in which the refrain is "Coming for to carry me home." In this spiritual, "home" can be taken as freedom—escape from enslavement on the plantation—and thus finding some degree of fulfillment while on earth. The idea of "home" can also be taken as representing the next life— that even if there is no hope of freedom or equality in this world, the afterlife promises deliverance from the suffering and oppression of earthly life.

    Difficulty: *Average*   **Objective:** *Essay*

Oral Response

15. Oral responses should be clear, well organized, and well supported by appropriate examples from the selections.

    Difficulty: *Average*   **Objective:** *Oral Interpretation*

Selection Test A, p. 77

Critical Reading

1. ANS: B	DIF: Easy	OBJ: Literary Analysis
2. ANS: D	DIF: Easy	OBJ: Interpretation
3. ANS: C	DIF: Easy	OBJ: Literary Analysis
4. ANS: C	DIF: Easy	OBJ: Reading Strategy
5. ANS: B	DIF: Easy	OBJ: Comprehension
6. ANS: A	DIF: Easy	OBJ: Reading Strategy
7. ANS: A	DIF: Easy	OBJ: Literary Analysis

8. ANS: D	DIF: Easy	OBJ: Interpretation
9. ANS: B	DIF: Easy	OBJ: Literary Analysis
10. ANS: B	DIF: Easy	OBJ: Reading Strategy

Vocabulary

11. ANS: A	DIF: Easy	OBJ: Vocabulary
12. ANS: C	DIF: Easy	OBJ: Vocabulary

Essay

13. Students' essays might suggest that "Swing Low, Sweet Chariot" is a lyrical and hopeful wish for freedom, while "Go down, Moses" is a demand for that same freedom. The first is a polite plea, while the second is a direct command.

    Difficulty: *Easy*

    Objective: *Essay*

14. Students' essays might explain any of the following codes: *chariot*—travel or a route on the Underground Railroad; *home*—a state without slavery; *Jordan*—the Ohio River, or a border between slave and free territories; *band of angels*—"conductors" on the Underground Railroad; safe houses; *get there*—reach freedom; *tell my friends*—tell those who have already escaped.

    Difficulty: *Easy*

    Objective: *Essay*

15. Students might note that the idea of a promised land is especially evident in "Swing Low, Sweet Chariot," in which the refrain is "Coming for to carry me home." In this spiritual, "home" might represent freedom, or escape from enslavement on the plantation. The spiritual, then, gives hope of a promised land on earth by escaping from slavery. The idea of "home" might also represent the next life. Even if there is no hope of freedom in this world, the afterlife promises an eventual relief from the suffering slaves experienced on earth. It thereby gives comfort as well as hope.

    Difficulty: *Easy*

    Objective: *Interpretation*

Selection Test B, p. 80

Critical Reading

1. ANS: C	DIF: Easy	OBJ: Comprehension
2. ANS: A	DIF: Average	OBJ: Literary Analysis
3. ANS: D	DIF: Challenging	OBJ: Reading Strategy
4. ANS: C	DIF: Average	OBJ: Comprehension
5. ANS: D	DIF: Easy	OBJ: Literary Analysis
6. ANS: C	DIF: Average	OBJ: Literary Analysis
7. ANS: A	DIF: Average	OBJ: Reading Strategy
8. ANS: D	DIF: Easy	OBJ: Literary Analysis
9. ANS: D	DIF: Average	OBJ: Interpretation
10. ANS: A	DIF: Average	OBJ: Literary Analysis
11. ANS: C	DIF: Challenging	OBJ: Comprehension
12. ANS: B	DIF: Average	OBJ: Literary Analysis

13. ANS: C   DIF: Average   OBJ: Reading Strategy
14. ANS: B   DIF: Challenging   OBJ: Literary Analysis

Vocabulary

15. ANS: A   DIF: Average   OBJ: Vocabulary
16. ANS: D   DIF: Challenging   OBJ: Vocabulary

Essay

17. Students should recognize that, in a veiled way, "Go Down, Moses" is about escaping slavery during life, whereas "Swing Low, Sweet Chariot" is about death's deliverance from hardship. The recurring refrain of "Let my people go" would have been more disturbing and worrisome to a slave owner than the references to Heaven and angels in "Swing Low, Sweet Chariot." Students may also cite the mention of violence (smiting the firstborn) in "Go Down, Moses" as part of the spiritual's undercurrent of rebellion.
    Difficulty: *Easy*
    Objective: *Essay*

18. For "Swing Low, Sweet Chariot," students should indicate that the release from hardship is not expected until after death. "Swing Low, Sweet Chariot" does not, therefore, have a "rebellious" feel to it. Students may say that faith in God and Heaven are an important part of the mood of the spiritual. For "Go Down, Moses," students should recognize that the spiritual speaks of the possibility of freedom during life by its recounting the story of Moses and the enslaved Israelites' escape from slavery. The mood of "Go Down, Moses," therefore, has elements of rebellion, bravery, and determination.
    Difficulty: *Average*
    Objective: *Essay*

19. Students may cite the fact that Tubman was called the Moses of her people. The repeated refrain, "Go down, Moses," could refer to Tubman's repeated trips from the North back *down* to the South to guide more people to freedom. Students may also mention that Tubman's repeated risking of her own life during her journeys paralleled the risk Moses took in standing up to the Egyptian pharaoh.
    Difficulty: *Challenging*
    Objective: *Essay*

20. Students might note that the idea of a promised land is especially evident in "Swing Low, Sweet Chariot," in which the refrain is "Coming for to carry me home." In this spiritual "home" can be taken as freedom—escape from enslavement on the plantation—and thus finding some degree of fulfillment while on earth. The idea of "home" can also be taken as representing the next life—that even if there is no hope of freedom or equality in this world, the afterlife promises deliverance from the suffering and oppression of earthly life.
    Difficulty: *Average*
    Objective: *Interpretation*

Benchmark Test 4, p. 83

MULTIPLE CHOICE

1. ANS: A
2. ANS: D
3. ANS: B
4. ANS: B
5. ANS: D
6. ANS: A
7. ANS: C
8. ANS: D
9. ANS: C
10. ANS: A
11. ANS: D
12. ANS: C
13. ANS: A
14. ANS: C
15. ANS: B
16. ANS: C
17. ANS: B
18. ANS: A
19. ANS: D
20. ANS: C
21. ANS: A
22. ANS: A
23. ANS: D
24. ANS: B
25. ANS: B
26. ANS: D
27. ANS: C
28. ANS: A
29. ANS: B
30. ANS: A
31. ANS: D

ESSAY

32. Students should clearly state the subject of the report. They should list media, such as music CDs, photographic slides, and posters, as well as explain how these will enhance the report.

33. Essays should describe a situation in which the student changed his or her mind. The essay should include a discussion of the impact and importance of the experience.

34. Reviews should begin with general information about a movie or television program. Next, students should describe the setting and characters before summarizing the plot. Reviews should end with an opinion supported with specific information and details.

Vocabulary in Context, p. 89

MULTIPLE CHOICE

1. ANS: A
2. ANS: A
3. ANS: D
4. ANS: D
5. ANS: B
6. ANS: B
7. ANS: D
8. ANS: C
9. ANS: B
10. ANS: B
11. ANS: D
12. ANS: B
13. ANS: B
14. ANS: D
15. ANS: B
16. ANS: C
17. ANS: C
18. ANS: A
19. ANS: B
20. ANS: A

"The Gettysburg Address" by Abraham Lincoln
"Letter to His Son" by Robert E. Lee

Vocabulary Warm-up Exercises, p. 93

A.
1. arrayed
2. conceived
3. retard
4. resolve
5. establishment
6. virtuous
7. patient
8. prosperity

B. Sample Answers
1. F; People usually avert their eyes when they are lying to someone.
2. T; You might still contend you were right even if someone disagreed.
3. T; Seeing someone you like after such a long absence might be fun to anticipate.
4. T; It is best not to get too excited about one side of a situation until you have heard all the facts.
5. F; If you are engaged in a project, you would be focused on it and not easily distracted.
6. F; Most people don't want to battle with their friends and family.
7. F; If you subject an article to careful perusal, you would have a good idea what it said.
8. T; A hurricane usually inflicts miseries on those in its path.

Reading Warm-up A, p. 94

Sample Answers
1. The use of the yell was created or thought up for a special purpose; John was so creative that he conceived of projects I could never have dreamed of.
2. The physical act of yelling would help release tension and retard stress; *increase, speed up*
3. the reputation of such shouting; Once he and his officers had finished the *establishment* of their priorities, they were able to begin their tasks.
4. to holler for the duration of their charge, minutes at a time; People often *resolve* to go on a diet and lose weight.
5. in long, neat lines in front of troops standing shoulder to shoulder; Books on shelves might be *arrayed* alphabetically.
6. The soldiers they commanded; George Washington is considered *virtuous* because he was a successful general and the first President of the United States.
7. steeds; I had to be *patient* when I waited for my parents to pick me up after the party.
8. Because now people can afford phones and computers; *Prosperity* signifies enough money to live and sometimes even signifies substantial wealth.

Reading Warm-up B, p. 95

Sample Answers
1. War often causes miseries and hardship for millions of people; *deprivation, suffering*.
2. Soldiers on both sides in the Civil War experienced the same type of suffering and separation from families and friends; The positions of the two sides were so far apart that *strife* seemed certain.
3. No; they were bored.
4. held back; There was nothing to do about the situation, so it was healthier for them to show *restraint* with their emotions.
5. (when battles would happen); I always anticipate my cousin's visits with pleasure.
6. assertions; Even after the judge found against her, she continued to contend that she was right.
7. on activities that provided entertainment; To *avert* the traffic jam, the car took an alternative route to work.
8. reading up on; *a book, a Web site*

Literary Analysis: Diction, p. 96

1. A; 2. B; 3. A; 4. B; 5. B; 6. A; 7. A; 8. A

Reading Strategy: Use Background Knowledge, p. 97

Sample Answers
1. Lee admired Washington and his policies, and had a great love for his country.
2. Lee's earlier freeing of his slaves demonstrated his willingness to act on principles, regardless of their popularity.

Unit 3 Resources: Division, Reconciliation, and Expansion

3. Lee was a patriot who had served the United States in its army for a long time.

Vocabulary Builder, p. 98

A. 1. bless; 2. honor; 3. chaos; 4. moral

B. 1. C; 2. B; 3. A; 4. A

Enrichment: Music, p. 100

Sample Answer

"Imagine" by John Lennon. *Lyrics:* ". . . Imagine there's no countries, / It isn't hard to do, / nothing to kill or die for, / No religion too, / Imagine all the people / living life in peace . . ." *Comparison:* The song describes a world without the political tensions leading to war, a world in which people are united by love. Its themes are similar to Lee's hatred of war and Lincoln's belief in equality for all, but contrast with Lincoln's passion about defending freedom to the death.

Open-Book Test, p. 101

Short Answer

1. The phrase "four score and seven years ago" reminds the audience of the history of the nation. The word "equal" reminds them of the ideals on which the nation was founded.
   Difficulty: *Challenging*   **Objective:** *Interpretation*

2. The phrase "eighty-seven years ago" would have made the diction less formal. Students might suggest that Lincoln chose the more formal diction to suit the solemn occasion of the dedication of a battlefield cemetery.
   Difficulty: *Easy*   **Objective:** *Literary Analysis*

3. Students might suggest that Lincoln is implying that giving their lives for their country makes the soldiers worthier people than those who have come to honor them.
   Difficulty: *Average*   **Objective:** *Interpretation*

4. Sample answers: Actions speak louder than words; It's easier to talk the talk than to walk the walk; Deeds are more important than words.
   Difficulty: *Easy*   **Objective:** *Literary Analysis*

5. Knowing the huge scope of the battle and the massive casualties suffered by both sides in the Battle of Gettysburg would help a reader to gain a deeper understanding of Lincoln's solemn tone and his deep respect for the sacrifices of the fallen soldiers.
   Difficulty: *Easy*   **Objective:** *Reading*

6. This ending shows that Lincoln hoped to inspire his audience to continue to support the war effort by reminding them that the Union was fighting to preserve the great ideals on which the country was founded.
   Difficulty: *Challenging*   **Objective:** *Interpretation*

7. The diction of these first two lines—with words and phrases such as "perusal" and "wreck of his mighty labors"—is more formal than the diction one would normally expect in a letter from a father to a son. Students might suggest that Lee chose this more formal

diction because he was writing about great historical events rather than about personal or family matters.
   Difficulty: *Average*   **Objective:** *Literary Analysis*

8. Students might suggest that Lee does not wish to fight either to preserve or split the Union. He will fight only in self-defense, as a last resort.
   Difficulty: *Average*   **Objective:** *Interpretation*

9. Sample Answers: Pro-Union arguments: "But I can anticipate no greater calamity for the country than a dissolution of the Union"; "Secession is nothing but revolution"; "It [the Union] was intended for 'perpetual union' . . . " Anti-Union arguments: "The South, in my opinion, has been aggrieved by the acts of the North, as you say"; "Still, a Union that can only be maintained by swords and bayonets, and in which strife and civil war are to take the place of brotherly love and kindness, has no charm for me."
   Difficulty: *Average*   **Objective:** *Interpretation*

10. The classroom atmosphere would not be orderly, because *anarchy* means "absence of order."
    Difficulty: *Average*   **Objective:** *Vocabulary*

Essay

11. Students might suggest that Lincoln means that the Union soldiers died at Gettysburg so that the Union could continue and not be split into two countries. By citing their noble spirit of ultimate sacrifice, he is trying to inspire the audience to continue to make lesser sacrifices to ensure the survival of the Union and the democratic ideals on which it was founded.
    Difficulty: *Easy*   **Objective:** *Essay*

12. Students might note that neither Lincoln nor Lee wanted civil war or secession. Both highly valued the Union and wanted to preserve it if possible. They might also note that Lincoln was determined to preserve it at all costs, whereas Lee was willing to preserve it only if it could be done peacefully. They might also note that Lee felt that the North had "aggrieved" the South, whereas Lincoln would take the opposite view.
    Difficulty: *Average*   **Objective:** *Essay*

13. Students might note that both men were highly principled, with strong convictions about what they considered the right course for their country. Both men were determined to act out of principle rather than personal convenience or advantage. Both believed in personal sacrifice on behalf of one's principles and ideals. Lincoln seemed to be more determined to use force to enforce his beliefs, whereas Lee believed in force only in self-defense. Both seem to be men of religious belief, because both make reference to God.
    Difficulty: *Challenging*   **Objective:** *Essay*

14. Most students will feel that Lincoln and Lee are both equally patriotic. Both Lincoln and Lee express concern for the preservation of the Union and its founding ideals. Lincoln, however, seems to believe that the

Union is worth preserving at all costs, whereas Lee expresses doubts about a Union that can be maintained only by force of arms. Some students might argue, however, that Lee ironically makes the best argument that not all viewpoints are patriotic when he states, "Secession is nothing but revolution"—and therefore a kind of treason. Here he makes it clear that some forms of dissent are regarded as betraying the interests of one's country and therefore cannot be considered patriotic.

Difficulty: *Average* **Objective:** *Essay*

Oral Response

15. Oral responses should be clear, well organized, and well supported by appropriate examples from the selections.

Difficulty: *Average* **Objective:** *Oral Interpretation*

Selection Test A, p. 104

Critical Reading

1. ANS: B	DIF: Easy	OBJ: Comprehension
2. ANS: D	DIF: Easy	OBJ: Interpretation
3. ANS: C	DIF: Easy	OBJ: Reading Strategy
4. ANS: B	DIF: Easy	OBJ: Literary Analysis
5. ANS: B	DIF: Easy	OBJ: Reading Strategy
6. ANS: C	DIF: Easy	OBJ: Reading Strategy
7. ANS: C	DIF: Easy	OBJ: Reading Strategy
8. ANS: A	DIF: Easy	OBJ: Interpretation
9. ANS: A	DIF: Easy	OBJ: Comprehension
10. ANS: B	DIF: Easy	OBJ: Comprehension

Vocabulary

11. ANS: D	DIF: Easy	OBJ: Vocabulary
12. ANS: B	DIF: Easy	OBJ: Vocabulary

Essay

13. Students' essays may reflect that Lincoln means to suggest that the Union soldiers who died at Gettysburg died so that the Union could continue and not be split into two countries. He is asking for support.

Difficulty: *Easy*

Objective: *Essay*

14. Students' essays should reflect that Lee agreed with his son that the North had acted aggressively toward the South. He also said he would sacrifice everything except honor to keep the Union intact. Students may suggest that the actions of the North were such that Lee finally felt he was honor bound to defend the Confederacy.

Difficulty: *Easy*

Objective: *Essay*

15. Most students recognize that answering the question of what is best for the country is neither simple nor

obvious. Even the most patriotic people, like Lincoln and Lee, disagreed. Lincoln, for example, seemed to believe that the Union is worth preserving at all costs. Lee, on the other hand, seemed to doubt whether a Union that must be preserved by war is best for the people.

Difficulty: *Easy*

Objective: *Interpretation*

Selection Test B, p. 107

Critical Reading

1. ANS: C	DIF: Easy	OBJ: Comprehension
2. ANS: B	DIF: Average	OBJ: Interpretation
3. ANS: B	DIF: Average	OBJ: Literary Analysis
4. ANS: C	DIF: Challenging	OBJ: Comprehension
5. ANS: C	DIF: Challenging	OBJ: Interpretation
6. ANS: A	DIF: Average	OBJ: Comprehension
7. ANS: B	DIF: Easy	OBJ: Comprehension
8. ANS: D	DIF: Average	OBJ: Interpretation
9. ANS: A	DIF: Easy	OBJ: Reading Strategy
10. ANS: B	DIF: Easy	OBJ: Literary Analysis
11. ANS: A	DIF: Challenging	OBJ: Reading Strategy
12. ANS: B	DIF: Challenging	OBJ: Reading Strategy
13. ANS: B	DIF: Challenging	OBJ: Comprehension

Vocabulary

14. ANS: A	DIF: Average	OBJ: Vocabulary
15. ANS: D	DIF: Average	OBJ: Vocabulary
16. ANS: C	DIF: Average	OBJ: Vocabulary
17. ANS: A	DIF: Average	OBJ: Vocabulary

Essay

18. Students should provide details to show that Lincoln and Lee both wished to preserve the Union at all costs. For example, they might include Lee's statement ". . . I can anticipate no greater calamity for the country than a dissolution of the Union" or Lincoln's attempt at Gettysburg to inspire new devotion to the Union.

Difficulty: *Easy*

Objective: *Essay*

19. Lincoln will likely be described as a humble, idealistic, God-fearing man. Lee will likely be described as a passionate, emotional, and extremely loyal man. However, accept any characterization that is well supported with details from the text.

Difficulty: *Challenging*

Objective: *Essay*

20. Most students will feel that Lincoln and Lee are both equally patriotic. Both Lincoln and Lee express concern for the preservation of the Union and its founding ideals. Lincoln, however, seems to believe that the Union is

worth preserving at all costs, whereas Lee expresses doubts about a Union that can be maintained only by force of arms. Some students might argue, however, that Lee ironically makes the best argument that not all viewpoints are patriotic when he states, "Secession is nothing but revolution"—and therefore a kind of treason. Here he makes it clear that some forms of dissent are regarded as betraying the interests of one's country and therefore cannot be considered patriotic.

Difficulty: *Average*

Objective: *Interpretation*

Contemporary Commentary

Nell Irvin Painter Introduces "An Account of an Experience with Discrimination"
by Sojourner Truth, p. 110

Sample Answers

1. Sojourner Truth served with a volunteer group of anti-slavery women who helped poor people from the battlefields of Virginia and from slaveholding Maryland.

2. She told how one streetcar conductor had not stopped for her and how another conductor had tried to push her from the platform of the car.

3. The first American history is that of Washington, D.C., a Southern city. The second American history is that of discrimination against African Americans throughout the United States.

4. It was national in scope because racial discrimination was national.

5. Frederick Douglass: traded blows with conductors who tried to push him out of his seat. Harriet Tubman: suffered shoulder injuries when she was dragged out of her seat and thrown into the baggage car. Frances Ellen Watkins Harper: experienced humiliating conflicts on streetcars and railroads.

6. Sample questions: What kinds of source material do you find most useful? What areas of research would you recommend to a young historian today?

Nell Irvin Painter

Listening and Viewing, p. 111

Sample answers and guidelines for evaluation:

Segment 1: Nell Irvin Painter's interest in history developed while she studied abroad in France and Africa and began to ask herself questions about her own country's history. Students may answer that historians write about significant events and people of the past. Their writings are important to society because they explain, clarify, and analyze past events for a modern-day audience.

Segment 2: Sojourner Truth was a preacher, an abolitionist, and a feminist who became an important national symbol during the Civil War. Nell Irvin Painter wants her audience to know that Truth was born and raised in New York, which

was then a slave state. She also did not say "Aren't I a woman?" at a convention, as she has been famously quoted for over a century.

Segment 3: Primary sources are documents that are intimate to an event and the people directly involved in the event; they are often more personal, emotional, and detailed than sources written by people many years later. These sources are important to Nell Irvin Painter's work because the information in her book must be as accurate as possible.

Segment 4: Nell Irvin Painter believes that it is important for students not to take the first thing they are told as fact but instead to look at it critically, realizing that there are many layers and that history is much more complicated. Students may answer that they can learn more about a historical event or era and get a more personal, intimate account of history from a different perspective.

"An Account of an Experience with Discrimination" by Sojourner Truth

Vocabulary Warm-up Exercises, p. 113

A. 1. streetcar
2. succeeded
3. company
4. dragged
5. ascended
6. clenching
7. platform
8. conductor

B. **Sample Answers**

1. T; If robbers are on video they would likely be *arrested* quickly.

2. F; An act of *violence* hurts someone.

3. T; Food and water are *necessities* of life.

4. T; A victim of *assault and battery* will likely have to go to the hospital.

5. F; If you react *furiously,* an insult really bothers you.

6. T; A person would be angry after having been *mistreated.*

7. T; If a dog is hit by a car, it would likely be *lame.*

8. F; If you have faith in *humanity,* you believe that people are basically good.

Reading Warm-up A, p. 114

Sample Answers

1. being very quiet right after dinner; *failed*

2. (his hands); *squeezing, clasping*

3. to the train station; no, there are no streetcars where I live.

4. (with only a few other early riders); my friends, some family

5. stepped on, climbed in; a small flat panel that you step on to get into something

6. (climbed the stairs); He *ascended* the mountain to see the view from the top.

7. (took their tickets and greeted them); streetcars

8. all the cars in the long train; Thomas *dragged* his back-pack along the hall.

Reading Warm-up B, p. 115

Sample Answers

1. his cow or his slave; *injured, crippled*

2. or other crimes; assault, any crime that injures some-one or something

3. things that are needed for life; food, shelter, clothing

4. a person; people, human beings

5. a slave; No one likes to be *mistreated* by other people.

6. *Assault and battery* means attacking and hurting someone.

7. (angrily); heatedly, crossly

8. because they have committed a crime or are thought to have committed a crime; Bruce was *arrested* after two witnesses said he had robbed the bank.

Literary Analysis: Author's Purpose and Tone, p. 116

Sample Answers

1. Truth's purpose is to inform readers about an incident of discrimination. Her purpose is clear because she gives specific, precise information about the incident, such as whom she was with and what exactly she was doing when the incident occurred.

2. Truth's tone is measured and calm, factual but not inflammatory. Words such as "I ascended the platform," "the conductor pushed me," and "I told I was not going off" are matter of fact, not passionate or angry.

3. Neither the author's purpose nor tone change in the course of the report. Truth's purpose throughout is to inform readers, and her language remains the same.

Reading Strategy: Identify Relevant Details and Facts, p. 117

Sample Answers

1. conductor of a streetcar; refused to stop his car for me

2. dismissed him; take the number of the car whenever I was mistreated

3. get a ride without trouble; with another friend

4. conductor pushed me; "Go back—get off here."

5. "Does she belong to you?"; "she belongs to humanity."

6. hard for the old slaveholding spirit to die; die it must.

Vocabulary Builder, p. 118

A. 1. Sojourner Truth *ascended* the steps to enter the streetcar.

2. The conductor denied that he had made an *assault* against Truth.

B. 1. A; 2. D

Enrichment: Personal Account versus Dramatic Account, p. 120

Student answers will vary, but students should recognize that the personal account is direct and to-the-point. The facts are given with little elaboration. Truth seems to deliberately avoid revealing her emotions or feelings of any kind while relating the events. On the other hand, the account remains personal, one person's view. The conductor or one of her companions might relate other facts or interpret them in other ways. A dramatic version of the incidents could both strengthen and weaken the telling. It would almost certainly inject more passion and feelings into the story. It might also add different viewpoints. By its nature, though, a film might appear more remote, the information being second-hand and being retold at a later date. The audience might feel less confident in its authenticity.

Open-Book Test, p. 121

Short Answer

1. Although the selection does contain a number of objectively reported facts, by the end of the piece it is obvious that Truth has gathered these facts to make a persuasive argument that discrimination is wrong and should be fought. So the expectation created by the title is not borne out by the end of the piece.
   Difficulty: *Challenging*   **Objective:** *Literary Analysis*

2. The reader can infer that Josephine was white.
   Difficulty: *Challenging*   **Objective:** *Interpretation*

3. Because Josephine reported the incident to the president of the streetcar company, one can infer that she was a compassionate, principled woman who stood up for the rights of African Americans.
   Difficulty: *Easy*   **Objective:** *Interpretation*

4. Truth's purpose is to carefully document instances of discrimination on the public-transit system so that the company president and the legal system can address them.
   Difficulty: *Average*   **Objective:** *Literary Analysis*

5. These details and facts allow the reader to conclude that Sojourner Truth was concerned not just about her own welfare but also about the well-being of others, especially those in need, such as patients in hospitals.
   Difficulty: *Easy*   **Objective:** *Reading*

6. Truth refuses to be put off the streetcar despite being physically assaulted by the streetcar conductor. Her refusal to be intimidated by words or force shows that she was a woman not only of great principle but also of great courage and fearlessness.
   Difficulty: *Average*   **Objective:** *Interpretation*

7. The question shows that even after the Emancipation Proclamation, many whites still assumed that African Americans were the property of whites.
   Difficulty: *Average*   **Objective:** *Interpretation*

8. The two incidents show that Truth believed in trying to assert her civil rights and, if they were denied, working patiently and peacefully within the legal system to gain these rights.
   Difficulty: *Average*   **Objective:** *Interpretation*

9. Truth's tone shifts only in the last two sentences. These two sentences strongly express a point of view, whereas the rest of the selection reports facts.
   Difficulty: *Challenging*   **Objective:** *Literary Analysis*

10. You would be coming from the first floor, because *ascended* means "moved upward."
    Difficulty: *Average*   **Objective:** *Vocabulary*

Essay

11. Sojourner Truth's encounters with the streetcar conductors show that in 1865 there was still considerable prejudice against blacks; the second streetcar conductor clearly exemplified "the old slaveholding spirit" when he asked Mrs. Haviland about Truth, "Does she belong to you?" But Truth's friendships with Josephine Griffing and Mrs. Haviland, and the firing of the two conductors by the streetcar company's president, show that there were white people of that time who supported the struggle of African Americans for freedom, equality, and civil rights.
    Difficulty: *Easy*   **Objective:** *Essay*

12. The selection shows first of all that Sojourner Truth was a woman of great determination. Just because she was kicked off the streetcar the first time, she did not become discouraged but attempted to board again on another occasion. The second attempt shows that she was a woman of great courage, because she resisted and held onto the platform even as the conductor tried to shove her off. She was also a woman of action—in both cases she took whatever measures she could to be sure that the offending conductors paid for their racism. But the selection shows that she was not concerned only about her own welfare—her work for the Freedman's Hospital shows that she was a compassionate person who cared about the welfare of all those in need.
    Difficulty: *Average*   **Objective:** *Essay*

13. Students might note that African Americans have made major strides since 1865 in the areas of civil rights, the right to use public accommodations, and recognition of their equal legal status. They might also note, however, that despite this progress on the legal front, many African Americans still fight against forms of racism that prevent them from enjoying the same opportunities for economic and social advancement as other Americans.
    Difficulty: *Challenging*   **Objective:** *Essay*

14. Students might argue that Martin Luther King, Jr., Malcolm X, and Nelson Mandela are examples of more recent figures who courageously and eloquently wrote, spoke out about, and acted against the injustices that prevailed in their day. On other issues, students might

mention Al Gore's stand on global warming, Elie Wiesel's on the Holocaust and antisemitism, and Jimmy Carter,s on issues of world peace.
Difficulty: *Average*   **Objective:** *Essay*

Oral Response

15. Oral response should be clear, well organized, and well supported by appropriate examples from the selections.
    Difficulty: *Average*   **Objective:** *Oral Interpretation*

Selection Test A, p. 124

Critical Reading

1. ANS: D	DIF: Easy	OBJ: Comprehension
2. ANS: B	DIF: Easy	OBJ: *Reading Strategy*
3. ANS: A	DIF: Easy	OBJ: *Comprehension*
4. ANS: B	DIF: Easy	OBJ: Comprehension
5. ANS: C	DIF: Easy	OBJ: Comprehension
6. ANS: C	DIF: Easy	OBJ: Comprehension
7. ANS: A	DIF: Easy	OBJ: *Interpretation*
8. ANS: B	DIF: Easy	OBJ: Comprehension
9. ANS: D	DIF: Easy	OBJ: Literary Analysis
10. ANS: A	DIF: Easy	OBJ: *Literary Analysis*

Vocabulary

11. ANS: A	DIF: Easy	OBJ: Vocabulary
12. ANS: B	DIF: Easy	OBJ: Vocabulary

Essay

13. Both women are white and are friends of Truth's. Truth describes them as friends. We can infer they are white because neither has trouble getting on the streetcar but Truth, who is with them, is not permitted on because she is black. We can also infer that both women are strong-willed and believe in equality because in both cases, they stand up for their friend and try to see that she is treated fairly and equally.
    Difficulty: *Easy*
    Objective: *Essay*

14. She means that the discrimination and inequality displayed in the two incidents she describes are a result of the attitude people had toward slaves and which has not ended even though the institution of slavery itself has ended. Many white people still treat her as a second-class human being in spite of the fact that she is free and equal to them in the face of the law.
    Difficulty: *Easy*
    Objective: *Essay*

15. Students might name Martin Luther King, Jr., Malcolm X, and Nelson Mandela as writers and activists who have spoken up about injustices in recent times. They might name Al Gore, who spoke out about global warming, and Rachel Carson, who spoke out about pollution. They might mention Jimmy Carter, who has worked for

world peace, and Elie Wiesel, who spoke out on the Holocaust.

Difficulty: *Easy*

Objective: *Essay*

Selection Test B, p. 127

Critical Reading

1. ANS: A	DIF: Easy	OBJ: Reading Strategy
2. ANS: C	DIF: Average	OBJ: Literary Analysis
3. ANS: B	DIF: Average	OBJ: Comprehension
4. ANS: C	DIF: Easy	OBJ: Comprehension
5. ANS: A	DIF: Average	OBJ: Comprehension
6. ANS: B	DIF: Average	OBJ: Interpretation
7. ANS: A	DIF: Easy	OBJ: Comprehension
8. ANS: D	DIF: Challenging	OBJ: Interpretation
9. ANS: B	DIF: Average	OBJ: Reading Strategy
10. ANS: C	DIF: Challenging	OBJ: Literary Analysis

Vocabulary and Grammar

11. ANS: A	DIF: Average	OBJ: Vocabulary
12. ANS: B	DIF: Average	OBJ: Vocabulary

Essay

13. Some people, such as the conductors, were extremely prejudiced and discriminated against African Americans. For example, they both tried to prevent Truth from riding their streetcars. Others, such as Truth's two friends and the president of the company, opposed these attitudes and practices and tried to ensure that Truth was treated fairly and equally. Truth's friends took active part in protecting Truth and in complaining to the streetcar company. The president of the company fired the two conductors and encouraged Truth to report any further problems.

Difficulty: *Average*

Objective: *Essay*

14. The conductor's question implied that Truth was a slave, someone who could be owned by someone else. This attitude—that one human could be owned by another—demonstrates the "old slaveholding spirit" that Truth insists must die.

Difficulty: *Challenging*

Objective: *Essay*

15. Students might argue that Martin Luther King, Jr., Malcolm X, and Nelson Mandela are examples of more recent figures who courageously and eloquently wrote, spoke out about, and acted against the injustices that prevailed in their day. On other issues, students might mention Al Gore on global warming, Elie Wiesel on the Holocaust and antisemitism, and Jimmy Carter on issues of world peace.

Difficulty: *Average*

Objective: *Essay*

"The Boys' Ambition" *from* Life on the Mississippi and "The Notorious Jumping Frog of Calaveras County" by Mark Twain

Vocabulary Warm-up Exercises, p. 131

A.
1. narrative
2. sociable
3. humbly
4. withstand
5. compliance
6. monotonous
7. deliberate
8. contribution

B. Sample Answers
1. A shy person or someone who really wanted to fit in would hate to be *conspicuous*.
2. I would rather have comfort than *grandeur* because I have to live there all the time.
3. Loud thunder makes a storm *impressive*, and so does lightning and a lot of wind and rain.
4. No, because I would get bored if I was *indifferent* about football.
5. Kids *loathe* bedtime because they don't want to miss any fun.
6. I don't think so, because why would they want to help hungry people if they were *ruthless*?
7. The phone ringing all the time makes life less *tranquil*, although it might make me feel more *tranquil* to know people could call me if they wanted to.
8. Exchange students are more *transient* because they go back home after not too long.

Reading Warm-up A, p. 132

Sample Answers
1. (books); A poem or short story could also be a *contribution* to literature.
2. (slow); The opposite of *deliberate* speaking might be "babbling" or "chattering."
3. (outgoing); Yes, because celebrities need to be *sociable* to deal with fans and reporters.
4. endless round of dinners and events; "Exciting" or "fun" could be the opposite of *monotonous*.
5. (fame); *Humbly* means "not in a conceited way."
6. tried to behave "properly"; A teacher or police officer might require *compliance*.
7. (whole last paragraph); Yes, because a *narrative*, or story, can be true or made-up.
8. her pleading; They might not be able to *withstand* peer pressure.

Reading Warm-up B, p. 133

Sample Answers

1. (awe, admiring); *Grandeur* means "magnificence."

2. recognize every landmark for twelve hundred miles, by day or by night; It's *impressive* because twelve hundred miles is a huge distance, and landmarks are hard to see at night.

3. (tree); A large snow bank, for instance, would be *transient*.

4. actually filled with hidden hazards; A person who is relaxing might be *tranquil*.

5. a "faint dimple" on the water's surface; A grizzly bear would be *conspicuous* in a classroom.

6. being awoken in the middle of the night to take over at the helm; "Love" or "adore" would be the opposite of *loathe*.

7. (mockery); If the pilot were not *ruthless*, he might be kind to Clemens instead of insulting him.

8. the scenic beauty of the Mississippi; *Indifferent* means "not caring much one way or another."

Twain Biography, p. 134

A. Sample Answers

Life on the River: Grew up along the Mississippi; loved it so much he took his pen name from a river boatman's term; became a riverboat pilot at a young age. Photograph: Mississippi River steamboat.

A Traveling Man: Traveled west and worked as journalist; his first story, "The Notorious Jumping Frog of Calaveras County," made him famous; Used his Western adventures and childhood on the Mississippi as ideas for his books. Photograph: Jumping frog contest in the Old West.

A Restless Soul: Traveled widely in his later years; lost his wife and three children; became pessimistic about people and society. Photograph: Twain giving a lecture before a crowd of people in Great Britain.

B. Sample Answers

Twain: No, I wasn't really serious, but you know the Mississippi always meant a lot to me. There's so much interesting life along that river—people and places—and of course it's always changing. Spending life as a riverboat pilot would have been a good life, a fascinating life.

Twain: Humor is at the heart of my writing. It's not the most important thing, perhaps, but the rest of it, all the ideas and people, would have been empty and dull creations without the humor.

Twain: Americans are impossible to define. There is every kind of person in America. You'll find the finest, most principled characters and the most flawed and ridiculous characters right here. That diversity is what makes Americans and this great country such a fascinating place for an observer of human nature to live in.

Literary Analysis: Humor, p. 135

1. dialect and sense of human foibles
2. dialect, hyperbole, sense of human foibles
3. dialect
4. dialect
5. incongruities

Reading Strategy: Understand Regional Dialect, p. 136

Sample Answers

1. He was so strange about betting that he would bet on anything. He would even bet the opposite of his original bet if he couldn't persuade anyone else to.

2. Smiley had a mare. Others called the mare the fifteen-minute nag, but only to tease. They called her that because naturally she was faster than that. Smiley used to win money by betting on that horse, even though she was slow and always seemed to have something wrong with her.

3. The dog didn't look like he was worth much. You wouldn't expect the dog to do much except lie around, look mean, and wait for a chance to steal something. But as soon as someone bet money on that dog, he seemed to become another dog entirely. His jaw would stick out like the front of a steamboat does, and his teeth would suddenly show and shine like the steamboat's burning furnaces.

4. Suddenly he would grab the other dog by the joint of its hind leg. He would freeze his jaw on that leg, not biting or chewing on it, but just gripping and hanging on. He would hang on until people stopped him, even if it took a year.

Vocabulary Builder, p. 137

A. 1. monolingual; 2. monoplegia; 3. monosyllable; 4. monosomic

B. 1. D; 2. G; 3. A; 4. F; 5. C; 6. B; 7. E

Grammar and Style: Fixing Misplaced and Dangling Modifiers, p. 138

A. 1. The steamboat that arrived at the landing was the first that day; steamboat

2. Waiting his turn, the man inspected the frog carefully; man

3. The gentlemen stood lost in thought; gentleman

4. Looking carefully at his frog, he realized something was wrong; he

5. The man who got the last laugh knew better than to stay around town; man

B. 1. Laughing heartily, the crowd cheered for the winning frog.

2. Correct

3. Eager to see the steamboat arrive, the boys left their chores undone.

4. Correct

5. He often exaggerated stories while he was working as a reporter.

Enrichment: Jargon, p. 140

Students should choose a job either that they have done themselves or with which they are very familiar (a parent's job that they've visited, for example). Students should choose several different words to fill out the chart and be able to give each word a specific definition.

Open-Book Test, p. 141

Short Answer

1. The steamboat's arrival was the high point of each day, and the large vessel always seemed imposing and glamorous.

   Difficulty: *Average*   **Objective:** *Interpretation*

2. He says that his father "could hang anybody that offended him."

   Difficulty: *Average*   **Objective:** *Literary Analysis*

3. The main impression is of a sleepy Southern town that comes to life only when the steamboat arrives. After the steamboat leaves, the town goes back to being sleepy.

   Difficulty: *Challenging*   **Objective:** *Interpretation*

4. Twain is jealous of the boy who gets a job as an engineer's apprentice. The humorous effect comes from Twain's claiming that the injustice of this situation shakes the foundation of his religious beliefs because a boy who was evidently ill-behaved ("worldly") enjoys a better fate than a well-behaved boy like Twain.

   Difficulty: *Challenging*   **Objective:** *Literary Analysis*

5. Twain ran away from home because his parents would not let him pursue his ambition of becoming a riverboat pilot.

   Difficulty: *Easy*   **Objective:** *Interpretation*

6. Sample answers: "I called on good-natured, garrulous old . . ."; he expected that Wheeler would "bore me to death" with a "tedious" remembrance that would be "useless" to Twain; the effort to trick Wheeler by using a name that will remind him of something else; Wheeler "backed me into a corner" and "blockaded" Twain; he "reeled off the monotonous" version that follows.

   Difficulty: *Average*   **Objective:** *Literary Analysis*

7. Sample answers: feller (man); warn't (wasn't); curiousest (most curious); uncommon lucky (unusually lucky); ary (any); foller (follow); resk (risk or bet).

   Difficulty: *Challenging*   **Objective:** *Reading*

8. Smiley is hoping to convince the stranger to bet on how well Dan'l could jump.

   Difficulty: *Average*   **Objective:** *Interpretation*

9. In telling the tale with such seriousness and earnestness, Wheeler obviously has no idea how ridiculous the story is.

   Difficulty: *Average*   **Objective:** *Literary Analysis*

10. You would probably have failed the test, because *conjectured* means "guessed; inferred from inconclusive evidence."

    Difficulty: *Average*   **Objective:** *Vocabulary*

Essay

11. Students might note that for boys living in a small town along a large river, working on a steamboat would have been an exciting life. It would have taken them to distant places and given them the opportunity to meet many new people and have new experiences.

    Difficulty: *Easy*   **Objective:** *Essay*

12. Students might note that each of the animals may have had a skill of some kind, but that none of them could do what Wheeler says they could do. For example, the dog probably was a tough fighter, but it is doubtful that it lay down and died when it lost a fight. Likewise, it is doubtful that anyone could train a frog to perform Olympian feats of jumping in the precise, predictable manner described in the story.

    Difficulty: *Average*   **Objective:** *Essay*

13. Wheeler is the main character—the person around whom the story revolves. Though he is not the subject of his own narrative, he drives the action of the story, and his interpretation and telling of the events give the story its humorous tone. In fact, it is Wheeler's deadly serious retelling of plainly preposterous events that lends the story its charm and makes of him an original character—a simple country man with a feverish imagination.

    Difficulty: *Challenging*   **Objective:** *Essay*

14. Students might note that the two selections by Twain evoke the uniquely American atmosphere of the nineteenth century—the small town full of quirky individualists and big dreamers with oversized ambitions. Students might also note that this picture does not express the truth of contemporary America, where small towns have been turned into suburbs and individuality has been ironed out by the sameness of mass merchandising and the uniform images of the mass media. Students might be hard pressed to think of artists who have evoked the American experience of our own day as effectively as Twain did in his, although some might mention figures such as Bob Dylan, Bruce Springsteen, and Alice Walker. Any figure should be accepted as long as the student's choices are supported by reasonable arguments and examples.

    Difficulty: *Average*   **Objective:** *Essay*

Oral Response

15. Oral responses should be clear, well organized, and well supported by appropriate examples from the selections.

    Difficulty: *Average*   **Objective:** *Oral Interpretation*

Selection Test A, p. 144

Critical Reading

1. ANS: A   DIF: Easy   OBJ: Comprehension
2. ANS: C   DIF: Easy   OBJ: Interpretation
3. ANS: B   DIF: Easy   OBJ: Literary Analysis
4. ANS: D   DIF: Easy   OBJ: Comprehension
5. ANS: B   DIF: Easy   OBJ: Literary Analysis
6. ANS: B   DIF: Easy   OBJ: Reading Strategy
7. ANS: A   DIF: Easy   OBJ: Literary Analysis
8. ANS: C   DIF: Easy   OBJ: Reading Strategy
9. ANS: A   DIF: Easy   OBJ: Interpretation
10. ANS: B   DIF: Easy   OBJ: Reading Strategy

Vocabulary and Grammar

11. ANS: B   DIF: Easy   OBJ: Vocabulary
12. ANS: C   DIF: Easy   OBJ: Grammar

Essay

13. Students' essays might reflect that for boys living in a small town along a large river, being a steamboatman would have been an exciting life. It would have taken them to distant places and given them the opportunity to meet many new people and have new experiences.

    Difficulty: *Easy*

    Objective: *Essay*

14. Students' essays may reflect that each of the animals may have had a skill of some kind, but that none of them could do what Wheeler says they could do. For example, the dog probably was a tough fighter, but it is doubtful that it lay down and died when it lost a fight. Writers use exaggeration to provide humor and make a story more interesting to the reader.

    Difficulty: *Easy*

    Objective: *Essay*

15. Students should realize that the two selections by Twain paint a picture of America as it was in the nineteenth century. Students should note that the landscape has changed dramatically in over 100 years. Cars, electric power, Interstates, and all the other trappings of contemporary America have forever altered the towns and cities of America. They should, however, realize that many of the same kinds of personalities that Twain described still decorate today's society; people never really change.

    Difficulty: *Easy*

    Objective: *Essay*

Selection Test B, p. 147

Critical Reading

1. ANS: C   DIF: Easy   OBJ: Interpretation
2. ANS: B   DIF: Challenging   OBJ: Comprehension
3. ANS: B   DIF: Challenging   OBJ: Interpretation
4. ANS: A   DIF: Average   OBJ: Reading Strategy
5. ANS: D   DIF: Average   OBJ: Interpretation
6. ANS: C   DIF: Challenging   OBJ: Interpretation
7. ANS: D   DIF: Challenging   OBJ: Literary Analysis
8. ANS: D   DIF: Average   OBJ: Literary Analysis
9. ANS: B   DIF: Easy   OBJ: Reading Strategy
10. ANS: A   DIF: Average   OBJ: Interpretation
11. ANS: D   DIF: Average   OBJ: Reading Strategy
12. ANS: C   DIF: Challenging   OBJ: Interpretation
13. ANS: A   DIF: Average   OBJ: Literary Analysis

Vocabulary and Grammar

14. ANS: B   DIF: Average   OBJ: Vocabulary
15. ANS: B   DIF: Average   OBJ: Vocabulary
16. ANS: D   DIF: Average   OBJ: Grammar
17. ANS: A   DIF: Average   OBJ: Vocabulary

Essay

18. Students should state that Simon Wheeler is the main character, as he tells the story from his unique point of view. Students should define the main character as the character around whom the story revolves or on whom it focuses. Though he is not the subject of his own narrative, he drives the action of the short story, and his interpretation and telling of the events give the story its distinctive humorous tone. Students should support their response with examples from the story, including how Wheeler's storytelling is humorous, and how the very premise of the story is derived from Wheeler's actions.

    Difficulty: *Easy*

    Objective: *Essay*

19. Students should give examples of all three techniques. Examples of exaggeration include the desire to kill the apprentice engineer in "The Boys' Ambition" and Simon Wheelers's tale in "The Notorious Jumping Frog of Calaveras County." Examples of embellishment include the apprentice engineer's escape from the steamboat accident as well as several statements made by Simon Wheeler. Many examples of regional dialect can be found in the dialogue from either story.

    Difficulty: *Average*

    Objective: *Essay*

20. Students' essays should explain why the unknown has a much greater appeal than the familiar, and give one or more of these examples from "The Boys' Ambition": instances of the boys' dreaming of different careers as the "perfect" career; and the idea that life on the Mississippi River in a steamboat would be idyllic.

    Difficulty: *Challenging*

    Objective: *Essay*

21. Students might note that the two selections by Twain evoke a uniquely American atmosphere of the nineteenth

Unit 3 Resources: Division, Reconciliation, and Expansion

century—the small town full of quirky individualists and big dreamers with oversized ambitions. Students might also note that this picture does not express the truth of contemporary America, where small towns have been turned into suburbs and individuality has been ironed out by the sameness of mass merchandising and the uniform images of the mass media. Students might be hard pressed to think of artists who have evoked the American experience of our own day as effectively as Twain did in his, although some might mention figures such as Bob Dylan, Bruce Springsteen, and Alice Walker. Any figure should be accepted as long as the student's choices are supported by reasonable arguments and examples.

Difficulty: *Average*
Objective: *Essay*

from The Life and Times of the Thunderbolt Kid
by Bill Bryson

Literary Analysis: Humor, p. 150
1. human foibles
2. regional behavior
3. human foibles, hyperbole
4. incongruity
5. hyperbole, human foibles

Vocabulary Builder, p. 151
A. 1. commence; 2. questionable
B. 1. D; 2. A

Selection Test, p. 153
Critical Reading

1. ANS: D	DIF: Challenging	OBJ: Interpretation
2. ANS: D	DIF: Average	OBJ: Literary Analysis
3. ANS: C	DIF: Average	OBJ: Literary Analysis
4. ANS: B	DIF: Easy	OBJ: Comprehension
5. ANS: A	DIF: Average	OBJ: Comprehension
6. ANS: C	DIF: Average	OBJ: Comprehension
7. ANS: A	DIF: Easy	OBJ: Literary Analysis
8. ANS: B	DIF: Average	OBJ: Interpretation
9. ANS: A	DIF: Challenging	OBJ: Literary Analysis
10. ANS: C	DIF: Average	OBJ: Literary Analysis

"To Build a Fire" by Jack London

Vocabulary Warm-up Exercises, p. 156
A. 1. methodically
2. aggressively
3. circulation
4. imperative
5. likewise
6. panicky

7. floundered
8. undesirable

B. Sample Answers
1. T; Three flat tires would cause *agitation* because that is a lot of bad luck and trouble for one week.
2. T; If you are a fly, *entanglement* in a spider's web is the first step in becoming the spider's dinner.
3. F; July in Texas is really hot, which is just the opposite of *arctic*.
4. F; Getting a *penalty* is bad news for the team.
5. F; Shakespeare's plays are the reason for his lasting fame, or *immortality*.
6. T; If I had always *yearned* to travel, I would like the chance to take a trip.
7. F; *Capsizing* the life boat could cause the passengers to drown.
8. T; She *asserted* her right to have a seat on the bus just like anyone else.

Reading Warm-up A, p. 157
Sample Answers
1. being lost alone in the wilderness, hungry, cold, and unprepared; Another *undesirable* situation would be arriving at a party in a costume and finding out that it is not a costume party.
2. Sit down, take a deep breath, and think carefully; The opposite of *panicky* would be "calm" or "relaxed."
3. (carefully); I could use a pencil and paper to make a list of everything I have with me or what I need to do, which would be thinking *methodically*.
4. Instead of *likewise*, you could say "similarly" or "also."
5. that you keep your body temperature up; Before riding a bicycle downhill, it is *imperative* that you know how to brake.
6. you can lose forty percent of your heat through your head; "Motion around" means the same thing as *circulation*.
7. getting even more lost; No, because *floundered* suggests aimlessness and clumsiness.
8. (wave); A soccer player might charge down the field *aggressively*.

Reading Warm-up B, p. 158
Sample Answers
1. barking madly; Babies usually show their *agitation* by crying.
2. (frozen); *Arctic* terrain would be dangerous because you could freeze to death.
3. No woman had ever won the Iditarod; Abraham Lincoln earned *immortality* by writing the Emancipation Proclamation.
4. they dragged her through the brush; *Capsizing* the sled would be bad because she might fall off and get hurt, and the sled might be damaged.

5. struggled to keep the lines clear; A dolphin in a fishing net would be an example of an *entanglement*.

6. Riddles might have *asserted* authority by calling out commands or pulling the dogs up short.

7. The "ultimate *penalty*" would have been dying in the blizzard.

8. became the first woman to win the "Last Great Race on Earth"; Someone might *yearn* to be elected President of the United States.

Literary Analysis: Conflict, Setting, Irony, p. 159

1. external; person against nature; setting is central; no irony

2. internal; person against himself; setting is not central to conflict; ironic because he is trying to contain his fear but situation is serious.

3. external; person against another character; setting is not central to the conflict; ironic because the dog senses the severity of the situation as well as the man does

4. external; person against nature; setting is central; ironic because readers know the fire represented safety but this accident will lead to disaster

5. external; person against nature; setting is central; no irony

6. external; person against himself; setting is not central; ironic because running will not save him

7. external; person against fate;; setting is not central; no irony

Reading Strategy: Make Predictions, p. 160

Students should cite specific clues from setting, predictions based on those clues, and the actual outcomes from the text. For example, Clue: . . . [the dog] experienced a vague but menacing apprehension that subdued it and made it slink along at the man's heels . . .; Prediction: the man may not realize how dangerous the cold really is; Outcome: the dog's instincts were correct.

Vocabulary Builder, p. 161

A. Sample Answers

1. *Depend* means to hang down or from something else. Going to the cabin hangs upon the weather.

2. *Appendix* is a section of a book that extends from the end of the book. Special words are often put in the appendix at the end.

3. To *suspend* something is to hang something from something else. You might suspend, or hang, a bird feeder from a branch.

B. 1. C; 2. D; 3. D; 4. C 5. C

Grammar and Style: Using Introductory Phrases and Clauses, p. 162

Sample Answers

A. 1. To build a fire in the snow and bitter cold, he worked carefully.

2. When he called to it, the dog avoided him.

3. When he called to it, he knew he could not survive.

4. In the warm cabin, his friends stayed warm and thought about their friend on the trail.

5. After his feet became soaked in the cold stream, he had to act quickly to save his life.

B. 1. Because he was alone in the wilderness, the traveler relied upon his dog.

2. On such bitter cold days, experienced Alaskans stayed inside.

3. With his matches gone, he could not build a fire.

4. When the snow put out the fire, he nearly panicked.

5. To keep warm, he walked quickly along the trail.

Enrichment: Films About Survival, p. 164

As students watch films that deal with survival under challenging conditions, they should keep the character traits and fate of the man in "To Build a Fire" in mind. For example, in a scene at the beginning of *Return of the Jedi*, Han Solo and Luke Skywalker are caught outside the shelter at night, where conditions are very cold and harsh. Solo finds Luke, who had been injured, and covers him in the entrails of a deceased mount until he has the chance to erect a shelter. Unlike the man in "To Build a Fire," they stay sheltered in one area until help arrives the next day. Han Solo's intelligence and cunning allow him and Luke to survive.

In their profiles of adaptable characters, students will probably include traits such as intelligence, forethought, and an ability to size up and react to new situations. They should support their points by citing events from "To Build a Fire" and the chosen film. For example, they might include as a trait the willingness to listen to others. The man in "To Build a Fire" did not listen to the advice of an old-timer who insisted that "no man must travel alone in the Klondike after fifty below."

Open-Book Test, p. 165

Short Answer

1. Possible response: The day was "cold and gray"; the man turned off the main trail; "an intangible pall"; "a subtle gloom."
Difficulty: *Challenging*   **Objective:** *Reading*

2. Sample answers: 1. London's clue: "He was a newcomer to the land . . . and this was his first winter"; Conclusion: He is inexperienced and thus likely to make mistakes. 2. "The trouble with him was that he was without imagination"; He will not be able to analyze and predict possible problems. 3. "He was quick and alert in the things of life but only in the things, and not in the significances"; He can perceive facts but cannot interpret them and so will ignore possible dangers. 4. He does not "meditate upon his frailty as a creature of temperature, and upon man's frailty in general"; He is overconfident about himself and human capabilities in general.
Difficulty: *Challenging*   **Objective:** *Reading*

3. Students might suggest that London wishes to show that the dog's ancient instincts for dealing with the challenges of nature are superior to a human being's perception of facts and use of reason—at least in the case of this man.

   Difficulty: *Average* **Objective:** *Interpretation*

4. The man is aware of the snow-hidden ice skins and their danger, which is why he sends the dog ahead to test the terrain. He moves quickly when he senses that he might be near an ice skin, and he listens for running water.

   Difficulty: *Average* **Objective:** *Literary Analysis*

5. The man's laughter shows a lack of awareness of how dangerously cold it is and how much trouble he could be in.

   Difficulty: *Average* **Objective:** *Literary Analysis*

6. This sentence implies that the man will have only a limited impact on the cold ("the moment"), and that he is facing a constant struggle with nature.

   Difficulty: *Average* **Objective:** *Literary Analysis*

7. The man experiences a conflict between emotions of hope that he will somehow get back to camp and resignation to/dread of his impending doom.

   Difficulty: *Average* **Objective:** *Literary Analysis*

8. The man treats the dog as an object, showing it only anger and authority, but no affection. He even has thoughts of sacrificing the dog at the end to save himself. These actions show that the man is devoid of compassion and underestimates the dog's natural instincts of self-preservation.

   Difficulty: *Average* **Objective:** *Interpretation*

9. Sample answers: At the beginning of the story, the narrator states that the man lacks imagination and an ability to interpret facts. He is also overconfident, so he lacks the humility to know his limitations in the face of extreme weather. He also lacks respect for the judgment of others, as is shown by his repeated mocking of the advice of the old-timer. Finally, he lacks respect for the primal power of nature to overcome the limited intellectual and physical powers of humans.

   Difficulty: *Challenging* **Objective:** *Interpretation*

10. No, it would mean that you were living in an area that normally gets very little rain, because *unwonted* means "unusual; unfamiliar."

    Difficulty: *Average* **Objective:** *Vocabulary*

Essay

11. Students' responses should draw on details of the story to create a credible, imaginative portrait of the dog's thoughts and feelings about the weather conditions, the problems they face, the man's character, and its treatment by the man.

    Difficulty: *Easy* **Objective:** *Essay*

12. Students might note that without names, the man and the dog can represent all humans and all animals, respectively. They might suggest that human beings

who confront nature without respect, humility, and knowledge do not survive. The dog represents the idea that animals' instincts give them a better chance of surviving the challenges of nature than humans have, with their false pride and flawed reasoning.

   Difficulty: *Average* **Objective:** *Essay*

13. Students who were uncertain for most of the story may mention details such as the man's generally cheerful state of mind, his powers of keen observation, and his ability to make a fire at lunchtime. Students who foresaw the outcome might mention the man's ignorance of the degree of the cold, his lack of imagination, his increasingly dangerous and stupid errors, and the instincts of the dog.

   Difficulty: *Challenging* **Objective:** *Essay*

14. Students might note that the conquest of nature has always been part of humankind's quest for survival—from the hunters who had to learn to kill for their food to the farmers who had to learn to grow their food. Some students might argue that with the industrial age, humankind's assault on nature—in the form of pollution and greenhouse gases—has brought humanity and all life on earth to the brink of extinction. Others might feel that humans have the right to tame and utilize the resources provided by nature. Students should support their opinions using examples from the story.

   Difficulty: *Average* **Objective:** *Essay*

Oral Response

15. Oral responses should be clear, well organized, and well supported by appropriate examples from the selections.

    Difficulty: *Average* **Objective:** *Oral Interpretation*

Selection Test A, p. 168

Critical Reading

1. ANS: B	DIF: Easy	OBJ: Literary Analysis
2. ANS: C	DIF: Easy	OBJ: Reading Strategy
3. ANS: B	DIF: Easy	OBJ: Comprehension
4. ANS: B	DIF: Easy	OBJ: Reading Strategy
5. ANS: B	DIF: Easy	OBJ: Interpretation
6. ANS: D	DIF: Easy	OBJ: Literary Analysis
7. ANS: A	DIF: Easy	OBJ: Interpretation
8. ANS: D	DIF: Easy	OBJ: Interpretation
9. ANS: B	DIF: Easy	OBJ: Comprehension
10. ANS: A	DIF: Easy	OBJ: Literary Analysis

Vocabulary and Grammar

11. ANS: B	DIF: Easy	OBJ: Vocabulary
12. ANS: C	DIF: Easy	OBJ: Grammar

Essay

13. Students may suggest that without names, both the man and the dog can represent all humans and all animals. The writer is suggesting that human beings who confront nature without knowledge do not survive. The dog represents all animals, whose instincts give them much more chance of surviving in the natural world than humans.
    Difficulty: *Easy*
    Objective: *Essay*

14. Students' essay should reflect that the man is skilled at building and lighting a fire, but he has not taken into account that he builds the second fire under a tree laden with snow. He cannot imagine the outcome: the killing of the fire by falling snow.
    Difficulty: *Easy*
    Objective: *Essay*

15. Students may note that except in rare instances, the nature described by London is seen by few people and only rarely in the contemporary world, where people are mostly isolated from the brunt of nature. Most people, they may say, live in cities where they are protected from nature by buildings and technology that protect them from the wild elements of nature. Other students will see nature as a omnipresent threat. They may cite the violence of hurricanes, ice storms, droughts, and floods as examples of the destructive side of nature that cannot be controlled and that can affect anyone at anytime.
    Difficulty: *Easy*
    Objective: *Essay*

Selection Test B, p. 171

Critical Reading

1. ANS: C	DIF: Average	OBJ: Literary Analysis
2. ANS: C	DIF: Average	OBJ: Comprehension
3. ANS: A	DIF: Average	OBJ: Literary Analysis
4. ANS: C	DIF: Challenging	OBJ: Interpretation
5. ANS: D	DIF: Easy	OBJ: Interpretation
6. ANS: D	DIF: Average	OBJ: Reading Strategy
7. ANS: B	DIF: Challenging	OBJ: Literary Analysis
8. ANS: A	DIF: Challenging	OBJ: Interpretation
9. ANS: B	DIF: Average	OBJ: Literary Analysis
10. ANS: B	DIF: Average	OBJ: Interpretation
11. ANS: C	DIF: Average	OBJ: Reading Strategy
12. ANS: C	DIF: Easy	OBJ: Reading Strategy

Vocabulary and Grammar

13. ANS: C	DIF: Average	OBJ: Vocabulary
14. ANS: C	DIF: Average	OBJ: Grammar
15. ANS: C	DIF: Easy	OBJ: Vocabulary

Essay

16. Students should describe their challenge in as much detail as possible. They should also mention the experience of the man, showing why respect for the power of what they are challenging is also important. They might mention learning about their challenge, welcoming advice from people who have experienced similar challenges, being careful and observant, and working at keeping—and using—their heads.
    Difficulty: *Easy*
    Objective: *Essay*

17. Students should mention that the man has no more respect for the cold than he does for the dog; he feels he can subdue them both simply by asserting his human power. His attitude toward taking extra precautions is that doing so would be a sign of weakness; he does not confront nature with the imagination or intelligence that successful humans muster in place of instinct. The dog, of course, follows instincts, which are more reliable than the thoughts of the man. The dog has no "ego"; he uses experience as a guide.
    Difficulty: *Average*
    Objective: *Essay*

18. Students who were uncertain for most of the story may mention details such as the man's generally cheerful state of mind, his powers of keen observation, his ability to make a fire at lunch time, etc. In opposition to these, they should mention the man's ignorance of the nature of the cold, his lack of imagination, his increasingly dangerous and stupid errors, and the instincts of the dog. Students who knew the outcome early in their reading should cite what details provided clues. They should also mention if they knew how the end would come, and which clues helped.
    Difficulty: *Challenging*
    Objective: *Essay*

19. Students might note that the conquest of nature has always been part of humankind's quest for survival—from the hunters who had to learn to kill for their food to the farmers who had to learn to grow their food. Some students might argue that with the industrial age, humankind's assault on nature—in the form of pollution and greenhouse gases—has brought humanity and all life on earth to the brink of extinction. Others might feel that humans have the right to tame and utilize the resources provided by nature. Students should support their opinions using examples from the story.
    Difficulty: *Average*
    Objective: *Essay*

"Heading West" by Miriam Davis Colt
"I Will Fight No More Forever" by Chief Joseph

Primary Sources: Personal History and Speech, p. 174

Sample Answers

1. The assumption is that farming implements will not be available where they are going.

2. The assumption is that travel by steamboat is dangerous.

3. The assumption is that the Georgians supported slavery and that they were dangerous if they found
someone among them who did not support that view.

4. The assumption is that houses and businesses
would be built, that the town would be much further
along toward thriving.

5. The assumption is that his children—his people—were
unprepared and have had a hard time trying to survive.

Vocabulary Builder, p. 175

A. 1. T; Shares represent portions of ownership.

2. F; A levee is an embankment built to prevent
flooding.

3. T; A foothold is a secure position from which they
could grow stronger.

4. F; A prairie is a grassland.

5. T; *Forded* means "crossed the river at a low point."

B. 1. There were *emigrants* from many lands in the West.

2. As far as the eye could see, the prairie was covered
by a *profusion* of wild flowers.

3. The feeling *pervading* the Nez Perce camp was
despair.

4. The people followed a *ravine* until they came to some
water.

5. The settlers *surveyed* before they built their homes
and settled the land.

Selection Test, p. 176

Critical Reading

1. ANS: C	DIF: Easy	OBJ: Comprehension	
2. ANS: C	DIF: Average	OBJ: Literary Analysis	
3. ANS: D	DIF: Average	OBJ: Interpretation	
4. ANS: A	DIF: Easy	OBJ: Comprehension	
5. ANS: A	DIF: Average	OBJ: Comprehension	
6. ANS: B	DIF: Average	OBJ: Interpretation	
7. ANS: D	DIF: Average	OBJ: Comprehension	
8. ANS: A	DIF: Easy	OBJ: Literary Analysis	
9. ANS: C	DIF: Average	OBJ: Reading Strategy	
10. ANS: B	DIF: Average	OBJ: Comprehension	

"The Story of an Hour" by Kate Chopin

Vocabulary Warm-up Exercises, p. 179

A. 1. intention

2. absolutely

3. powerful

4. revealed

5. significance

6. paralyzed

7. countless

8. perception

B. Sample Answers

1. T; A dictionary provides *illumination* because it
explains the meaning of words.

2. F; That much salt would give the food a very strong
taste, not a *subtle* one.

3. T; The *inability* to tell colors apart is known as color-
blindness.

4. T; Trying again in the face of failure shows *persistence*.

5. F; A house's *eaves* are the overhanging parts of its roof.

6. F; Begging and pleading are the same thing as
imploring.

7. F; *Trivial* problems are not important and would not
upset an easygoing person.

8. T; Reading self-help books can be a sign that someone is *striving* to change.

Reading Warm-up A, p. 180

Sample Answers

1. (many); "Few" could be the opposite of *countless*.

2. (definition); To find out the *significance* of a word, I
might look in a dictionary or ask someone.

3. Her tone of voice; If my *intention* was to spend a lot of
money, I would start by taking a long trip around the
world.

4. run out and buy that; No, when people are *absolutely*
full, they do not have room for dessert.

5. (motionless); No, because if I were *paralyzed*, I could
not move.

6. You see things differently; If the person started acting
differently, or you learned something new about the
person, that could change your *perception*.

7. (showed); I feel annoyed when a movie's ending is
revealed to me before I see it, because that can ruin the
movie for me.

8. (strong); The smell of a perfume could be described as
powerful.

Reading Warm-up B, p. 181

Sample Answers

1. (important); No, I do not think taking a pet for a
checkup is *trivial*, because it is important to be sure
your pet is healthy.

2. by the porch, resting in the shade under the eaves; An
igloo or a teepee does not have *eaves*.

3. he dropped it at my feet, then pushed at me with his
nose; I showed *persistence* when I finished reading a
book that I thought was hard.

4. No, symptoms such as sneezing and a runny nose are
obvious rather than *subtle*.

5. Blue may be seriously ill; The opposite of *striving* might
be achieving something without effort, or it might be not
trying at all.

6. (pet him); *Begging* or *pleading* are other words for
imploring.

7. He showed his *inability* to take a hint by trying to get Kevin to throw the ball even after Kevin said, "Not now."

8. (entire next-to-last paragraph); I might look for *illumination* in a book on pet care or ask someone who has a lot of experience caring for pets.

Literary Analysis: Irony, p. 182

1. Situational irony: Students should choose a passage that illustrates how the outcome of an action or a situation is different from what the reader expects.

2. Dramatic irony: Students should choose a passage that illustrates how the reader is aware of something that a character in the story does not know.

Reading Strategy: Analyze the Philosophical Argument, p. 183

Students should recognize Chopin's philosophical argument about women being the equal of men but not being giving their full humanity in the society of Chopin's day. They may cite various details from the story and should relate them to this philosophy. Here are two examples:

Detail: Mrs. Mallard is troubled by the her husband's death but in the end becomes relieved and almost joyful about it.

How It Relates: It shows how repressed and unfulfilled Mrs. Mallard's life as a woman has been and how much she will relish some independence.

Detail: The narrator describes the typical marriage as one in which the man, no matter how much he loves his wife, will exert his will and dominate her.

How It Relates: The narrator is questioning this traditional relationship and implying that the wife should have equal share in decisions and should not be dominated over.

Vocabulary Builder, p. 184

A. 1. A; 2. C; 3. B; 4. D

B. 1. repression
2. tumultuously
3. forestall
4. elusive

Enrichment: Social Studies, p. 186

Pre-discussion questions:

1. Students should recognize the differences between husband-and-wife relationships in the era of the story and today. For example, is the idea that a woman could feel imprisoned in a marriage still valid, and if so, is it valid for the same reasons?

2. Students should recognize the similarities in customs between the era of the story and today—for example, the way bad news is broken and the conduct of family and friends.

3. Students should recognize the differences in the roles of men and women and how, if the roles were reversed, a man might not have to hide his true feelings. A man

might also not feel as trapped in the marriage as a woman because of the gender roles of the time.

Post-discussion questions:

1. Students should arrive at a group answer for each question, and record each answer on a sheet of paper.

2. Students should recognize the differences between their own answers and the group answers, and that the differences stem from students' different experiences and opinions. They should also recognize how the answers differ due to gender, age, or family background.

3. Students should be aware of gender differences in the answers, and what they say about how each gender views marriage. Students should also be aware of how each group views the appropriateness of Mrs. Mallard's actions.

4. Students should share their views on marriage and what it takes to make a marriage work. They should also comment on the Mallards' marriage and, from the reaction of Mrs. Mallard, draw conclusions about how it worked.

Open-Book Test, p. 187

Short Answer

1. Sample answer: most people of that era would have expected a wife to greet news of her husband's death with pure grief and sorrow, not with the sense of renewal and independence that Mrs. Mallard expresses.
   Difficulty: *Average*   **Objective:** *Reading*

2. As she sits at her open window, Mrs. Mallard notices signs of renewed life. These signs of vibrant life contrast ironically with the news of her husband's death.
   Difficulty: *Challenging*   **Objective:** *Interpretation*

3. In her room, Mrs. Mallard begins to feel a sense of relief, renewal, and independence in the wake of her husband's death. This response is an example of situational irony, because it contradicts the reader's expectations that she will be grief-stricken.
   Difficulty: *Average*   **Objective:** *Literary Analysis*

4. Mrs. Mallard needs to be alone so that she can express and work through her real feelings about her husband's death.
   Difficulty: *Challenging*   **Objective:** *Interpretation*

5. Josephine's statement is an example of dramatic irony, because the reader is aware of the fact that Louise is, in fact, happy rather than upset or ill.
   Difficulty: *Average*   **Objective:** *Literary Analysis*

6. Sample answers: verbal—"veiled hints that revealed in half concealing"; "a monstrous joy"; "the joy that kills"; dramatic—the reader knows, unlike Josephine and Richard, that Louise feels relief at her husband's death; the reader knows, unlike the doctors, that her husband's reappearance is not a pleasant surprise; situational—Louise feels free instead of in deep despair; Louise dies instead of her husband.
   Difficulty: *Average*   **Objective:** *Literary Analysis*

7. The doctors assume that Louise's joy at the sight of her husband is so intense that it kills her. In reality, she is shocked and disappointed that he is still alive because

she has already begun to relish the thought of her independence.

Difficulty: *Average*   **Objective:** *Interpretation*

8. Some students might find the title appropriate because it shows how dramatically people's lives can change within an hour. Others might claim that it is not a good title, because it understates the emotional impact of the story.

Difficulty: *Easy*   **Objective:** *Interpretation*

9. It is an example of situational irony, because the reader expects neither the return of the husband nor the sudden death of Louise.

Difficulty: *Easy*   **Objective:** *Literary Analysis*

10. He would be implying that you are avoiding your fate, because *forestall* means "prevent by acting ahead of time."

Difficulty: *Average*   **Objective:** *Vocabulary*

Essay

11. Some students will argue that Louise was trapped in an unhappy marriage, so her feelings of relief and renewal are appropriate and promise a new life of independence and self-expression that she could not have known in her marriage. Others will argue that her concern with her own happiness and her relief at not being concerned with someone else comes off as selfish and self-indulgent, because people often find their happiness in making others happy.

Difficulty: *Easy*   **Objective:** *Essay*

12. Sample answer: Chopin is suggesting that marriage signals the end of personal freedom for one or both of the parties. The fact that the parties in question are kind, rather than cruel, makes no difference to her.

Difficulty: *Average*   **Objective:** *Essay*

13. Students might note that in the first part of the story, the term implies that Louise is delicate—this is ironic because she turns out to be strong emotionally. At the end of the story, Richards and Josephine once again try to protect this delicate creature who, ironically, collapses at what would normally be regarded as joyful, rather than disastrous, news. Louise's "heart trouble" seems to be that she has placed her heart with her husband rather than with her own best interests for many years.

Difficulty: *Challenging*   **Objective:** *Essay*

14. The quoted comment reflects a belief that independence in marriage is not possible—that one or both partners will attempt to bend the other to his or her will. This pessimistic view about the possibilities for happiness and autonomy in marriage does seem to imply advice: if maintaining your sense of freedom and independence is important to you, approach marriage with caution. To this extent, this story both reflects a social reality and seeks to influence people's reactions to it.

Difficulty: *Average*

Objective: *Essay*

Oral Response

15. Oral responses should be clear, well organized, and well supported by appropriate examples from the selections.

Difficulty: *Average*   **Objective:** *Oral Interpretation*

Selection Test A, p. 190

Critical Reading

1. ANS: B	DIF: Easy	OBJ: Comprehension
2. ANS: A	DIF: Easy	OBJ: Literary Analysis
3. ANS: D	DIF: Easy	OBJ: Literary Analysis
4. ANS: C	DIF: Easy	OBJ: Literary Analysis
5. ANS: C	DIF: Easy	OBJ: Interpretation
6. ANS: A	DIF: Easy	OBJ: Reading Strategy
7. ANS: D	DIF: Easy	OBJ: Comprehension
8. ANS: D	DIF: Easy	OBJ: Literary Analysis
9. ANS: B	DIF: Easy	OBJ: Comprehension
10. ANS: D	DIF: Easy	OBJ: Literary Analysis
11. ANS: A	DIF: Easy	OBJ: Literary Analysis

Vocabulary

12. ANS: B	DIF: Easy	OBJ: Vocabulary
13. ANS: B	DIF: Easy	OBJ: Vocabulary

Essay

14. Students' essays should reflect that the words are ironic because the doctors think Mrs. Mallard died of the shock of joy, not horror, of seeing her husband still alive. Some students may also suggest that the cause of death being called "heart disease" is ironic because Mrs. Mallard's feelings might seem heartless.

Difficulty: *Easy*

Objective: *Essay*

15. Students' essays should reflect that Chopin, in this story, suggests that marriage signals the end of personal freedom for one or both of the parties. The fact that the parties in question are kind, rather than cruel, makes no difference to her.

Difficulty: *Easy*

Objective: *Essay*

16. The plot elements reflect a belief that marriage can place limits on a person's independence because of the need to consider someone else's needs and desires. This pessimistic view of marriage does seem to imply advice: If you value freedom above all else, approach marriage with caution. In this way, this story both reflects a social reality and seeks to influence people's reactions to it.

Difficulty: *Average*

Objective: *Essay*

Selection Test B, p. 193

Critical Reading

1. ANS: A	DIF: Easy	OBJ: Reading Strategy
2. ANS: C	DIF: Average	OBJ: Literary Analysis
3. ANS: B	DIF: Average	OBJ: Literary Analysis
4. ANS: C	DIF: Easy	OBJ: Comprehension
5. ANS: B	DIF: Average	OBJ: Comprehension
6. ANS: C	DIF: Average	OBJ: Interpretation
7. ANS: B	DIF: Easy	OBJ: Literary Analysis
8. ANS: D	DIF: Average	OBJ: Reading Strategy
9. ANS: A	DIF: Challenging	OBJ: Interpretation
10. ANS: D	DIF: Challenging	OBJ: Literary Analysis
11. ANS: A	DIF: Easy	OBJ: Literary Analysis
12. ANS: C	DIF: Challenging	OBJ: Literary Analysis
13. ANS: C	DIF: Challenging	OBJ: Literary Analysis

Vocabulary

14. ANS: A	DIF: Average	OBJ: Vocabulary
15. ANS: B	DIF: Average	OBJ: Vocabulary
16. ANS: D	DIF: Average	OBJ: Vocabulary

Essay

17. Students who admire Mrs. Mallard should mention that she felt trapped in her marriage, that in accepting her feelings she is throwing off hypocrisy, and that her desire to face the world alone reflects strength of character. Those who condemn her should stress that her joy is selfish, that her thoughts about weeping as she sees her husband's body seem hypocritical, that her freedom has come from the death of another human being, one she supposedly loved.

    Difficulty: *Easy*

    Objective: *Essay*

18. Students should back their conclusions using details from the story and their own knowledge of prevailing Victorian attitudes. Whether they argue that Josephine would support her sister or think her wicked, they should realize that Josephine would be deeply shocked at first. Students should conclude that Richards would probably be totally uncomprehending of and scandalized by Mrs. Mallard's feelings and cite one or more of the following reasons: He is a close friend of the husband; he has the Victorian attitude that women need men to shelter them from the shocks of life; and he may believe that women don't want freedom from marriage.

    Difficulty: *Average*

    Objective: *Essay*

19. Students who agree that Mrs. Mallard is a victim should mention the irony that her only escape from the strictures of Victorian marriage is the death of her husband. Freedom for a married woman is simply not a choice.

Those who disagree may mention that the reason she feels joy so soon after her husband's presumed death is that she did not let herself be completely victimized by marriage. In her heart, she did not buy into the prevailing attitudes. As a widow, she will probably be stronger and live a more enjoyable life than others in her position, who are true victims.

Difficulty: *Challenging*

Objective: *Essay*

20. The quoted comment reflects a belief that independence in marriage is not possible in marriage—that one or both partners will attempt to bend the other to his or her will. This pessimistic view about the possibilities for happiness and autonomy in marriage does seem to imply advice: if maintaining your sense of freedom and independence is important to you, approach marriage with caution. To this extent, this story both reflects a social reality and seeks to influence people's reactions to it.

Difficulty: *Average*

Objective: *Essay*

"Douglass" and "We Wear the Mask"
by Paul Laurence Dunbar

Vocabulary Warm-up Exercises, p. 197

A.
1. devious
2. tortured
3. grins
4. mask
5. passionate
6. swarm
7. tempest
8. harsh

B. Sample Answers
1. T; A *bark* is a boat or ship, so it would typically be located on the water.
2. T; *Dissension* connotes conflict.
3. F; *Ebb* refers to a withdrawing tide, not an advancing one.
4. F; *Guile* would normally suggest that a person wouldn't be trustworthy.
5. F; *Myriad* connotes large numbers.
6. T; A *salient* argument is prominent.
7. F; By definition, *subtleties* are often hard to identify.
8. T; People who are *vile* should probably be avoided.

Reading Warm-up A, p. 198

Sample Answers
1. happily; *smiles*
2. (wearing the . . . brave cheerfulness); figuratively
3. rages a . . . painful emotions; *storm*
4. (scolds); *gentle, soft*

5. (filled the air) (angry bees); Locusts are insects that *swarm*.

6. <u>punishing</u>; "You look *pained*, Karen. You have to stop punishing yourself."

7. <u>try to trick</u>; We have to be *devious* when we are planning a surprise party.

8. (truly love); *uninterested*, *passive*

Reading Warm-up B, p. 199

Sample Answers

1. <u>probably beyond counting</u>; The hive contained *myriad* bees, and their droning hum was clearly audible.

2. (one of the most important . . . features); The opposite of *salient* is *minor* or *insignificant*.

3. <u>hideous</u>; *beautiful, lovable*

4. <u>warships . . . terrifying mask was fixed to the prow of the . . . to frighten opponents</u>

5. (conflict); The opposite of *dissension* is *agreement, harmony,* or *concord*.

6. <u>elaborate, complex</u>; We found it difficult to follow the *subtleties* of the philosopher's argument.

7. <u>or cunning, and naughty pranks</u>

8. (and flow); figuratively

Literary Analysis: Formal Verse, p. 200

1. *abbaabba*
2. *cdcdcd*
3. *aabba*

Reading Strategy: Interpret, p. 201

Sample Answers

1. The "we" stands for African Americans. Some students may think it stands for all honorable people who value freedom.

2. Students will probably answer that it is the public sentiment on African Americans' position in society.

3. The "shivering bark" is the African American people as a group.

4. The "lonely dark" is the hard times the African Americans are living in.

5. He addresses it to Douglass because Douglass was known as a fighter for freedom for all African Americans.

6. The mask is hiding the true feelings of African Americans.

7. The cheeks and eyes must be hidden so that no one can see the true emotions of African Americans.

Vocabulary Builder, p. 202

A. 1. *beguiled* (misled by deceit or craftiness)

2. *guileless* (innocent or naive, not exposed to guile)

3. *beguiler* (one who misleads by deceit or craftiness)

4. *beguiling* (misleading by deceit or craftiness)

B. 1. A; 2. D; 3. A; 4. B; 5. C

Enrichment: Art, p. 204

Students should describe the image or emotion, outline characteristics of their masks that portray the desired image or emotion, and then complete a drawing of their masks. Students should share their masks with classmates and describe the different features of the mask (eyes, nose, mouth) and how they convey the image or emotion.

Extension activity: Have students build their designed masks out of papier-maché and other suitable materials. They may then act out skits with their masks, or put them together with other students' masks for a classroom display.

Open-Book Test, p. 205

Short Answer

1. The boat in a storm-tossed sea evokes the turmoil and hardships African Americans were still facing after the abolition of slavery.
   Difficulty: *Challenging* **Objective:** *Reading Strategy*

2. African Americans are facing trials and injustices that are even more severe than those that prevailed in the days of slavery.
   Difficulty: *Average* **Objective:** *Reading Strategy*

3. It is abbaabba cdcdcd.
   Difficulty: *Easy* **Objective:** *Literary Analysis*

4. It is a fourteen line poem with a regular rhyme scheme.
   Difficulty: *Average* **Objective:** *Literary Analysis*

5. In "Douglass," Dunbar speaks of the injustice and difficult times still faced by African Americans. The phrase "lonely dark" therefore refers to that era as a kind of dark age of racial prejudice and injustice.
   Difficulty: *Average* **Objective:** *Interpretation*

6. The mood is upset and agonized. The exclamations "O great Christ," "oh the day is vile" and "We wear the mask" and the rhymes stressing "cries" and "vile" contribute to the mood.
   Difficulty: *Challenging* **Objective:** *Literary Analysis*

7. The mask represents the human tendency to hide one's true feelings.
   Difficulty: *Easy* **Objective:** *Interpretation*

8. "Them" is white people and "we" is black people. The lines mean that whites recognize or "see" blacks as people only if they wear a mask of good cheer or good will that hides their rage and suffering.
   Difficulty: *Challenging* **Objective:** *Reading Strategy*

9. Sample answer: "Douglass": know, ago, flow, fro; storm, form; stark, bark, dark. "We Wear the Mask": guile, smile; otherwise, sighs; cries, arise; vile, mile.
   Difficulty: *Average* **Objective:** *Literary Analysis*

10. No, you would expect to find a wide range of styles represented, because *myriad* means "countless."
    Difficulty: *Average* **Objective:** *Vocabulary*

Essay

11. Dunbar pays tribute to Douglass as all three. Sample examples: Douglass as a visionary—"Saw, salient, at the cross of devious ways"; as a great orator—"and all the country heard thee with amaze" and "thy voice high-sounding over the storm"; and as a great political leader—"thy strong arm to guide the shivering bark," "the blast-defying power of thy form," "to give us comfort through the lonely dark."

    Difficulty: *Easy*   **Objective:** *Essay*

12. Students might note that when one group of people has power and another group does not, the powerless must be careful not to show negative feelings in order to survive and function in society on a day-to-day basis. Dunbar points out that for African Americans, showing their inner anger over the inequality and injustice of their circumstances was dangerous. If they expressed their anger to the powerful, who were usually their employers, they could lose their jobs and more. These circumstances forced them to suppress their real feelings in order to survive in an unjust world.

    Difficulty: *Average*   **Objective:** *Essay*

13. Some students might argue that "Douglass" is the more effective protest, since it holds up the example and ideals of a great antislavery crusader, Frederick Douglass, and decries the fact that conditions for African Americans, far from moving toward Douglass's ideals of justice, have grown even worse. Others might argue that "We Wear the Mask" is the more powerful and effective cry of protest, because it gives a glimpse of the inner emotional anguish suffered by African Americans who feel inner rage about their conditions but who must maintain a civil exterior "mask" to survive in everyday society.

    Difficulty: *Challenging*   **Objective:** *Essay*

14. Students might suggest that these poems are both a record of the social realities faced by African Americans and a cry of protest against them. "Douglass," for example, both reflects injustice and expresses a strong judgment in speaking of "evil days" and the need for a strong, inspiring leader like Douglass to lead African Americans out of "the lonely dark." "We Wear the Mask" also reflects a social reality—the need for African Americans to appear cheerful in the face of their oppression—but it also decries the state of these "tortured souls." So the writer of these poems is both social analyst and social critic, both analyst and judge.

    Difficulty: *Average*   **Objective:** *Essay*

Oral Response

15. Oral responses should be clear, well organized, and well supported by appropriate examples from the selections.

    Difficulty: *Average*   **Objective:** *Oral Interpretation*

Selection Test A, p. 208

Critical Reading

1. ANS: B	DIF: Easy	OBJ: Interpretation
2. ANS: D	DIF: Easy	OBJ: Literary Analysis
3. ANS: A	DIF: Easy	OBJ: Literary Analysis
4. ANS: A	DIF: Easy	OBJ: Reading Strategy
5. ANS: C	DIF: Easy	OBJ: Interpretation
6. ANS: D	DIF: Easy	OBJ: Literary Analysis
7. ANS: B	DIF: Easy	OBJ: Reading Strategy
8. ANS: C	DIF: Easy	OBJ: Comprehension
9. ANS: B	DIF: Easy	OBJ: Interpretation
10. ANS: D	DIF: Easy	OBJ: Interpretation

Vocabulary

11. ANS: B	DIF: Easy	OBJ: Vocabulary
12. ANS: D	DIF: Easy	OBJ: Vocabulary

Essay

13. Students' essays may reflect that when one group of people has power and another group does not have power, the powerless must be careful not to show anger. Otherwise, the powerful will get angry in return and make the lives of the powerless much harder.

    Difficulty: *Easy*

    Objective: *Essay*

14. Students' essays should reflect that the poet imagines Douglass as the captain of a boat of African American passengers, caught in a storm—the strife caused by racial inequality. This scene imagines a captain guiding his ship safely through the dangers of a life of injustice.

    Difficulty: *Easy*

    Objective: *Essay*

15. Students might suggest that these poems are both a record of the social realities faced by African Americans and a cry of protest against them. "Douglass," for example, both reflects injustice and expresses a strong judgment in speaking of "evil days" and the need for a strong leader like Douglass to lead African Americans out of "the lonely dark." "We Wear the Mask" reflects the need for African Americans to appear cheerful in the face of their oppression, but it implies a criticism of these awful conditions. So the writer of these poems is both recording social realities and making judgments about them.

    Difficulty: *Average*

    Objective: *Essay*

Selection Test B, p. 211

Critical Reading

1. ANS: B	DIF: Average	OBJ: Reading Strategy
2. ANS: B	DIF: Average	OBJ: Interpretation
3. ANS: D	DIF: Challenging	OBJ: Reading Strategy
4. ANS: D	DIF: Easy	OBJ: Interpretation
5. ANS: D	DIF: Average	OBJ: Interpretation
6. ANS: B	DIF: Average	OBJ: Literary Analysis

Unit 3 Resources: Division, Reconciliation, and Expansion

7. ANS: C	DIF: Average	OBJ: Literary Analysis
8. ANS: C	DIF: Easy	OBJ: Comprehension
9. ANS: D	DIF: Challenging	OBJ: Interpretation
10. ANS: C	DIF: Average	OBJ: Reading Strategy
11. ANS: B	DIF: Challenging	OBJ: Reading Strategy
12. ANS: A	DIF: Challenging	OBJ: Interpretation
13. ANS: A	DIF: Easy	OBJ: Literary Analysis

Vocabulary

14. ANS: A	DIF: Challenging	OBJ: Vocabulary
15. ANS: C	DIF: Average	OBJ: Vocabulary
16. ANS: B	DIF: Average	OBJ: Vocabulary

Essay

17. Students should indicate that the poem expresses the needs of African Americans who are pretending to be happy with their position instead of showing their true feelings. Students should use details from the poem to support their position, including how they wear masks that "hide" their eyes and cheeks and present a smile instead, and how the world does not see the tears and sighs of the people.

Difficulty: *Easy*

Objective: *Essay*

18. Students' answers will vary but should indicate that Dunbar was keenly aware that despite emancipation and victory in the Civil War, the struggles of the African American community went on and, in some ways, got worse. Details from the selections that support this include his plea to Douglass for his leadership, his statement in "Douglass" that the community is still awash in a tempest, and that they have to hide their true feelings in "We Wear the Mask."

Difficulty: *Average*

Objective: *Essay*

19. Students' answers will depend on the position they choose, but they should defend their positions with citations from one or both of the selections and any other knowledge they have of Dunbar's life and other works. Most students will probably feel the poem is about concealed racial fire, although the poem may be applied more universally to any group of people who face discrimination. Supporting examples include the bitter tone of "We Wear the Mask," the use of the word *guile* and the statement that African Americans are in "debt," and the line "but let the world dream otherwise," which suggests the foolishness of the outside world.

Difficulty: *Challenging*

Objective: *Essay*

20. Students might suggest that these poems are both a record of the social realities faced by African Americans and a cry of protest against them. "Douglass," for example, both reflects injustice and expresses a strong

judgment in speaking of "evil days" and the need for a strong leader like Douglass to lead African Americans out of "the lonely dark." "We Wear the Mask" reflects the need for African Americans to appear cheerful in the face of their oppression, but it implies a criticism of these awful conditions. So the writer of these poems is both recording social realities and making judgments about them.

Difficulty: *Average*

Objective: *Essay*

"Luke Havergal" and "Richard Cory"
by Edwin Arlington Robinson
"Lucinda Matlock" and "Richard Bone"
by Edgar Lee Masters

Vocabulary Warm-up Exercises, p. 215

A.
1. memorable
2. rambled
3. medicinal
4. discontent
5. weariness
6. chiseled
7. schooled
8. repose

B. Sample Answers
1. No, someone who walked *imperially* would probably be proud or even arrogant.
2. I would give him the red one because *crimson* is red.
3. Water would *quench* a fire, while gasoline would make it burn hotter.
4. The hero behaves more *admirably*; the villain does evil things.
5. No, grades of *A* and *B* are more *consistent* with college plans.
6. No, someone who is *pessimistic* makes you feel bad about the future.
7. If she was *arrayed* in her best clothes, I would think she was going to a party.
8. Yes, if somebody has very little money, he or she would be strongly *influenced* by price.

Reading Warm-up A, p. 216

Sample Answers
1. strong, brown, weather-beaten hands; The most *memorable* thing about my seventh-grade English teacher was her pointy high-heeled shoes.
2. (stray); Instead of *rambled*, you could say "wandered" or "moseyed."
3. the idea that a boy with a few minutes of free time was a boy looking for trouble; Someone might be *schooled* in the belief that kids need free time to develop their imaginations.
4. (exhaustion); Taking a nap is a good cure for *weariness*.

5. hospital room; Cough syrup is *medicinal*.

6. <u>He rested on his back, eyes closed, his hands folded across his chest</u>; No, he dislikes *repose* and would rather be doing things all the time.

7. (unhappy); Frowning and complaining are typical signs of *discontent*.

8. <u>wooden cow</u>; You could say "carved" instead of *chiseled*.

Reading Warm-up B, p. 217

Sample Answers

1. Her parents probably *influenced* her, and also her director and other actors she worked with or admired; *affected*

2. (toga); *Arrayed* means "dressed."

3. *Crimson* might be a school's team color.

4. (strode); A school principal might behave *imperially*.

5. (taught) (acted); An Olympic skater would skate *admirably*.

6. <u>the memory of Ms. Graham</u>; *Consistent* means "all the time, not just sometimes."

7. She might have felt *pessimistic* because the competition for movie roles is fierce, and lots of actors do not succeed even if they have talent.

8. If I wanted to do the opposite of *quench* a fire, I would light one, or feed one that was already going.

Literary Analysis: Speaker, p. 218

Sample Answers

1. The speaker must be a ghost, because he or she speaks "out of a grave."

2. It is likely that the woman is dead, since messages about her are brought by one who speaks from the grave, and because she can only be reached through leaves that whisper or by listening to the wind.

3. The speaker seems to be providing advice about a supernatural journey, one that would make it possible to contact a woman who cannot be contacted in the physical world. The meeting or contact Havergal seeks is likely to be supernatural, because the woman will call him "if [he] trusts her." The leaves cannot physically whisper to Havergal, and a kiss cannot be literally flaming on his forehead. In addition, the speaker is a ghost, and would seem to be more qualified to speak about the supernatural than the natural.

4. No, the speaker advises Havergal that "there is not a dawn in eastern skies/To rift the fiery night that's in your eyes," and that "the dark will end the dark, if anything," suggesting that there is no hope for Havergal, and that the only route he can take is a "bitter" one.

5. Something terrible must have happened to Luke Havergal, leaving him with a "fiery night" in his eyes. The speaker advises Havergal on how to contact or reunite with the woman he seeks or misses, so perhaps Havergal was separated from the woman, possibly by her death. It's possible that Havergal may have done something terrible, such as contributing to the woman's death, because the speaker

seems to feel that there is no hope for him. The speaker may be suggesting that Havergal meet his death willingly.

Reading Strategy: Comparing and Contrasting, p. 219

Sample Answers

"Luke Havergal": *aabbaaaa* rhyme scheme, iambic pentameter; third-person point of view; loss of a loved one.

"Richard Cory": *abba* rhyme scheme, iambic pentameter; third-person point of view; suicide and how little we know of the troubles of others.

"Lucinda Matlock": unrhymed iambic pentameter; first-person; living and loving life fully.

"Richard Bone": unrhymed iambic pentameter; first-person; the parallels between life as it is and life as we wish it to be.

Vocabulary Builder, p. 220

A. 1. existing at birth

2. kind or type of literature

3. of the original kind

4. the people born at a certain time

B. degenerate, repose, epitaph, chronicles

Enrichment: Dance, p. 222

Sample Answers

Luke Havergal

Body movements: looking around, head often bowed, wandering aimlessly, wobbling while walking, slumped posture; **sounds:** howling winds, thunderstorm.

Richard Cory

Body movements: head held high, walking stiffly and in a definite direction, hands held behind back while walking, stopping to shake hands or nod at people; **sounds:** silence except for the sound of Richard Cory's heels as he walks briskly across a hard surface, like a floor or sidewalk.

Lucinda Matlock

Body movements: formal dances such as square dancing, stooping to garden or attend to a sick person, cleaning house (i.e., sweeping, making beds, washing dishes), sitting and sewing; **sounds:** lively, fast folk music.

Richard Bone

Body movements: lifting, carrying, chiseling, standing and listening, looking; **sounds:** mournful, funeral music, possibly bagpipes.

Open-Book Test, p. 223

Short Answer

1. The speaker is a ghost that comes from a grave in the cemetery. Some students might suggest that it is the ghost of his lover, who refers to her old identity as "her" and "she." This possibility is suggested by this line: "Out of a grave I come to tell you this."

   Difficulty: *Average*   **Objective:** *Literary Analysis*

2. "She" was Luke Havergal's lover, and she died.
   Difficulty: *Average* **Objective:** *Interpretation*

3. Robinson uses this repetition to emphasize the poem's key theme: that life is a dark and tragic experience in which true love can find lasting fulfillment only in death.
   Difficulty: *Challenging* **Objective:** *Interpretation*

4. The speaker is a person in the town, and the speaker's views seem to reflect those of other average residents of the town.
   Difficulty: *Easy* **Objective:** *Literary Analysis*

5. The ending is surprising because Richard Cory, who seems favored by life's circumstances in so many ways, ends up killing himself. The theme that is underscored by this ending is that being wealthy, admired, and handsome does not necessarily add up to inner peace or happiness.
   Difficulty: *Challenging* **Objective:** *Interpretation*

6. Students might suggest that Cory might have lacked true love or human attachments. They also might suggest that because he was born with every material advantage—money, good looks, etc.— he lacked a sense of personal achievement and worth.
   Difficulty: *Challenging* **Objective:** *Interpretation*

7. He was uncomfortable chiseling messages that might not have reflected the truth of people's lives.
   Difficulty: *Easy* **Objective:** *Interpretation*

8. Richard Bone is implying that historians often do not know whether they are giving a true account of the past, or that they can even intentionally shade the truth if someone pressures them to do so.
   Difficulty: *Average* **Objective:** *Interpretation*

9. Matlock's outlook is optimistic—at the end of the poem, she reproaches the younger generation for its pessimism. Bone's outlook is pessimistic—he sees the hypocrisy of others' epitaphs.
   Difficulty: *Challenging* **Objective:** *Reading Strategy*

10. She would likely not be interested in going out for a three-mile run if she were longing for *repose*, because repose means "state of being at rest."
    Difficulty: *Average* **Objective:** *Vocabulary*

Essay

11. Students might suggest that when we see someone only in public, we are apt to judge him or her by external appearances rather than the truth of their inner lives. The townspeople envied Cory's wealth, look, and grace, but they did not stop to think whether he had an emotionally satisfying or enriching life beneath that glittering surface.
    Difficulty: *Easy* **Objective:** *Essay*

12. Students should choose one of the four title characters and write a biographical essay on him or her. They can imagine details not mentioned in the poem, but their answer should be based at least in part on details from

the poem. They should also draw on the tone of the poem—for example, from the tone of the portrait painted of him in the poem, Luke Havergal seems to have had a sad and mournful life.
   Difficulty: *Average* **Objective:** *Essay*

13. The western gate symbolizes death. Some students may feel that the speaker might therefore be encouraging Havergal to accept the death of his beloved and the accompanying sadness. Others may say that the speaker might be suggesting that Havergal himself accept death as the only path to being reunited with the woman. Some might suggest that the speaker is even urging Havergal to hasten his own death to bring about this reunion. In any case, the speaker makes it clear that Havergal can expect no happiness in this life— perhaps only in the life to come.
   Difficulty: *Challenging* **Objective:** *Essay*

14. Students might note that all of these poems paint a portrait of life in American small towns. "Luke Havergal" evokes a sense of despair and longing out of the loneliness and desolation of a small-town cemetery; "Richard Cory" conveys the secret despair lurking behind even the most superficially privileged and successful members of small-town society; "Lucinda Matlock" speaks of a simple life of hard work and devotion to family that sustain a long life in a small town; and "Richard Bone" hints at the hypocrisies that lurk behind the simple surface of life in a small town.
   Difficulty: *Average* **Objective:** *Essay*

Oral Response

15. Oral responses should be clear, well organized, and well supported by appropriate examples from the selections.
    Difficulty: *Average* **Objective:** *Oral Response*

Selection Test A, p. 226
Critical Reading

1. ANS: B	DIF: Easy	OBJ: Comprehension
2. ANS: A	DIF: Easy	OBJ: Interpretation
3. ANS: C	DIF: Easy	OBJ: Interpretation
4. ANS: C	DIF: Easy	OBJ: Literary Analysis
5. ANS: B	DIF: Easy	OBJ: Interpretation
6. ANS: B	DIF: Easy	OBJ: Interpretation
7. ANS: C	DIF: Easy	OBJ: Literary Analysis
8. ANS: D	DIF: Easy	OBJ: Interpretation
9. ANS: B	DIF: Easy	OBJ: Reading Strategy
10. ANS: B	DIF: Easy	OBJ: Comprehension
11. ANS: C	DIF: Easy	OBJ: Comprehension

Vocabulary

12. ANS: C	DIF: Easy	OBJ: Vocabulary
13. ANS: C	DIF: Easy	OBJ: Vocabulary

Essay

14. Students' essays should reflect that when we only see someone in public, we really don't know him or her. The townspeople envy Cory's wealth, looks, grace, and an admired place in the town. They do not look underneath that image.

    Difficulty: *Easy*

    Objective: *Essay*

15. Students' essays should reflect that both carvers of epitaphs and historians give the birth and death dates of the people about whom they write. Students might also suggest that in both occupations, the writers might be tempted to portray the people as better or more accomplished than they actually were.

    Difficulty: *Easy*

    Objective: *Essay*

16. Students might note that all of these poems paint a portrait of life in American small towns. "Luke Havergal" tells of the despair felt by a man mourning his lost love in a bleak small-town cemetery; "Richard Cory" hints at the unhappiness that exists even for rich people who appear to have it all; "Lucinda Matlock" speaks of a simple life of hard work and devotion to family that sustain a long life in a small town; and "Richard Bone" hints at the false picture of reality that is reflected in the epitaphs of a small-town cemetery.

    Difficulty: *Easy*

    Objective: *Essay*

Selection Test B, p. 229

Critical Reading

1. ANS: B	DIF: Average	OBJ: Comprehension
2. ANS: D	DIF: Average	OBJ: Interpretation
3. ANS: A	DIF: Average	OBJ: Comprehension
4. ANS: C	DIF: Easy	OBJ: Literary Analysis
5. ANS: B	DIF: Easy	OBJ: Literary Analysis
6. ANS: A	DIF: Easy	OBJ: Interpretation
7. ANS: A	DIF: Average	OBJ: Interpretation
8. ANS: C	DIF: Average	OBJ: Comprehension
9. ANS: A	DIF: Average	OBJ: Reading Strategy
10. ANS: B	DIF: Average	OBJ: Literary Analysis
11. ANS: D	DIF: Challenging	OBJ: Literary Analysis
12. ANS: B	DIF: Challenging	OBJ: Literary Analysis

Vocabulary

13. ANS: B	DIF: Average	OBJ: Vocabulary
14. ANS: D	DIF: Easy	OBJ: Vocabulary
15. ANS: A	DIF: Average	OBJ: Vocabulary

Essay

16. Students should choose one of the four title characters and write a biographical essay on him or her. They can imagine details not mentioned in the poem, but they should support their imaginings with details from the poem. They should also draw biographical information from the tone of the poem—for example, from the tone of the portrait painted of him in the poem, Luke Havergal can be said to lead a sad and mournful life.

    Difficulty: *Easy*

    Objective: *Essay*

17. Students should recognize that Lucinda Matlock's tone is not bitter or angry, but in fact lovingly chiding of the younger generation. Students can support this statement with such details from the poem as her gentle tone, her life-loving attitude despite terrible tragedy, and her open and friendly demeanor, as portrayed by Masters.

    Difficulty: *Average*

    Objective: *Essay*

18. As it is unclear exactly what the speaker wants Luke Havergal to do, many interpretations are possible, provided they are supported by the text. The speaker tells Luke to go to the western gate, which might be a real gate or a symbolic one. The speaker may want Luke to accept the death of the woman and the sadness that goes with it, or the speaker may be suggesting that Luke will have to die in order to be with the woman. The speaker seems to want Luke to take action without expecting that any happiness will come from it.

    Difficulty: *Challenging*

    Objective: *Essay*

19. Students might note that all of these poems paint a portrait of life in American small towns. "Luke Havergal" evokes a sense of despair and longing out of the loneliness and desolation of a small-town cemtery; "Richard Cory" conveys the secret despair lurking behind even the most superficially privileged and successful members of small-town society; "Lucinda Matlock" speaks of a simple life of hard work and devotion to family that sustain a long life in a small town; and "Richard Bone" hints at the hypocrisies that lurk behind the simple surface of life in a small town.

    Difficulty: *Average*

    Objective: *Essay*

"A Wagner Matinée" by Willa Cather

Vocabulary Warm-up Exercises, p. 233

A. 1. conjuror
    2. alight
    3. vainly
    4. comprehend
    5. eluding
    6. pitiless
    7. haggard
    8. legacy

Unit 3 Resources: Division, Reconciliation, and Expansion
© Pearson Education, Inc. All rights reserved.
302

B. Sample Answers

1. F; *Absurdities* are illogical and irrational, so they would not be taken seriously.
2. T; *Characteristically* describes generally predictable behavior.
3. T; A person in a state of *frenzy* might act wildly.
4. F; Nations willing to sign a peace treaty would expect peaceful or *harmonious* relations.
5. T; Paralysis is virtually synonymous with lack of motion, or *immobility.*
6. T; A *pathetic* situation would arouse a feeling of compassion or pity.
7. T; Statues and sculptures are often found on a base, or *pedestal.*
8. F; *Wholly* means "entirely," so the entire house would have been renovated.

Reading Warm-up A, p. 234
Sample Answers

1. streamed off ships from Europe to . . . on American soil; Mary wanted to *alight* on the platform as soon as the train had come to a stop.
2. (could help the new arrivals . . . the challenges of building a new life . . . they could assist with learning an unfamiliar language . . .); *understand*
3. scorching summers and freezing winters; *merciful*
4. (passed down to their descendants); *inheritance*
5. (was so harsh . . . worn out with fatigue); The opposite of *haggard* is *rested* or *flourishing.*
6. struggle . . . and are crushed by the obstacles they encounter; *successfully, productively*
7. (are luckier . . . disaster and disappointment); *Eluding* their pursuers, the robbers managed to escape.
8. magical abilities; A *conjuror* always captures people's imagination, appealing to the audience by suggesting that the impossible is possible.

Reading Warm-up B, p. 235
Sample Answers

1. in an ideal performance, all these elements exist in a . . . balanced combination; The opposite of *harmonious* is *unbalanced* or *discordant.*
2. (some critics mock . . . that no reasonable person can take seriously); *illogical*
3. *typically; atypically, rarely*
4. which depend on coincidence so much that they are . . . unbelievable; *entirely*
5. (wild emotions); The opposite of *frenzy* is *calm* or *tranquility.*
6. static; *motionlessness*
7. unduly glorifying opera; *figuratively*
8. (ranging from the triumphant to the . . .)

Literary Analysis: Characterization, p. 236

1. Clark thinks his Aunt Georgiana's appearance is unsightly.
2. Aunt Georgiana was not an outwardly beautiful woman.
3. Aunt Georgiana eloped with her husband and moved with him to the Nebraska frontier, thus avoiding local criticism of her for marrying him.
4. Aunt Georgiana looked out for Clark when he was a boy.
5. Aunt Georgiana had lost something (music) that she loved very much.
6. The concert was an emotional experience for Aunt Georgiana.
7. Aunt Georgiana's hands, which once played the piano so well, are now deformed because of hard work.
8. Aunt Georgiana does not want to leave the life she remembers in Boston for her life in Nebraska.

Reading Strategy: Clarify, p. 237
Sample Answers

1. A chilblain is a painful swelling or sore caused by exposure to cold.
2. The trip started in Red Willow County, Nebraska, and ended in Boston, Massachusetts.
3. The Green Mountains are in Vermont.
4. Aunt Georgiana had been a music teacher at the Boston Conservatory years earlier.
5. Venusberg is a legendary mountain in Germany where Venus, the Roman goddess of love, held court.
6. It reminded her of a young man she knew who used to sing the song.

Vocabulary Builder, p. 238

A. 1. nonmusical
2. nonmusical
3. musical
4. musical

B. 1. overture; prelude
2. with a quivering voice; tremulously
3. unable to move; inert
4. light-hearted joking; jocularity
5. very respectful; reverential

Enrichment: Music, p. 240

Students may choose any song they are familiar with or write one of their own. Students should be able to justify their choices by citing lines from the songs they have chosen or written and linking them to their own personality or self-image.

Open-Book Test, p. 241
Short Answer

1. She strikes her nephew as a withered, sad, and spiritually starved person.
   Difficulty: *Easy* **Objective:** *Literary Analysis*

2. The text of the story does not explain why Clark went to live with his aunt.
   Difficulty: *Average*   **Objective:** *Reading Strategy*
3. Readers might infer that she has deep regrets about leaving the cultured, vibrant, varied life of a major city like Boston for the monotonous chores of life on a farm. Clark recalls how, back on the farm, she would fondly recall performances of classical music she had seen in Paris in her youth, or how she would speak of the Mozart she had once heard.
   Difficulty: *Challenging*   **Objective:** *Literary Analysis*
4. Details that clarify the hardships of train travel a century ago: She had to wear a duster (according to the footnotes), a smock to prevent dust from getting on the clothes. The duster had become black with soot, apparently from the exhaust of the coal-fueled steam locomotive, and her black bonnet was gray with dust that evidently streamed in through open windows.
   Difficulty: *Easy*   **Objective:** *Reading Strategy*
5. The passage shows that Aunt Georgiana has been conditioned to focus more on her daily chores and responsibilities—even when she has traveled far from the farm—than on the pleasures and attractions of a major city like Boston. This gives evidence that her soul has withered under the pressure of decades of daily responsibilities and cultural deprivation on the farm.
   Difficulty: *Challenging*   **Objective:** *Literary Analysis*
6. He is clearly observant and perceptive, and has a great love of music. Aunt Georgiana fostered this love in his early years by exposing him to great music, singing to him, and teaching him to play instruments.
   Difficulty: *Challenging*   **Objective:** *Literary Analysis*
7. Sample Answers:
   Painful memories: he suffered from chilblains and shyness; his hands became raw from corn husking; he fell asleep while studying; he had to plow "forever and forever." Pleasant memories: he read Shakespeare with his aunt; he learned mythology from her; she taught him to play the organ; she talked to him about music.
   Difficulty: *Average*   **Objective:** *Reading*
8. Because it has been so long since she has experienced classical music, he does not know whether she still can appreciate or understand it.
   Difficulty: *Challenging*   **Objective:** *Interpretation*
9. The teacher would likely have a good sense of humor, because *jocularity* means "the condition of being given to joking or playfulness."
   Difficulty: *Average*   **Objective:** *Vocabulary*
10. Sample answers: The pain of realizing what one has lost; the richness of city life vs. the desolateness of farm life; the follies of young love; the ability of music to touch the deepest recesses of even the most withered soul; the resiliency of the human spirit, even after decades of cultural deprivation and boredom on a farm.
    Difficulty: *Average*   **Objective:** *Interpretation*

Essay

11. Examples of Aunt Georgiana's retaining her love of music: helping young Clark learn music, worrying that Clark may also have to sacrifice music, keeping some music books, enjoying the music of the young cow puncher, and all of her reactions during the Wagner concert.
    Difficulty: *Easy*   **Objective:** *Essay*
12. Students might note that although he is trying to be helpful, it appears that Clark has ironically done the opposite. He has exposed his aunt to something that was dead in her; at the end of the story, she is in pain, not wishing to return to her desolate life on the farm.
    Difficulty: *Average*   **Objective:** *Essay*
13. Students might note that in her youth, Aunt Georgiana was a musician. When she let romance take her away from that life, she was left with a love of music but no way to express it—only a lifetime of drudgery on a desolate farm. She warns Clark against having the same thing happen to him. She is warning him about the devastating effect of coming to the realization that one has let one's true passions and talents go to waste.
    Difficulty: *Challenging*   **Objective:** *Essay*
14. Students might note that in the culturally vibrant atmosphere of Boston, Georgiana developed a passion for listening to and performing serious music. Although she never loses her love of music, there are few outlets for her to cultivate this passion on the lonely Nebraska farm where she spends most of her adulthood. When she returns to Boston and hears the Wagner concert, her sense of lost opportunities is devastating to her. Place, then, is a decisive factor in shaping her character.
    Difficulty: *Average*   **Objective:** *Essay*

Oral Response

15. Oral responses should be clear, well organized, and well supported by appropriate examples from the selections.
    Difficulty: *Average*   **Objective:** *Oral Interpretation*

Selection Test A, p. 244

Critical Reading

1. ANS: B	DIF: Easy	OBJ: Literary Analysis
2. ANS: D	DIF: Easy	OBJ: Reading Strategy
3. ANS: D	DIF: Easy	OBJ: Literary Analysis
4. ANS: C	DIF: Easy	OBJ: Comprehension
5. ANS: B	DIF: Easy	OBJ: Interpretation
6. ANS: A	DIF: Easy	OBJ: Comprehension
7. ANS: B	DIF: Easy	OBJ: Literary Analysis
8. ANS: C	DIF: Easy	OBJ: Reading Strategy
9. ANS: A	DIF: Easy	OBJ: Reading Strategy
10. ANS: B	DIF: Easy	OBJ: Interpretation

Vocabulary and Grammar

11. ANS: C   DIF: Easy   OBJ: Vocabulary
12. ANS: D   DIF: Easy   OBJ: Vocabulary

Essay

13. Students' essays should reflect that in her youth, Aunt Georgiana was a musician. When she let romance take her away from that life, she was left with a love of music but with no way to express it. She warns Clark against having the same thing happen to him.
    Difficulty: *Easy*
    Objective: *Essay*

14. Students' essays should reflect that Aunt Georgiana's home is not really just outside the concert hall, but it might as well be. For when she leaves the hall and leaves Boston, she has nothing to look forward to except her empty life in Nebraska.
    Difficulty: *Easy*
    Objective: *Essay*

15. Students might note that in culturally rich Boston, Georgiana developed a love of listening to and performing music. Although she never loses her love of music, there are few outlets for her to pursue her talents on the lonely Nebraska farm where she spends most of her adulthood. When she returns to Boston and hears the Wagner concert, her sense of lost opportunities makes her terribly sad. So the places she lived in have had a strong influence on her character.
    Difficulty: *Average*
    Objective: *Essay*

Selection Test B, p. 247

Critical Reading

1. ANS: B   DIF: Average   OBJ: Literary Analysis
2. ANS: A   DIF: Average   OBJ: Reading Strategy
3. ANS: D   DIF: Easy   OBJ: Interpretation
4. ANS: D   DIF: Average   OBJ: Reading Strategy
5. ANS: D   DIF: Average   OBJ: Interpretation
6. ANS: B   DIF: Average   OBJ: Interpretation
7. ANS: C   DIF: Challenging   OBJ: Reading Strategy
8. ANS: C   DIF: Average   OBJ: Comprehension
9. ANS: C   DIF: Challenging   OBJ: Literary Analysis
10. ANS: D   DIF: Average   OBJ: Comprehension
11. ANS: D   DIF: Easy   OBJ: Reading Strategy
12. ANS: A   DIF: Easy   OBJ: Interpretation
13. ANS: B   DIF: Challenging   OBJ: Literary Analysis

Vocabulary and Grammar

14. ANS: D   DIF: Average   OBJ: Vocabulary
15. ANS: B   DIF: Easy   OBJ: Vocabulary
16. ANS: A   DIF: Challenging   OBJ: Vocabulary

Essay

17. Students should give some or all of the following examples of Aunt Georgiana's retaining her love of music: helping young Clark learn music, worrying that Clark may also have to sacrifice music, keeping some music books, enjoying the music of the young cow puncher, and all of her reactions during the Wagner concert.
    Difficulty: *Easy*
    Objective: *Essay*

18. Students should recognize that Aunt Georgiana's reluctance to leave the concert is really a desire to cling to a time and place in her life when she was once happy: when she lived in the cultured city of Boston and taught at the Conservatory. Now that she has been reawakened to the beauty of the life and music she gave up so long ago, she is desperate not to return to her hard, bleak life in Nebraska.
    Difficulty: *Average*
    Objective: *Essay*

19. Students should describe Clark on the basis of the selection. They may at first feel he is shallow because he seems to be ashamed of his aunt, but they should also recognize his sensitivity; he loves his aunt and appreciates the tremendous sacrifices she has made. Students may observe that Clark callowly takes for granted that which his aunt misses so dearly and seems to want to prove his cultural superiority, but they should also realize that he comes to understand and regret the depth of the pain awakened in his aunt.
    Difficulty: *Challenging*
    Objective: *Essay*

20. Students might note that in the culturally vibrant atmosphere of Boston, Georgiana developed a passion for listening to and performing serious music. Although she never loses her love of music, there are few outlets for her to cultivate this passion on the lonely Nebraska farm where she spends most of her adulthood. When she returns to Boston and hears the Wagner concert, her sense of lost opportunities is devastating to her. Place, then, is a decisive factor in shaping her character.
    Difficulty: *Average*
    Objective: *Essay*

Writing Workshop—Unit 3

Research Report: Integrating Grammar Skills, p. 251

Sample Revision

  Two early American writers who promoted a spirit of individualism were Ralph Waldo Emerson and Henry David Thoreau, who were neighbors in Concord, Massachusetts. Fourteen years older than Thoreau, Emerson was a major influence on his younger friend. ***For example,*** Emerson's essay, called "Self-Reliance," inspired Thoreau to trust his own instincts about right and wrong.

Like Emerson, Thoreau believed in self-reliance. *Unlike Emerson,* he put his ideas to the test in more extreme ways. *For instance,* he lived by himself in a cabin at Walden Pond for two years, where he observed nature and wrote his best-known book, *Walden. Furthermore,* he once spent a night in jail rather than pay a tax that might help support a war he did not believe in. This experience led to his famous essay "Civil Disobedience," which has inspired generations of social activists, including Martin Luther King, Jr.

Vocabulary Workshop 3, p. 253

A. Sample Answers

1. An *atlas* is group of maps.
2. *Cereal* is made from grain.
3. A *gorgon* is terrifying.
4. People imagined America to be *edenic* because they envisioned it as a natural paradise.

B. Sample Answers

1. In Greek mythology, an oracle foretold the future. By correctly predicting the outcome of the game, she proved to be *oracular.*
2. In Roman mythology, Vulcan was the god of fire. The *volcano* belched fire from deep under the earth's surface.
3. In Greek mythology, the Chimera was a monster with a lion's head, goat's body, and serpent's tail. His design for the new building was a *chimera,* an impossible and foolish fancy.

Benchmark Test 5, p. 255

MULTIPLE CHOICE

1. ANS: D
2. ANS: D
3. ANS: C
4. ANS: A
5. ANS: B
6. ANS: C
7. ANS: B
8. ANS: B
9. ANS: D
10. ANS: B
11. ANS: A
12. ANS: B
13. ANS: C
14. ANS: B
15. ANS: D
16. ANS: D
17. ANS: B
18. ANS: D
19. ANS: B
20. ANS: D
21. ANS: A
22. ANS: B
23. ANS: C
24. ANS: D
25. ANS: C
26. ANS: D
27. ANS: C
28. ANS: A

ESSAY

29. Field reports should be detailed, factual, and based on observation.
30. Students should present a clear point of view on one of the pressures that young people face and support it with realistic examples. The ideas and language should be persuasive in nature.
31. Essays should discuss both similarities and differences in content, viewpoint, and presentations between two media with a similar subject. Ideas should be supported by examples.